Mary Queen of Scots
The Fair Devil of Scotland

Daughter of James V of Scotland, Mary Stuart was born in 1542 and succeeded to the throne when she was six days old. Her childhood, however, was spent in France at the Court of Henry II and Catherine de' Medici; affianced to the Dauphin Francis, Mary was pampered and adored, and at seventeen became Queen of France. After Francis's premature death she returned to Scotland, unprepared for the quagmire of Scottish politics. All went well until she married her cousin Lord Darnley: arrogant and feckless, he soon became a nuisance and many of the Scottish Lords connived at his murder. But when Mary married the murderer-in-chief, the ruthless Earl of Bothwell, the lords turned against her. As a last resort, Mary fled to England, where Queen Elizabeth immediately had her imprisoned. Even nineteen years later, Mary was still considered a threat, and in 1587 Elizabeth signed the warrant for her execution at Fotheringhay.

Mary
Queen of Scots

The Fair Devil of Scotland

JEAN PLAIDY

A STAR BOOK

Published by
the Paperback Division of
W. H. ALLEN & Co. Ltd

A Star Book
Published in 1978
by the Paperback Division of
W. H. Allen & Co. Ltd.
A Howard and Wyndham Company
44 Hill Street, London W1X 8LB

This edition reprinted 1978

First published in Great Britain by
Robert Hale & Company, 1975

Printed in Great Britain by
C. Nicholls & Company Ltd,
The Philips Park Press, Manchester

ISBN 0 352 39504 4

Contents

Illustrations

The English Succession

Henry VII 1485-1509 m. Elizabeth of York

Margaret m.1 James IV m.2 Archibald   Henry VIII 1509-47   Mary
              of Scotland 6th Earl   m.1 Katherine   m.1 Louis XII
              1488-1513   of Angus   of Aragon   of France
                                                                 m.2 Charles
                           Lady Margaret   Mary I 1553-8   Brandon
    James V   Douglas   Duke of Suffolk
    of Scotland   m.   m.2 Anne Boleyn
    1513-42   Mathew Earl   Lady Frances
    m.2   of Lennox   Elizabeth I 1558-1603 Brandon
    Mary of Guise   m.
                     Lord Charles   m.3 Jane Seymour   Henry Grey,
                     Stuart   Duke of Suffolk
  Mary Queen m.2 Henry,   Edward VI 1547-53
  of Scots   Lord Darnley   Lady   Lady   Lady Mary
  1542-87   1546-67   Earl of Lennox   Jane   Catherine Grey   Grey
                                                     Grey   m.   m.
                         m.   m.   Edward Seymour   Thomas
  James VI   Elizabeth   Guildford Earl of Hertford Keys
  of Scotland 1567,   Cavendish   Dudley
  I of England   Edward Seymour Thomas Seymour
  1603-25   Arabella
                         Stuart

The Scottish Succession of Stewarts, Lennox Stuarts and Hamiltons

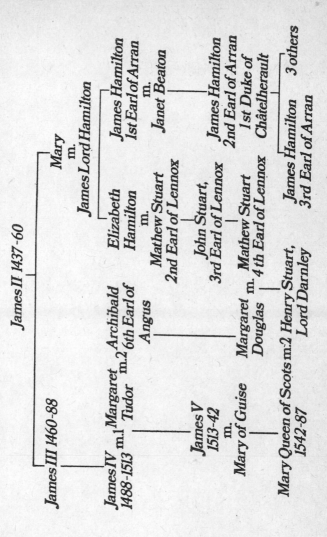

Parentage

When James V of Scotland heard that his wife had given birth to a daughter, he declared this to be the greatest disaster in his calamity-laden life. It was December – one of the most bleak Decembers Scotland had known; and not only climatically. James, the thirty-year-old King, had led his armies into battle against the old enemy, and had suffered a defeat which was only to be compared with that of Flodden Field in 1513. At Solway Moss, James's armies had been routed; his hopes were in ruins; he saw nothing but disaster. The birth of the longed-for son would have raised his spirits even if he could not hope to raise his standard for a while; but this boon was denied him.

On 8th December 1542, he, the father of numerous bastards – and sons among them – heard the news that at the palace of Linlithgow, his French wife had given birth to a girl. There had been two previous children, both sons and neither had survived, so there he was, a defeated King, with death very close and the knowledge that he was leaving his kingdom to a baby girl. He turned his face to the wall and bemoaned the fate of his dynasty. "The Devil go with it," he said. "It came with a lass and will go with a lass."

James was the son of Margaret Tudor and James IV; and his arch-enemy, who wished to add the Scottish crown to his own, was his mother's brother, King Henry VIII. This wicked uncle had a very personal reason for desiring the defeat of James. The King of England was a vengeful man and he had never forgiven James for his French marriage. Henry had been in need of a wife having rid himself of his first Queen, Katherine of Aragon, after a wearisome legal struggle which had

13

resulted in the most cataclysmic event of the century – the break with Rome. He had married the lady of his choice and beheaded her, to make room for the third wife who, having presented him with the son he so urgently craved, had died – some said fortunately for her – in childbed.

He had heard of the charms of a French widow some twenty-two years of age who had already proved herself fruitful. Tall, good-looking, she belonged to the second most important family of France, that of the notorious Guises. The widow's father was Claude, Duke of Guise; her mother was Antoinette of Bourbon, daughter of Francis of Bourbon, Count of Vendôme. All this set Henry's eyes sparkling with antici-pation. Unfortunately for him, Mary of Guise, as a widow, had the privilege of deciding where she would or would not marry; hers was a very handsome head and she wished to keep it where it belonged – on a very handsome pair of shoulders; she declined the much-married monarch in favour of his far less powerful nephew. To choose to share the crown of Scotland when that of England was offered could mean one thing: she was refusing the King of England because she preferred the King of Scotland. Henry rarely forgot and never forgave. This was an insult to the King of England, and more-over he was to take instead of this handsome Frenchwoman, the sister of the Duke of Cleves who turned out to be not to his liking at all. She was a great Flanders mare, he grumbled; but he succeeded in divorcing her – much to her relief, for she had begun to fear that her head was not very safe; and although he had found the fascinating, alluring Katherine Howard, who pleased him mightily, he still would not forgive the woman who had refused him in order to share the poor little crown of Scotland rather than the mighty one of England.

So while the King of Scotland mourned for the loss of his army and suffered great humiliation at the rout of Solway Moss, the King of England rejoiced not only on account of the victory but because at Linlithgow the woman who had refused him had given birth to a puny girl instead of the lusty boy for whom she and her husband had hoped and prayed.

James was a handsome man, his good looks marred only by a small mouth and weak chin. His blue-grey eyes were almond

14

shape, his face oval – features which his daughter was to inherit. An aquiline nose gave a touch of strength to his face in contrast to the chin, and like all contrasts was appealing; his red hair was curly and abundant; he was neither tall nor short; and the over-all effect was one of charm.

When he became King of Scotland on the death of his mother, Margaret Tudor, he had two objectives. One was to preserve Scotland from falling under the rule of the King of England; the other was the pursuit of women. His mistresses were numerous, and he had begotten several children; his favourite was a son by Margatet Erskine: James Stewart, who was to become the Earl of Moray, known as the Regent Moray, and was to play a leading part in the drama of the King's legitimate daughter, Mary Queen of Scots.

For help against the English, James looked across the water to France, England's perennial enemy. Francis I, who had always kept a sharp eye on his neighbour, could not deny a helping hand to a King who could weaken that neighbour's position – if only by forcing Henry to keep an army on the Border. So Francis was very much inclined to listen to James's request.

There was nothing like marriage to strengthen the bonds between countries and Francis had a daughter, a pretty, dainty fifteen-year-old. James was delighted at the prospect of marriage with the tender Magdalene. There was one drawback: she was delicate and the climate of Scotland was notoriously harsh. Under the aesthetic lecher, Francis I, the Court of France was the most intellectual and cultivated in the world. Francis had given his patronage to the world's greatest artists. Leonardo da Vinci had received a salary of 700 crowns from him and Benvenuto Cellini, the greatest goldsmith of the Renaissance, was also on his payroll. The golden salt-cellar which Cellini made for Francis – although it was originally intended for the Duke of Ferrara – still exists. Francis and his sister Margaret, with whom it was said he was incestuously in love, surrounded themselves with artists, poets, and musicians. Francis was fastidious; his linen was kept in scented cabinets. He had a passion for architecture, and he built or reconstructed some of the finest palaces ever to have been created. His manners were gracious; his conversation witty; and he naturally set the fashion for his Court.

Francis was uneasy at the thought of his daughter's leaving France for Scotland, but he was the first to see the political advantage and he knew of course that the prospect of the marriage would set Henry grinding his teeth with rage and apprehension. Moreover sons and daughters of kings had one main duty and that was to marry and produce children who in their turn would become pawns in the game; and the more pieces there were to be moved advantageously about the board, the better the chance of winning. So poor little Magdalene had no choice; she must be given to the King of Scotland.

Henry, as might have been predicted, viewed such a proposition with alarm and offered James his own daughter by Katherine of Aragon as bait. If Henry's daughter became Queen of Scotland then that rapacious monarch would indeed strengthen his claim. James decided on the French marriage, and when he saw the lovely young girl he was more determined than ever. She was delectable, though fragile; she brought with her a magnificent dowry; and the marriage was obnoxious to Uncle Henry. What more could he ask? For a less fragile bride, perhaps? But the mists and snows of Scotland would harden her; she would give him many sons who would grow in strength to protect Scotland from that predatory old bird below the Border.

The marriage took place in January 1537. At the celebrations was a young woman, Mary of Guise, daughter of Claude, Duke of Guise, and Antoinette of Bourbon, with her husband the Duke of Longueville to whom she had already borne a son and was at the time pregnant with another. James may have noticed her cursorily; for she was of an important family and the King of France – as he sometimes did with favoured well-born children – had adopted her as his daughter. But it may well be that James's attention was so taken up with his pretty little bride that he had no time to notice a contentedly married young woman, personable and rich though she might be.

Feasting and celebrations for the marriage continued through the winter months of February, March and April, and it was May by the time Magdalene sailed with her husband for her new home. Poor little Magdalene – nurtured in the hot-house ambience of the French Court – wilted immediately in the harsh atmosphere of Scotland. In two months she was dead and James was looking for a new wife.

There was another who did not long survive the wedding of James and Magdalene, and this was the young Duke of Longueville. He was only some twenty-seven years of age and his death was an unexpected tragedy; but in the sixteenth century it was easy to die. A cold which turned to congestion of the lungs, a disorder or the internal organs, some ailment which proved beyond the skill of medical knowledge of the day to deal with, and a young life came to an abrupt and mysterious end. Thus it was with the Duke of Longueville. He left a sorrowing pregnant widow with a two-year-old son to console her. Mary was indeed sorrowful, as her marriage had been a happy one; for two months she might shut herself away from society, enjoying the company of her little son Francis, named after the King, but she knew very well that her respite would be short. She was too important a *parti* to be allowed to remain a widow.

She was right. In August her second son was born and she named him Louis after her husband, but by December the child was dead. This made her a free bargaining counter. There would be a good dowry from her "father", the King of France; she was an important member of the Guise family; she had proved that she was fertile and moreover could bear sons. Henry turned lascivious eyes in her direction, which act she was allowed to flout, for there was little the King of France enjoyed more than irritating his Brother England. But what of Scotland? A Queen, no less! The King of France approved and so did her ambitious family. A crown – albeit a not very grand one – was welcome to the Guises. Mary must consider her family. She had seen the young King of Scotland at his wedding. He was a handsome young fellow; she could do worse.

But what of her little boy, her Francis? Mary was a maternal woman and loved her son. It was inconceivable that he should go to Scotland, but she could trust his grandmother Antoinette to look after him.

The King of France would give her half her dowry of 150,000 *livres*, the other half being provided by her powerful family. There was one drawback: she was related to the royal family and therefore to the King's previous wife. But this disadvantage was soon swept away; a dispensation could be easily obtained. It was duly provided by Pope Clement VII.

In January 1538 – exactly a year after James's first marriage – the marriage contracts were signed; by May the marriage by proxy took place in the Cathedral of Notre-Dame. Gnashing his teeth in the royal palace, Henry refused her the necessary permission to travel through England to her new home. It was therefore necessary for James to send a large fleet to bring her to Scotland. It was June when she arrived and on the 14th Mary of Guise and James V of Scotland were married by Cardinal Beaton in the Cathedral of St Andrews.

Mary was quickly disillusioned. The happy first marriage with a man of her own nationality, taste and customs, had ill-prepared her for what she found in Scotland. She had been forced to leave behind her beloved son; and Mary, who was to prove herself a good mother, missed him sorely, although she had left him in what she considered the best possible hands, those of his grandmother Antoinette of Bourbon. The crude manners of her husband's Court were in sharp contrast to those to which she was accustomed; but the chief complaint was her husband's absorption with his mistresses. He was not going to change his habits, and if Mary did not like his way of living she must put up with it.

She hoped for a child which would have been a compensation but in this she was for more than a year disappointed. Her forceful mother was in constant correspondence, following her daughter's progress with concern and plenty of advice. It was a great joy, therefore, when Mary at length became pregnant and on Friday 22nd May 1540 gave birth to a son. There was exultation both in Scotland and in the family circle of France, especially as almost immediately she was once more pregnant, and in April of the following year gave birth to another son. Alas, two days after his birth this child died, and a few days later the year-old Prince followed his little brother. There was then no heir to the Scottish throne.

This must have been the most unsatisfactory period of her life. Her marriage had brought her no happiness; if her two little boys had lived they would have provided her with the compensation she so desperately needed. She had a husband who was crude by French standards, and who lived with her for the sole purpose of getting an heir for the Scottish throne, clearly preferring any one of his many mistresses to his wife; she was in a foreign country, apart from her family. A child would have meant so much to her; for this reason alone she must welcome her husband to her bed.

She had introduced a few French refinements into her court. Her mother was clearly anxious for her welfare; the Guises were a family who looked after each other. Her brother Francis, their father's eldest son, was growing into a man of strength and ambition; he would be a worthy head of the family. Her brother Charles, destined for the Church, was brilliantly clever. They were devoted to her, and they wished to make sure that all went well with her. She knew she had only to ask and they would come over to see her; and she was well aware that they would disapprove of James's treatment of her.

The English were restive. Some of the most powerful houses in Scotland were in conflict with James, mainly on a religious issue. There were some who were determined to break away from Rome and others who wished to remain under Papal jurisdiction; another group preferred to keep to the old Church while agreeing that some reforms were necessary. Henry sent a peremptory order to James, in September 1541, to join a conference at York. Suspecting treachery, James declined the invitation. Henry was determined on war.

In March 1542, to her great joy, Mary became pregnant once more. The uneasy situation below the Border, the disaffection of the Lords of Scotland, and the grumbling threats of the English could not suppress her delight. Even James believed that with the birth of a son all his troubles would begin to evaporate. It seemed likely that the child would be a boy – after all, the Queen had already given birth to two. When this one arrived they must take the utmost care to preserve it. The fact that the two little boys had died within a few days of each other had given rise to rumours of poison. In fact, any death which could not be explained came under this suspicion.

In November came the great battle of Solway Moss – a rout for the Scottish armies which went to pieces before the advancing English. Rarely had there been such a débâcle. Sick in heart and body, James fled the field knowing himself utterly defeated. He was so certain that he was about to die that he prophesied this event. He returned to the Queen for comfort. Their hopes were in the child whose birth was imminent. But James was a beaten man; because he believed he could not hold up his head again after the defeat of Solway Moss he desired death.

He left the Queen at Linlithgow and went to Falkland Palace; there he retired to his bed prophesying that he would never rise from it. It was while he was at Falkland that the news came to him of the birth of the child. The final calamity, a girl. There he turned his face to the wall and made his famous remark, "It came with a lass and will go with a lass." In this prophecy he was wrong, for although the House of Stewart had been founded by Marjorie Bruce when she married Walter Stewart in 1315, the Stuarts were to be royal for years to come.* His own grandson James VI of Scotland became James I of England, and the Stuarts were set to reign for a hundred years until the death of Queen Anne, and only then gave place to the House of Hanover because Anne had no direct heir to follow her.

The other prophecy concerning his own death, however, came true. Six days after the birth of his daughter James died; and the puny little girl born in Linlithgow Palace became Mary Queen of Scots, who was to be the most romantic, fascinating and controversial Queen in history.

*Mary was born a Stewart but became known as *Stuart* during her stay in France; she then properly became a Stuart through her marriage to Darnley. Their descendants were therefore Stuarts, but Mary's half-brothers of course remained Stewarts.

Escape to an Enchanted Island

Fortunately for Scotland, Henry VIII was a very superstitious man, and although the rout at Solway Moss left the road to Edinburgh wide open he declined to proceed along it because he feared the curses of the dead king; so he called a halt to the fighting and decided to rely on negotiations. There was a little Queen of Scotland and he had his son by Jane Seymour, Prince Edward, who was at this time five years old. What could be more desirable than a match between the heir of England and the heiress of Scotland? Such a marriage could be a convenient settlement of the troubles, and if Scotland was to come under his rule it was better that the land should not be devastated by fighting.

In those early months of 1543, the baby of Linlithgow Palace was a very important person both in England and Scotland. Mary of Guise could not deeply mourn a husband when by his death a power was placed in her hands which, as such a forceful woman, she must have long coveted. Her eyes were turned immediately to her native land. She would have chosen a French prince to be her daughter's husband if there had been one available; but only one of the highest rank would suffice.

The Dauphin of France, a gauche young man, was married to Catherine de' Medici, the Italian merchant's daughter who had only been accepted into the royal House of France because she brought with her one of the greatest fortunes in Europe. They had been married for ten years and the marriage had so far been sterile. Henry, the Dauphin, was a man who would do his duty by his wife even though he had no love for her and was deeply enamoured of the fascinating Diane de Poitiers, the mistress to whom he had been faithful for many years – and fidelity was something of a phenomenon in the French Court. Had he and Catherine de' Medici had a son, Mary of Guise would have done everything possible – and so would her influential family – to bring about a match between that son and her daughter.

It was characteristic of the Scottish nobles that they could not agree amongst themselves let alone with other statesmen, and the death of James leaving an infant Queen made a highly inflammable situation. There were two men who were determined to become the baby's Governor, which was another way of saying Regent, and Regents governed kingdoms during a monarch's minority, disability, or absence from the scene. One of them was Cardinal Beaton – the wiliest of men; the other was the Earl of Arran, one of the simplest. The Cardinal believed his superior mental powers designated him for the role; Arran was of the opinion that his birth made it his by right.

There can be no doubt of the superior powers of the Cardinal. He had studied at the universities of St Andrews and Glasgow and at the age of sixteen had gone to Paris, where he became a student of civil and canon law. He was suave, cultivated, proud, cruel and immoral. An ardent Catholic, his policy was pro-French and therefore directed against England: he was a zealous persecutor of those who followed the Reformed religion – and it was this which was to prove fatal to him. In 1539 he succeeded his uncle as Archbishop of St Andrews; he had been one of the chief negotiators in the marriage of James and Magdalene, and the leader of the mission which went to France to bring Mary of Guise to Scotland.

In direct contrast was James Hamilton, 2nd Earl of Arran and later Duke of Châtelherault. His grandfather had married the sister of James III and the family was very proud of this strain of royal blood. Arran himself was no ruler. He was too weak in character; he was lazy and disinclined to take decisions. It was clear that he would have no chance against the scheming Cardinal.

When James V died, the Cardinal professed to have in his possession a will made by the late King in his last hours in which he, the Cardinal, and the Earls of Arran, Argyll and Huntly were appointed joint Regents. It was declared by the Cardinal's opponents that this will was a forgery which had been fabricated by the Cardinal himself. Beaton's story was that when James lay dying he had gone to him and urged him to appoint a regency; the notary Henry Balfour had drawn up the will. Whether James was aware of what he was doing is another matter, and it may have been that Beaton guided his hand as he signed.

Mary of Guise, recognizing the strength of the Cardinal, his friendship for her native land, and his determination to uphold the Catholic faith in Scotland where the Reformed religion was beginning to take hold, gave him her support. This was the signal for the enemies of the Dowager Queen and the Cardinal to circulate scandal about them, although there was no evidence to justify this except for the fact that Beaton's private life, in spite of his vows of celibacy, was far from moral and he had several children.

Henry VIII was naturally making the most of the situation. At Solway Moss he had captured certain influential noblemen, among them Fleming, Cassillis, Maxwell, Glencairn, Angus and Oliver Sinclair. Handsome Sinclair, commanding the army, owed his position to the favour of the King, a fact which rankled with those who considered themselves more capable of leading the Scots into battle. Henry ordered that these captives should be brought to London and there he prevailed upon them to sign a marriage treaty between Mary and his son Edward. He even inveigled some of them into promising him help if, on the little Queen's death, he took the crown of Scotland. Mary was in fact a healthy child, but there had been rumours that she was sickly and unlikely to live long. In consequence, Henry sent an envoy to Scotland to report on the child's condition; and the little Queen was unswaddled and revealed in her three-month-old nakedness. The English envoy could only report to his master that Queen Mary was a goodly child and likely to live.

Henry was well aware that the Earl of Arran had wanted Mary for his own son; in an endeavour to prevent trouble over the agreement which was about to be drawn up, he offered

Arran his daughter Elizabeth – Anne Boleyn's girl. Elizabeth was ten years old and it seemed hardly likely that she would ever come to the throne, for in addition to being of dubious legitimacy she had Jane Seymour's boy Edward and Katherine of Aragon's Mary ahead of her. Arran sulked, but even he was wise enough to know he could not pit his strength against that of the King of England. So an agreement was drawn up at Greenwich and the little Queen of Scots was promised to Edward.

Since she was affianced to his son, Henry wanted Mary in England. He declared that if she were to have an English bridegroom, she must have an English upbringing. The last thing Mary of Guise would agree to was to pass her daughter over to a man who had already beheaded two of his wives – for by this time Katherine Howard, sharing the fate of her cousin Anne Boleyn, had laid her head on the block. Mary of Guise declared that she would take her child to France rather than let her fall into the hands of that royal murderer.

Henry's brutal enforcement of his will in England had led him to believe that he could use the same methods on a country which had suffered humiliating defeat as the Scots had at Solway Moss. He was amazed at the refusal to send Mary to his Court.

Arran was a poor ally – a man who swayed this way and that, and changed his mind when he changed company. Cardinal Beaton would have made a better ally, and it was unfortunate that he was a Cardinal since Henry had broken with Rome. He intimated that if the Cardinal would abandon his allegiance to the Pope he might then become a friend of the King of England. Henry had forgotten that Beaton was beyond his reach and it was of no avail to offer him the choice of saying goodbye to his Cardinal's hat or his head.

Henry had missed his chance. The Scots were recovering after the débâcle of Solway Moss. Cardinal Beaton was in league with the French. Mary had been moved from Linlithgow to Stirling Castle and on 9th September 1543 was crowned Queen of Scotland.

A year after the coronation an event occurred at the French court which set the secret hopes of Mary of Guise soaring.

Catherine de' Medici, who it had been prophesied would never produce a child, gave birth to a son. Catherine was already acquiring an unsavoury reputation in France. In the first place she was Italian and in some French circles the word Italian was synonymous with that of poisoner. Deeply concerned by her inability to bear children she had, it was said, called in the aid of sorcery and the result was a son. The boy, as the eldest son of the Dauphin, was in direct line to the throne of France. Alas, he was puny; but every effort would be made to keep him alive; and the Dowager Queen of Scotland could trust her ambitious family to keep their eyes open for the advantage. As for herself she was going to do everything in her power to get her daughter married into France – Greenwich agreement or not.

Cardinal Beaton was firmly behind her. He deplored the insidious advance of the Reformed religion. England was still Catholic in spite of the break with Rome. The only difference was the new head of the Church: the King in place of the Pope. In England, heretics – those who dabbled in the teachings of Martin Luther – were burned at the stake, while those who declared themselves for the Pope died the traitor's death. There was only one law in England – the King's will, and every Englishman must obey that law or lose his head.

Incensed by the treachery of those prisoners whom he had released and who had changed their allegiance once they were back in their native land. Henry sent a punitive army into Scotland under his brother-in-law Edward Seymour, Earl of Hertford. The Scots had broken faith with him, and they were in league with the French. English soldiers invaded the land across the Border. Edinburgh was pillaged, Holyrood Palace overrun. These were uneasy days for Mary of Guise who knew full well that one of the main objects of the invading armies was to seize the little Queen and carry her off below the Border.

There was another anxiety. Throughout Europe at this time the Reformed religion was being discussed often in secret. Cardinal Beaton, with the aid of the Queen Mother, was determined to keep Scotland loyal to the old faith. John Knox was already thundering away and denouncing the iniquities of the royal and sinful. Scotland was ripe for the Reformed faith; but Cardinal Beaton and his friends were determined to prevent its adoption. In 1546 George Wishart, one of the most prominent preachers of the Reformed faith, was arrested and, on the order of the Cardinal, burned at the stake for heresy. Wishart had been greatly admired for his religious way of life and his death gave the Cardinal's enemies the opportunity they were waiting for.

Beaton was living rather more luxuriously and voluptuously than his cloth warranted. At his castle of St Andrews he was said to be entertaining his favourite mistress. How significant to seize him while he was actually in bed with the lady. A party of lairds posing as workmen entered the castle, broke into his bed-chamber, stabbed him to death and, dragging his body from the apartment, exposed it in the most obscene manner they could think of outside the castle walls.

The Cardinal's murderers believed that having slain the Cardinal, who was clearly working for the French, Henry VIII would help them. But Henry did no such thing, and the French acted instead. They sent a punitive expedition to Scotland, laid seige to the castle, captured the murderers and took them to France, where they were severely dealt with and sent to the galleys. Among the prisoners was the fiery preacher, John Knox.

The year 1547 was a momentous one. During it two Kings died: Henry VIII and Francis I. The passing of these Kings changed a way of life in both countries. Little Edward, now a boy ten years old, was King of England; and Henry II had become King of France which meant that his sickly little first-born was the immediate heir to the throne. The anxious mother in Stirling Castle, well aware of the implications of the situation was more determined than ever on a French marriage; and her influential parents and brothers showed equal determination.

The new ruler of England was in fact the young King's uncle, Lord Hertford, who immediately delcared his intention of carrying on with the punitive expedition into Scotland, his idea being to bring the little Queen of Scots to England and in due course unite the two crowns. Scottish resistance was fierce and the climax was the battle of Pinkie Cleugh which resulted in a disaster to Scotland almost as great as those of Solway Moss and Flodden Field.

In the castle of Stirling, hearing of the rout, and that Hertford was within striking distance of Stirling Castle, the Queen Mother trembled for her daughter's safety.

At the centre of the storm was the little Queen. Although not yet five years old she must have begun to be aware of the conflict swirling about her. It was impossible for such a child to have a normal upbringing. She could not help learning at a very early age of her importance. She was too young at the time it had taken place to remember her coronation, but at the death of the Cardinal it was necessary for her to receive the oath of allegiance from the loyal lairds.

There, in the questionable safety of Stirling Castle, she, not yet four years old, was required to sit in the chair of state while hoary old chieftains knelt and kissed her hand – crafty, ambitious and treacherous men, such as Arran who was not clever enough to hide his longing to wear the crown, and her half-brother James Stewart who would have been in her place – and there would be many to say that a strong young man was a better proposition than a wee lassie – if his father had been married to his mother. Both Arran and James Stewart had their pretensions to royalty. There was Patrick, Earl of Bothwell, a wild giant who had long had his eyes on the widowed Queen Mother. Marriage with her would have been his way to power. There was George Douglas, condemned by many Scotsmen as a traitor, the diplomatic leader of the pro-English party in Scotland. Before the death of James he had been exiled in England and he took a prominent part in negotiating the proposed marriage between Prince Edward and Mary. He had been guilty of submitting plans of Scotland to English generals when they proposed an invasion of Scotland; and he was ever ready to come to terms with Scotland's greatest enemy. These were the men who knelt before the child in the chair, kissed her hand and cynically swore loyalty. Mary of Guise was well aware of the nature of these men and apprehensive, but doubtless to the little girl it was no more than a rather tiresome game.

In the castle of Stirling she had been provided with four

playmates who strangely enough were all named Mary and who were to become famous as the Four Maries. They were Mary Fleming, Mary Seton, Mary Beaton and Mary Livingston, and they had all been chosen because they were the children of influential houses.

Mary Fleming was the daughter of Janet Stewart, herself a natural daughter of James IV, and therefore had royal blood and was related to the little Queen. Her mother had married Lord Fleming and had been appointed governess to the four Maries.

Mary Beaton was one of the Cardinal's family; Mary Seton was the daughter of Lord Seton, one of the noblest of Scottish families; and Mary Livingston was the daughter of Lord Livingston. All these highly born little girls were therefore considered worthy to enter the royal hierarchy. But while they were in Stirling Castle they could have caught only a glimmer of the conflict and would only now and then be aware of the little Queen's importance. Doubtless they pursued their games of hide-and-seek and battledore and shuttlecock as noisily and carelessly as any others of their age.

Lady Fleming was a very pretty woman, by no means learned, for it was her birth rather than her scholarship which had earned her her important place in the Queen's nursery. She was frivolous, loved admiration and missed her husband Lord Fleming who was away with the army. She was to prove herself singularly lacking in discretion; and it seems highly probable that she must have betrayed to the Maries the true reason why they were shut up in Stirling Castle and never allowed to go beyond the castle walls. It is certain that the young Queen heard of the wicked English who were wreaking such damage on her country and who planned to carry her off to England to be with the little King of England, a sort of cousin who was destined to change the relationship to that of husband.

This was the situation in Stirling Castle at the time of the the battle of Pinkie Cleugh, when the English were advancing and were in fact within six miles of the castle. Lady Fleming was in despair because her husband was killed in that battle.

She was not a woman to control her distress, and it was after all little Mary Fleming's father who was dead, so the tragedy was brought into the royal household.

But the great shadow which hung over the castle was the proximity of Hertford's men. In the night, the little Queen awakened to learn that she was leaving Stirling. The haven was such no longer. Wrapped in a warm robe she was taken from her bed. Half asleep as she was, the adventure must have seemed to her like a dream in which the thudding horses' hooves mingled with the gentle swish of oars on water, then to be handed to a tall cowled figure with a kindly voice who bade her be at peace.

She had been brought to the island with the magical name of Inchmahome.

It is uncertain how long Mary spent on the island. Its hauntingly beautiful name, the fact that a defenceless child had ridden through the dark night to safety with a cruel army only a few miles distant, held all the ingredients for romance.

It may well have been that she was there only while the English Army was in close proximity; on the other hand it may have seemed wise to keep her on this island which was the last place her enemies would expect to find her. Inchmahome – set in the middle of Lake Menteith – is still surely one of the most romantic spots in Scotland. There could be found perfect peace. Who would have expected the little Queen of Scotland to be shut away in an ancient monastery with the old abbot and his monks? The English remained close at hand for some three weeks, but it seems likely that the Queen was kept at Inchmahome for longer than that; and the stories that there she began to learn French, Spanish and Italian under the monks' tuition, as well as Latin, may well be true. One imagines the Maries joining her there and playing their games round the old grey walls, charming the old monks with their childish ways and the Queen's beauty which was already becoming apparent. She must have loved that island with the enchanting name.

It was the following June when the envoy of Henry II landed

in Scotland – his object being to arrange for the voyage of the Queen of Scots to France.

The defeat at Pinkie Cleugh and the lack of cohesion between the Scottish nobles had convinced the Queen Mother that she needed immediate help from France. Her daughter was still safe in her care but the flight to Inchmahome following on the disastrous battle of Pinkie Cleugh was a warning. There was no time to be lost; they could not hope to be fortunate every time. Mary must be taken away to safety, and safety was France where she would be brought up in the French Court in a manner acceptable to her mother, with the prospect of a marriage into the royal family which would in time secure her the crown of France. The King of France would treat her as his daughter; she would be watched over by her ambitious and powerful relations, the Guises. The way was clear.

Mary of Guise loved her daughter dearly. To part with her would be a personal tragedy; but personal feelings must not be allowed to influence royal actions. She knew that Mary would sooner or later be captured if she stayed in Scotland; she would be taken to the English Court and who could guess what might become of her there? There was only one course open to the Dowager Queen. Her daughter must leave Scotland for France. It was a policy with which all those who wished Scotland well must agree.

So very shortly after her return from Inchmahome Mary Queen of Scots was on her way to France.

The French Court

The French Court at the time Mary came to be a member of it was dominated by the King's mistress, Diane de Poitiers. Living in the shadows, biding her time, as yet a woman of little influence but of great ambition, was Queen Catherine de' Medici, known as "The Italian Woman".

Diane was seventeen years older than the King – a charming cultured woman. Henry had suffered as the son of a brilliantly witty father. After the battle of Pavia he and his elder brother had been sent as hostages to Spain and had lived there for some four years. At the beginning of his captivity Henry was five years old. Those were impressionable years, and on returning to his father's Court he had had little French at his command, been gauche, unable to understand his father's wit and slow to think, in effect a dullard which was the very characteristic Francis I found most unattractive. His brother Francis, the Dauphin, being a little older, had been less affected by those years of captivity and on his return to the Court of France better able to adjust himself. Consequently Henry was left to himself; after all he was only the Duke of Orleans, the second son.

But there is a story which in view of the character of Francis I seems plausible. Anxious to put a veneer on this gauche son of his, it is said that the King provided him with a mistress who was older than himself, a cultured, experienced woman of the world, Diane de Poitiers. At the time her friendship with young Henry began, Diane was some thirty-one years old; Henry was just past fourteen. They were not lovers immediately but it was at that time that the tremendous fascination she exerted began.

Diane de Poitiers had, at the age of fifteen, been married to the Grand Sénéchal of Normandy, a man reputed to be one of the richest – and one of the ugliest – in France. He was at that time middle-aged and a widower. She had been noted then for her virtue; but there was a rumour that she had had one lover, the King of France himself. It seems hardly likely that this was the case, although Francis appears to have made advances.

The fact was that her father, the Count of Saint-Vallier, became involved in the Constable of Bourbon's conspiracy against the King. Bourbon escaped but Saint-Vallier was captured and imprisoned in the gruesome dungeons of Loches, and sentenced to death. Diane at this time – 1524 – had been married for eight years to the Sénéchal of Normandy and had borne him two daughters. She came to plead with the King for her father's life. As her father's life was spared, when Diane became the most important woman in France because of the utter devotion of Henry II, rumours were set in motion to the effect that she had become the mistress of Francis I in order to save her father's life. Edith Sichel quotes the evidence of a follower of Margaret of Angoulême (the sister to whom Francis was devoted) to the effect that it was solely Diane's eloquence, her prayers and tears which preserved her father's life. However, one version of the story – and one which seems possible – is that Francis offered Diane her father's life if she would become his mistress. Diane thanked the King and her father's sentence was commuted to one of imprisonment, but when Francis claimed his reward for clemency Diane pretended that she had misunderstood the King's meaning. Francis admired cleverness and it would have been characteristic of him to concede that she had outwitted him. The fact that Diane's father remained a prisoner for many years does suggest that there might be some truth in this story. And if it is a fact that Francis arranged for a woman to teach his son some of the graces expected of his rank, it seems likely that this clever woman would be the one he would choose.

Diane was even more attractive in her early thirties than she had been as a young girl. She had become a rich widow and had a reputation for chastity. She had poise, wit and experience of the world. She was just the woman to "tutor" the King's graceless son. It is easy to imagine that the young boy despised for his gauche manners was enchanted when this cultured, beautiful woman sought his company. Quite naturally he was very soon head over heels in love, and by the time his young bride Catherine de' Medici, a girl a few months younger than himself, arrived in France he had no eyes or thoughts for anyone but Diane.

History has given too little sympathy to Catherine, who found herself in a deeply humiliating position. Coached by her relatives, including the Pope, on the enormity of her good fortune and the need to provide heirs, she must have wondered how she could hope to succeed with a husband who showed no desire for her company. Moreover, she appears to have had a deeper regard for her husband than she ever felt for any other person throughout her life, with the possible exception of her son who became Henry III. But that was later, when as the Queen Mother she came into power for which she had worked all through the humiliating years – for humiliated she undoubtedly was; and it seems likely that some aspects of her complex and sinister nature began to form during those trying years. She was young, it was true; but even at the age of fifteen she possessed a Machiavellian quality; she appeared quiet, demure and eager to please, but she was biding her time. Displaying humility as though begging not to be reminded that she was merely the daughter of Italian merchants, a fact of which she was deeply aware, as she was of the honour done her by bringing her into the French royal family, she sought the favour of Francis I and gained it to a certain extent. She was piquant in his eyes and she flattered him with her humble devotion; and all the time she must have been praying for a child, knowing that her future depended on her supplying the heirs to the royal house.

Meanwhile Diane and Henry had become lovers. Far from this arousing public sympathy for Catherine, the young wife found that her position in the French Court was becoming more and more difficult. People simply did not like Catherine. She was an Italian and the French did not like foreigners, least of all Italians. She was barren; they had forgotten that she had brought a fortune with her and bemoaned the fact that there were no children. Henry occasionally did his duty but there were no results, and being in love with Diane he could not bear to tear himself away from her to sleep with his wife. He was becoming more confident; Diane had done her work well, and she had grown fond of him.

Henry, the Duke of Orleans, was at this time the second son; his brother Francis stood between him and the throne. When the Dauphin died suddenly and mysteriously Catherine de' Medici began to acquire the evil reputation which was to cling to her throughout her life.

The circumstances of the Dauphin's death were certainly strange. He had been playing tennis in the sun, and being thirsty had asked his cup-bearer to bring him a drink. It was well known that he drank only water and when this was brought he drank it and asked for another. Almost immediately he began to feel ill. He left the court for his bed and he never rose from it again. In a very short time he was dead.

During the sixteenth century, when a man or woman died suddenly the first thought was poison; and since by the Dauphin's death his brother Henry became Dauphin, and since Henry's wife was an Italian, certain conclusions were drawn. It was remembered that the Dauphin's cup-bearer was an Italian, so it seemed a foregone conclusion that the young man was a victim of an Italian plot to kill him and put the Italian Dauphiness on the throne.

Within a short time the cup-bearer, Count Sebastiano di Montecuculi, was arrested and submitted to the cruel torture of the boot, in which the feet were crushed, in the hope that he would incriminate his accomplices. And there was one accomplice whom the people wished to see incriminated more than any other: the Italian wife of Henry, who was now the Dauphiness. It was said she had every reason to have plotted the death of her brother-in-law. She had doubtless recommended the Italian cup-bearer to the poor dead victim and she stood to gain a crown by the young man's death. This would be remembered against her for as long as she lived. Whether or not she was involved in a plot to eliminate the Dauphin and thus make way for her ascent to the throne, one cannot be

34

certain. Montecuculi did not implicate her even under the direst torture. He confessed to his tormentors that two Spanish generals had given him instructions to kill the King and all his sons. This seemed absurd, but at least Catherine was not mentioned.

Later she was obliged to sit in the pavilion and watch the execution by quartering of the Italian cup-bearer, for it was the custom of the French Court to make a spectacle of these gruesome events. On this occasion each limb was tied to a wild horse; when this was securely effected a great fanfare of trumpets was blown causing the startled horses to gallop away, each carrying with it a part of the condemned man's body.

One imagines the covert glances that were turned on Catherine de' Medici sitting there beside her husband, who had now become Dauphin of France. The whispering campaign swelled against her. She was "The Italian Woman", the poisoner, who was on the way to becoming Queen of France. There was one fact, however, which could prevent her reaching this high eminence: she seemed unable to bear a child. In such circumstances a divorce could be arranged, for now that Henry was indeed heir to the throne it was imperative that he produce an heir.

Politics, which always played a big part in court affairs, came into this. As Catherine was related to the Pope, there were some who would like to see her replaced. Politically aware as she was, Catherine must have been at this period a very frightened woman. She had an ally in the King of France, but Francis was never a very reliable ally; and she would know him well enough to realize that even as he soothed her with comforting words he might well be planning to have her replaced. It seems that Diane, like most people at Court, was unaware of the cunning of the Dauphiness, and accepted the face which Catherine showed the world. It doubtless occurred to her that if Henry had a wife who was beautiful he could become attracted to her. Far better for him to continue with the Italian whom he clearly found somewhat repulsive. Diane it appears. decided that Catherine must stay, and the only way she could make her position secure was by bearing children. Diane took charge of Henry's domestic affairs with great effect when he became King, and as he confided in her completely she would understand as no one else could his feelings for his wife. Diane certainly appears to have arranged for Henry to spend more time with Catherine. The miracle happened. A year or so after the birth of the Queen of Scots, Catherine gave birth to a son. He was called Francis after his grandfather and although he was puny, Catherine had proved that she was capable of bearing children.

The bad luck was broken. She then began to produce children regularly, and between the years 1543 and 1556 she gave birth to ten. Three of them died – Louis and the twins Jeanne and Victoire. After Francis, the first-born, came Elizabeth and Claude, then Louis, Charles, Edward-Alexander (who was known as Henry and became Henry III), Margaret, Hercule (known as Francis on the death of his brother) and the twins Jeanne and Victoire. All but Claude and Hercule were to wear crowns. Elizabeth that of Spain through her marriage with Philip II (she was his third wife), Charles was Ninth of that name (the poor little mad King who is remembered for his part in the Massacre of St Bartholomew), Henry who was known for his love of his minions, and the even more notorious Margaret (*la Reine Margot* whose amatory exploits have delighted the readers of romantic history ever since).

The great point was that Catherine was secure in her position; her husband might dislike her, the people of France might hate her, but she was the mother of *les Enfants de France* and that meant that no one could shift her from her position.

She still suffered the humiliation of knowing that Henry merely tolerated her and was devoted to his mistress, who was becoming a great power in France and would wield the greatest possible influence with the Dauphin when he mounted the throne. A rumour persisted that Catherine took an apartment in the palace of Saint-Germain immediately above that of Diane de Poitiers, and that she had a hole made in the floor above Diane's bedroom through which she used to watch her husband and his mistress making love. Considering her devious nature and the complexities of her character it seems plausible. Accounts of her life are littered with eavesdropping, secret cabinets, working in the dark; and even when she came to great power she clung to these methods. To understand the nature of this strange woman who no doubt at times earned the name of poisoner (although many evil deeds have been laid at her door for which she could not possibly have been responsible), one must consider her upbringing in the Medici Palace, her separation from her cousin Ippolito whom she was reputed to have loved and hoped to marry, her arrival in France at the early age of fourteen, an unwanted bride, despised for her lack of royal birth, and the continual humiliation she was forced to suffer in those early years. Relying on her own considerable resources, forced to hide her true feelings, this clever and ambitious girl grew as her character dictated she should into one of the most sinister (one might say *the* most sinister) women in history.

This was the state of affairs in the fateful year in 1547. The King of England had died and this had its effect on the King of France. They had been young together; they had been constant enemies and all-important to each other since that period when they had feigned friendship and wrestled together (symbolically and actually) at the Field of Cloth of Gold. Francis I's health deteriorated. He was a victim (like his brother of England) of that disease prevalent among those whose lives were a succession of amatory adventures, suffering from what ironically his countrymen called *la maladie Anglaise* while on the other side of the Channel it was known as the "French disease". Francis knew that his end was near and as others before him he began to repent of his misdeeds. He began to weigh the advantages he had brought to France against the somewhat scandalous life he had led. He had encouraged writers, painters and musicians as few other monarchs ever had; he had made the Court of France the most intellectual in the world. He had scattered the countryside with châteaux which would be the admiration of generations to come. That surely would be recorded in his favour. But alas, his sins were great.

He was anxious too about his country; he was leaving this in the hands of a son whom he had always regarded as something of an oaf. Henry was a good soldier, it was true, and at last he had produced offspring. He had a clever little wife who was not attractive enough or skilled in the arts of love to win and hold her husband; but he had a clever mistress. And there were the Guises, that powerful family – the most ambitious in France – whose fingers were always in the political pie, and whatever loyalty they swore were constantly wondering how they could put the House of Guise where that of Valois now stood. Lying on his deathbed in the palace of Rambouillet he saw events more clearly than he had had time to during a life spent largely in the pursuit of pleasure. There was a little girl in Scotland – a Queen who was half Guise. That wily family would have plans for her. They wanted her for little Francis. They wanted to see her Queen of France as well as Scotland. He must warn Henry.

Time was running out. He sent for his eldest son. His last words were a warning to beware of the Guises, to be considerate to the sex which Francis had always loved and respected (his mother and sister were the two women to whom he owed everything, he knew, and in spite of his numerous amours he was more devoted to them than any others, so devoted that they had been known as "The Holy Trinity") but not to be ruled by them.

Then he died. Henry had become the King, Catherine the Queen; but the most important person in France was Diane de Poitiers. This was the state of the French Court when Mary Stuart became a member of it.

The Golden Days

When Mary left the peace of Inchmahome it was to be plunged into the bustle which preceded departure. And what a departure! To leave home to go and join a prospective bridegroom when one was not quite six years old was an ordeal even for royalty. Mary of Guise must have suffered agonizingly at the prospect of losing her daughter, for naturally she could not accompany her; her great comfort would be in the knowledge that her family would look after Mary.

The Guises were determined to dominate France for the King was no Francis I, and Queen Catherine, all believed at that time, counted for nothing. There was Diane, of course; but the Guise clan would be a match for any mistress whose position, by the very nature of her status, was insecure. It was that she was clever; that the King had been extraordinarily faithful to her for many years, but she was considerably his senior. Though she was still beautiful, she was nearly fifty and her power could not last forever. In the meantime their little protégée, the Queen of Scots, would marry the future King; and this alliance would give the family the hold over affairs they had long craved.

Reports of Mary must have excited her maternal relations. She was, by all accounts, a fascinating creature. Little Francis was not robust. So much the better, as long as he did not die. Francis *must* be kept alive and at the same time remain weak in character so that he could be dominated by his pretty little wife who in her turn would be dominated by her magnificent, brilliant, powerful family, the Guises.

Mary had been brought up to realize that even though she was the heiress of Scotland she was also a member of the House of Lorraine. The gold agraffe which held her scarf in place was engraved with the arms of that House as well as those of the Stuarts. She would have heard of the glories of France and no doubt Scotland suffered in comparison. At least Mary would believe that she was going to a superior country; she was also going to grandparents who loved her; and her uncle Francis of Guise must have sounded like one of the gods from Olympus. Moreover, a journey was always exciting; and she was to have with her four Maries and with them, as their governess, would travel Lady Fleming – Mary Fleming's mother, who had been with them in Scotland, that easy-going, rather frivolous, pretty young widow. The parting quickly became an exciting adventure for Mary. And indeed she was about to embark – not only for the shores of France but on the happiest period of all her life.

The Queen Mother accompanied her daughter to Dumbarton and handed her over to the care of the Sieur de Brézé who was to guard her with his life until she was handed over to the King of France. Like most Frenchmen he quickly became enchanted by Mary Stuart. With the party were three of her half-brothers, members of her father's numerous family of bastards: James, John and Robert. It is not difficult to guess at the thoughts of these ambitions young people who were there in the train of their little sister. Surely they resented the fact that because of a simple ceremony, she was their mistress whom they must swear to obey. Lords Livingston and Erskine, Mary's guardians, were also of the party.

The journey was a trying one and storms buffeted the ship as it sailed down the west coast of England. Mary appears to have been the only member of the party who did not suffer from acute sea-sickness. Lady Fleming was so ill that as they passed the coast of Cornwall she begged to be put ashore, declaring that she would rather face the wicked English than go on in her misery. The Admiral was in no mood to humour her; the rudder of his ship had been damaged in the violence of the storm and he was deeply concerned for his precious royal cargo; he told Lady Fleming peremptorily that she would either go to France or drown for he was certainly not putting her ashore. So poor Lady Fleming had no help but to continue in her wretchedness.

At last they reached the port of Roscoff in Brittany. Here Mary was indeed made welcome for the King of France had sent an order through his country that the Queen of Scots must be regarded as though she were already his daughter. It seems that Mary Stuart had only to appear to be adored. The people shouted *"Vive La Reinette"* as they had been commanded to; but it was obvious that they were very willing to welcome such a pretty creature to their shores.

Having arrived in Brittany she must make her journey across France. Mary either rode a small horse or was carried in a litter, and it must indeed have seemed to her like a glorious adventure. She was half French and she immediately felt a rapport with these people which she could not feel for the dour Scots. Through every town she went she was greeted with genuine pleasure and at Nantes she found a decorated barge waiting for her. It must have been a delightful voyage sailing up the Loire, passing the vineyards and towns and villages, through Anjou and Touraine.

At Tours she found her grandparents waiting for her: Claude, Duke of Guise, and his Duchess. Uncle Francis of Guise was not there. Her mother would most certainly have told her stories of this great man who was already famous throughout France. He was at this time, however, with the King and his armies. Grandmother Antoinette must have been quite formidable enough for Mary to cope with. One can imagine how their hopes soared when they first gazed on this enchanting creature on whose fragile shoulders rested the hopes of the House of Guise.

The Duchess immediately took charge and she did not think very highly of her grand-daughter's entourage. With the exception of the very pretty governess Lady Fleming, they were a dowdy crowd and she feared not over-clean, but it was clear that she was pleased with her grand-daughter. She intended to travel with the party and, as they progressed, tutor Mary into the ways of the French and do all in her power to groom the child for that important day when she should meet her future bridegroom – and more important still the occasion when she should be presented to the King of France.

It seems certain that Grandmother Antoinette primed Mary

on how she must behave. It was imperative that she charm the French. She must particularly like the Dauphin; she must take care of him because he was younger than she was and rather delicate, so she must not be rough with him, and so on.

The Court was at Moulins and the meeting with the children was to be at Carrières, with their governor and governess, the Maréchal and Madame d'Humières. The only children in the nursery at this time were Francis the Dauphin and Elizabeth who was three and a half. Claude and Louis (who was not to survive infancy) were too young to join the other two.

It must have been rather a touching scene when the children met. Mary, primed by her grandmother and perhaps feeling rather tender towards the frail little boy, won his heart by her kindness. From the moment they met the Dauphin loved Mary. It could rarely have happened that a royal prince was as delighted with his bride as this five-year-old boy was with his.

The Duchess of Guise would have felt very gratified when watching the children meet, for Elizabeth as a princess (though daughter of the King and Queen of France) must kneel to the Duchess' grand-daughter because she was a queen. There would certainly have been a subtle change in the manner of the Maréchal and Madame d'Humières; they would have always been eager to please the Guises but now even more so than before, for with the coming of the Queen of Scotland the great Guises had shown that they could become of even more significance than they were already.

Mary's charm even at this stage made itself felt. When studying her portraits it is difficult to understand this over-whelming attraction which made itself felt from her earliest years and which she seemed to have for everyone with whom she came in contact. We hear of the almond-shaped eyes, the glowing complexion, the abundant reddish-gold hair, but the pictures are disappointing and have little to distinguish them from those of other beauties of the day. But the fascination must have been there. It is continually referred to; later poets (for example Ronsard) wrote in glowing eulogies of her charms. The King of France on beholding her said: "This is the most perfect child I have ever seen". She became his darling and that of Diane; she was beloved of the Dauphin and adored by

Elizabeth. Not only did the King of France make this comment but Mary's uncle, the Cardinal of Lorraine, who was a connoisseur of women, declared that he had never seen anyone to rival her – noble or commoner. Yet this does not strike one in the portraits. It may well have been that, like another Queen of France, Marie-Antoinette, as ill-fated as Mary herself, the Queen of Scots possessed a charm which it was impossible for an artist to recapture. Her attraction doubtless lay in her vitality, her grace and an indefinable aura, which must be seen to be recognized.

She was an accomplished musician. Brantôme wrote that she possessed a sweet and rich voice and accompanied herself gracefully on the lute; and her elocution won admiration from the Court when she delived a Latin oration at the age of twelve. The glowing reports from all sides leave us in no doubt that Mary was unique in her charms. It was natural that the French who set great store on grace and charm should have adored her. Great good fortune had set her youth in France. She was, in any case, half French; and this Court with its airs and graces, its artistic finesse, its culture, was the rightful setting for Mary. All her luck came in the early years of her life. In after years there was nothing but ill luck. But as has been said by the poet whose commentaries on human nature are rarely to be disputed, the fault is not in our stars but in ourselves, and Mary's ill fortune and later years of tragedy can largely be traced to her own actions. She seemed to have a genius for making mistakes. Impulsive, uncalculating, she forms a great contrast to her kinswoman Elizabeth, who was to dominate the English scene and have such an effect on Mary's later life. The first of these mistakes was made in the nurseries before she was seven years old.

Diane de Poitiers had made herself aware of all that went on in the royal nurseries. The children's ailments, their education, their food, their general upbringing, was her affair. They were her lover's children, and everything that touched him was of the greatest moment to her. They were the children of France, and, in all but name, she was the Queen of France.

Catherine smiled in her docile manner, accepting the advice of Diane, but there can be no doubt that in private she ground her teeth in fury. What did she now plan when she watched the lovers through that hole in the floor? What vengeance did she brood on when she saw this woman take over the direction of her children? Knowing Catherine's character as later revealed when after Henry's death she did come to power, we can well believe that if it had been possible to slip what had become known as the *morceau italianisé* into Diane's wine it would have been done.

When the King visited the nurseries as he often did, for he was fond of children and popular with them, he was able to show his affection for Mary as a child, as men who are shy with adults often can. All his children loved him although they were all (perhaps with the exception of young Henry) terrified of their mother. They loved Diane too; and seeing her come to the nurseries with the King, Mary assumed that she was the Queen. Often she would have seen the entwined initials, which since the accession of Henry had been in evidence everywhere. These were two D's placed back to back and overlapping, and joined by a horizontal stroke to make an H – ⬚ – H and D to represent Henry and Diane. This was a sixteenth-century royal custom, and Henry VIII, for instance has left evidence of his brief loves in his various palaces; in his case, however, hardly was one pair of initials set up than new ones were needed. It was different with the faithful Henry II. He even had those initials on his clothes so anxious was he for the whole world to know in what esteem he held his mistress. The relationship between them was built on such a firm foundation that it was tantamount to marriage, and Henry wished everyone to know that that was how he regarded it. Thus it is likely to suppose that without giving the matter very much thought Mary accepted Diane as Queen.

The first meeting with Catherine was unfortunate. One version is that the Queen of France came into the nurseries without ceremony and stood quietly watching the children. Mary taking an instant dislike to her – as people did to Catherine – demanded to know if she realized she was in the presence of the Queen of Scotland. Catherine deflated Mary by asking if she was aware that *she* was in the presence of the Queen of France. Dislike was instantaneous. Mary had made a mistake which may well have had a lasting effect on her life.

It is interesting to imagine Elizabeth of England in a similar situation. One finds one is constantly comparing the two Queens; their position was not dissimilar; their characters as different as they possibly could be. Mary's emotions dictated her actions; Elizabeth's cool shrewd brain governed hers. Elizabeth lived through the most hazardous childhood and girlhood which could befall anyone – even in dangerous Tudor times – and survived very often through her own cool wits. Mary, the pampered darling of the French Court, was unprepared for the harsh future which was awaiting her. Had she been in Elizabeth's place she would never have lived through the dangers, yet Elizabeth emerged from near disaster to become the triumphant Gloriana, while Mary left her triumphs ill-prepared for harsh adult life. One feels sure that had Elizabeth been in Mary's place she would never have made an enemy of anyone as Mary did of Catherine de' Medici.

Having made that fatal mistake, it might have been supposed that instinct at least would have led Mary to rectify it, for neglected as she was Catherine was yet Queen of France. Mary, however, went from bad to worse. No doubt feeling secure in the doting approbation of the King, Diane, her bridegroom-to-be and her powerful family, she failed to see the significance of the woman who was to become as powerful – and far more deadly – than anyone else in France. Even after that first mistake Mary was overheard referring to Catherine as having no breeding and being merely the daughter of Italian merchants. No doubt she was thoughtless and too young to be blamed for this unkind outburst and touch of snobbery. But the insult was remembered by Catherine who promised herself that when the day came for her to repay it she would be ready.

Meanwhile Mary made the acquaintance of the uncles who were to have such an effect on her youth. The most important of these to her was the Cardinal of Lorraine, Charles of Guise. His elder brother Francis was the dashing hero. Dramatic and dominating, wearing his battle scars as though they were medals, he was known as *le Balafré* because of the scar on his cheek which he had received in battle. By a strange coincidence, his son Henry of Guise, even more handsome, equally dominating, destined to play his part in the history of France, was similarly scarred on the cheek and was known by the same sobriquet. It was to become at one time the most honoured name in France. Francis was ruthless and brutal, but he was a soldier of the sixteenth century so could scarcely have been anything else. It was because he was so often absent fighting his country's wars that his brother, the Cardinal, became Mary's mentor. The other Guise brothers, the Marquis of Elboeuf, the Cardinal of Guise (on whom this title was bestowed when Charles became Cardinal of Lorraine) and the Duke of Aumale (who married one of Diane de Poitiers' daughters), though distinguished in their way, were pale shadows of their two elder brothers. The family was the most ambitious in the land; every member of it possessed a vibrant vitality which was rare in the effete House of Valois. They were a race of rulers and none was more aware of their ability to govern than themselves. Thus they sought every opportunity to advance the numerous members of their family; and in their opinion the House of Guise-Lorraine stood equal with that of Valois.

At the time of Mary's arrival, Francis was head of the House in all but name for Duke Claude, Mary's grandfather, was ailing and soon to die; but Francis was the soldier and Mary's tuition was therefore entrusted to the second brother.

The Cardinal emerges as a somewhat sinister character. His features were clear-cut in the style of Greek heroes and he was more handsome than his flamboyantly virile brother Francis. He was cultured – a clever theologian, a brilliant scholar, linguist and statesman. He was a dandy who loved to surround himself by luxury; his linen was scented, his manners suave. He was a sensualist; and because of his extreme good looks and courtly manners he was very popular with women. He made full use of his popularity, and has been accused of an eroticism which he had developed to such an extent that he found it hard to satisfy with normal sensations, and was continually devising new methods of titilating his senses. This was the man who undertook to win Mary's confidence –

and he succeeded completely in doing so during the early years of her life in France. It is not surprising, in view of the Cardinal's reputation, that he has been accused of an incestuous relationship with Mary because it is clear that she adored him. Mary was susceptible to flattery. He was her beloved uncle; one can imagine the tender schemes between them; but it is impossible to accept the suggestion that the affection between them diverged from that which conforms to the standards set down as respectable between an uncle and his niece. The Cardinal was too much of a Guise to imperil the family's ambitions for the sake of a new sensation. Between them he and his brother Francis intended to govern France and they were going to do it through this enchanting little girl from Scotland.

So the Cardinal undertook Mary's education; he won her affection by his own tenderness and exerted all his considerable charm. He would have made her realize the importance of her family; he would impress on her that her duty was to enslave the Dauphin which she was doing successfully. Francis, who was so sickly, already doted on her; and although he was inclined to be peevish and, aware that he was the future King of France, perhaps somewhat arrogant, he could always be subdued by Mary, and it was clear that he was never happy when she was not with him. Excellent progress had been made by the child, and all she had to remember was to go on dominating the Dauphin and to do everything that Grandmother and Uncles told her to. Then she would be a good little Dauphiness when the time came – and in due course a Queen – and what was more important a worthy member of the House of Guise.

Mary was eight years old when her mother paid a visit to France. Mary of Guise was received royally by the King and was delighted to see that her daughter was growing into such a charmer. Mary's manners had improved under the guidance of Uncle Charles and her affection for her maternal family was gratifying. For a year Mary of Guise enjoyed the amenities of the French Court and very sadly returned to dour Scotland where the seeds of future trouble were being lavishly sown.

Before she left the French Court, a rather alarming incident occurred. An archer of the guard was arrested and accused of attempting to poison the Queen of Scots. The man confessed to this. It is a mysterious affair and it is not clear who were the instigators of such a plot or indeed whether there even was one. There was a hint that Robert Stuart (who was quite a different person from the Queen's brother of the same name) was an English spy. Although the matter is wrapped in obscurity, we do know that Robert Stuart suffered a traitor's death by being hanged, drawn and quartered. Precautions for Mary's safety were strengthened; and, since the death of the first Dauphin and the execution of the cup-bearer Montecuculi, whenever the word poisoner was mentioned, people looked to Queen Catherine. However, there seems no reason for Catherine to have wanted to be rid of Mary at this stage, save personal dislike, and Catherine was never a woman to allow personal grudges to come between her and good political sense. Her revenge on Diane – when she was in a position to take it – was in the circumstances a very mild one.

About this time Diane fell ill and returned alone to her beautiful château of Anet, there to recuperate doubtless because she would not wish her lover to see her looking anything but her best, and although he was devoted enough to follow her there, on this occasion he did not do so.

Anet, one of the most beautiful châteaux in France, had been built by that most brilliant of architects, Philibert de l'Orme. Situated in the valley of the river Eure it was accessible by barge. Diane had beautiful taste, and in the early days of their relationship Henry had found more peace there than anywhere in the world. It had been his favourite spot in those days, and as he was almost always a faithful man it probably remained so. Diane's colours, which the King wore on every possible occasion, were black and white, and these were in evidence through the château.

The King was melancholy and as it turned out Diane might have been wise to allow him to accompany her even though she was not well enough to entertain him in her accustomed manner. Mary's governess, Lady Fleming, had caught the King's eye from the first and he had always been exceptionally gracious to her. Pretty as she was, although not over-endowed

48

mentally, she was the type to appeal to the King when Diane was away. She bore no resemblance to that clever woman, of course, but Henry would not be looking for a pale shadow of his incomparable goddess. However, he was in great need of comfort and finding a willing collaborator in the frivolous Fleming he indulged in rare infidelity to Diane. This would have passed the time pleasantly until Diane's return to Court; but there were to be results. Lady Fleming discovered herself to be pregnant. She had never been noted for her discretion; nor was she very far-seeing. It is reported by Brantôme, that gossipy recorder of the times, that she boasted of her condition and announced in her Scottish-French: "God be thanked. I am with child by the King and very honoured and happy about it." She gleefully added that the royal blood must contain some magic for she felt in such glowing health.

At last it must have seemed that the power of Diane was waning. And it is in this incident that the strange character of Catherine emerges. A lesser woman might have been unable to resist crowing over the apparent downfall of a hated rival; not so Catherine. She did not wish to see Diane replaced by a frivolous, indiscreet Scottish beauty. Diane conducted her life with the King in the most discreet manner possible. Catherine was clever enough to know that the displacement of Diane by a succession of mistresses (for Lady Fleming would certainly not be able to hold the King), could prove a great trial to her; so she and Diane put their heads together. The King, with the return of Diane, showed only a desire to be back on the old terms with his beloved mistress, the lapse forgotten and forgiven. Diane immediately forgave and forgot; but Catherine and Diane agreed that Lady Fleming must be banished to Scotland. So she was, where she gave birth to the King's illegitimate son who became known as the Bastard of Angoulême.

It was Catherine's custom to distil the utmost benefit from anything that might befall from this incident and she saw the possibility of replacing the flighty Fleming by a governess of her own choosing who could act as her spy in the royal nurseries. This was the first little cloud that had appeared since Mary's arrival in France: the loss of Lady Fleming –

gay, frivolous, flirtatious and lenient – for the sly Madame de Paroys who was without doubt the Queen's woman. Mary protested, but after having received such help from Catherine over the delicate matter of Lady Fleming's dismissal which had helped so much to mitigate the scandal, the King and Diane graciously permitted her to have this concession.

The Fleming affair had ended in a small – a very small – triumph for the Queen; Diane's position had suffered not a whit. She had emerged as the tolerant mistress who understood full well that her lover had needed this trivial diversion while she recovered from her indisposition. The King's devotion had not diminished; the letters H and D glowed as brightly as ever.

Even the surveillance of Madame de Paroys could not for long cast a shadow on that golden childhood, and as she grew to her teens Mary was regarded as one of the brightest ornaments of the Court. Poets wrote their verses to extol her charms. Young Charles conceived a wild passion for her – everything Charles did was wild for his mind showed signs of the taint of madness from his early childhood – and he would be aware that if his elder brother died it might well be that the powerful Guises would choose him as their niece's bridegroom. He was eight years younger than Mary – but what was age in royal marriages? The Guises had made up their minds that Mary was to be Queen of France.

The Court was a hotbed of intrigue kept in rein by the character of the King and the steadiness of his devotion to Diane de Poitiers. The poets of the day flourished there; and two of them, Ronsard and du Bellay, had been chosen to be literary tutors in the royal nurseries. It was apparent that Mary was the favourite pupil, for apart from that all-conquering charm she had some literary ability. Her beauty inspired the poets and Ronsard wrote a verse commanding his eyes to be contented for they had never seen, nor ever would see, anything in the world to equal the beauty of the Queen of Scots.

A coterie of poets had been formed under the name of the Pléiade led by du Bellay and Baïf. They had decided to make

France the centre of literature. They had in the beginning of their movement suffered great hardship, but having been discovered and some of their members being brought to Court they were enjoying the fruits of fame and the royal patronage. Mary was the darling of this group.

The royal children who were her companions in the schoolroom were beginning to show marked characteristics – Francis's weakness and reliance on Mary had been apparent from the beginning, but this intensified as he grew older; Elizabeth and Claude were the most normal of the children and close friends of Mary; Charles would suddenly break into a frenzy and kick his dogs and servants, after which he would often repent and sink into deepest melancholy; Edward-Alexander, whom his mother always called Henry and who was indeed to become Henry III, already showed signs of effeminacy and bore a strong resemblance to his mother. He was her favourite; he looked Italian and that set him apart from the other children. He liked to adorn himself with jewels and was fond of wearing ear-rings. Catherine on occasions betrayed her emotions as far as he was concerned, as she had in the case of her husband. Her two Henrys appear to be the only two people who ever touched her heart. The rest were counters in a game to be moved this way and that according to the most advantage they could give her.

The most fascinating person in the nursery – next to Mary and later she might be said to have been more so – was Margaret, nicknamed Margot. Margot was at this stage quite young but already showing signs of her turbulent, passionate nature. Margot was a rebel; she was precocious and her vivacity vied with Mary's charm. The other member was Hercule (who took the name of Francis on the death of his brother, and later became Duke of Alençon), too young as yet to make much impact. But the children were growing up; under the surveillance of those ever watchful Guises, the health of Francis began to give them great concern. They despised the boy while admitting his weakness was an asset. What they needed for their beloved niece was a sickly young fellow, entirely dependent on his wife; but life was essential; and Charles, the next on line, was too young and unstable –

not that madness in itself would have been considered a drawback, for a wife was no less a Queen because she had a mad husband. The ideal husband for Mary was, however, weak Francis, yet sometimes his health was so poor that it seemed as though death might beckon at any moment. The Guises decided the marriage must take place without delay.

The marriage would be entirely to the glory of the Guises, and Diane and Catherine could see no great advantage to themselves from it. The last thing Catherine wished was to see the powerful family become more so. The King was inclined to feel more friendly towards her at this time. She had behaved with the utmost decorum over the case of Lady Fleming and had in fact taken upon herself the delicate task of dismissing the woman; moreover, now that they had so many children it was not necessary for him to share her bed as it once had been, a fact which made her more tolerable to him. Catherine was able to point out to her husband that the Guises were anxious for the marriage for their own glory, but the Dauphin and Mary were children as yet. To marry them might be to spoil that tender companionship which was charming. The King agreed. His character comes over clearly as a family man. Before he came under Diane's influence he had been inclined to be timid and rather sullen; but Dandolo of Venice wrote of him at the age of twenty-three: "He has a presence which is passing comely and he is rather tall than short, neither stout nor thin, but so well-knit that one would think he is all muscle ... He hath a nature which one cannot but call taciturn and sombre. Rarely doth he laugh or give sign of laughter and those at court assure me that they have not seen him laugh a single time." He could, however, laugh with the children; and as he grew older he showed a strength of character which was formidable, and his Court was far more respectable than that of his father. It was true he was unfaithful to his wife, and his mistress was the first lady of the Court; but such an example did the King and his mistress set that it had its effect on those about them. Henry was a man of simple tastes, and for his times a good man, though unimaginative, bigoted in religious matters and lacking the graces of his father. He was always courteous to women and would not allow coarse conversation or so-called jokes in their presence.

A few years after Dandolo set down the above of him Cavalli wrote "He is of robust constitution but of a melancholic humour." So that trait in his character appears to have persisted. But went on the observer: "He is no *beaudiseur* in his repartees but he is most clear-cut and firm in his opinions." From these eye-witness accounts his character emerges more clearly than usual, largely because of his uncomplicated nature, and there is no doubt of his love for children and theirs for him.

Henry knew that the marriage would be no fearful ordeal to the boy who had been brought up with his young bride and obviously adored her, but in view of the sickly condition of Francis, the marriage could not be consummated; therefore it seemed better to wait. This displeased the Guises; and it was a situation they could not allow to continue. The clever Cardinal therefore prepared a scheme which he laid before the King. Mary was the Queen of a country which it was true was scarcely a prosperous one, but a country nevertheless. It was the gateway to the old enemy England and, all things considered, a rich prize. It was ready to fall into the King's hands. Mary's signature on a few documents could make it his. But a marriage would be necessary.

The King of France was an ardent Catholic and religion was important to him. The Cardinal of Lorraine pointed out that the vitriolic preacher John Knox – freed from the galleys and back in Scotland – was preaching hell-fire against the Church of Rome. The Protestant party was stronger in Scotland than almost anywhere else in the world. James Stewart, the Queen's bastard brother, most certainly had his eye on the crown. He was supported by some of the most powerful men in Scotland, Argyll, Erskine, Morton, to name a few. Was the King of France going to stand aside and watch heretics take command of the domains which belonged to his little daughter of Scotland when by a marriage ceremony he could make himself ruler of the barbaric northland of that enemy island?

The King saw the point. The wedding must take place. Mary had passed her fifteenth birthday; the Dauphin was a year or so younger; she could be counted marriageable even if he were a little young. He salved his conscience and the necessary documents were prepared.

The public marriage document which Mary signed on 19th April 1558 guaranteed the independence of Scotland; but on the 4th of that month Mary had put her signature to three other documents which robbed the public one of its validity. In the first she agreed that in the event of her death without heirs, Scotland would pass to France; in the second she assigned the revenues of Scotland to the King of France until he had recovered the money he had spent in defence of that country; and in the third she renounced any agreement which contradicted what she had agreed to do in the two previous declarations.

By signing these Mary disposed of rights which were not hers to dispose of. Mary cannot be blamed entirely for what happened. It may be said that she knew very well that she was a Queen and that a Queen had responsibilities; we have heard eulogies of her intelligence so it was clearly not beyond her power to grasp the meaning of a case set out quite lucidly; she should have known that she was signing away her birthright – and that of which she had no right to dispose. One must remember, however, that her beguiling uncle the Cardinal of Lorraine had asked her to put her signature to these documents. She trusted him absolutely. Had not her kind uncles Francis and Charles, her beloved grandmother Antoinette, watched her interests, guided her, loved her, worked only for her good – and theirs? Why should she not believe that in signing these documents she was doing what was right for herself, her family, for France and for Scotland? For even if she knew that she was giving Scotland to the crown of France it would seem to her that it was very good for Scotland to be placed under the control of such a great country as France with such a good and benevolent man as its King.

The wedding was naturally celebrated at the Cathedral of Notre-Dame. Mary's wedding garments were a masterpiece of *haute couture*, but so heavy, studded as they were with priceless gems, that she could scarcely carry them. Her wedding dress was made of white damask, decorated with jewels. Her mantle and train were a subtle mingling of blue and grey and in velvet decorated with pearls. As if this were not enough for her shoulders to support, a crown of gold was placed on her head containing diamonds, pearls, sapphires, and rubies; in the centre was suspended a carbuncle which was worth 500,000 crowns. So it was a weighty fortune that Mary carried on her person that day. Brantôme wrote: "She appeared a hundred times more beautiful than a goddess".

The royal family spent the night at the palace of the Archbishop of Paris; and from there they made their way to the cathedral. A gallery had been set up between palace and cathedral to make the way easy; and it was the King himself who led her along this gallery holding her right hand while her kinsman the Duke of Lorraine held her left. The King of Navarre led in the Dauphin and they were followed by the Dauphin's brother Charles, who must have been feeling envious as he himself loved Mary, and Edward-Alexander (Henry) who would enjoy the occasion because already he had betrayed a passionate love of clothes and jewellery, and like everyone else would have been particularly finely clad on that occasion.

At the door of the cathedral Mary stood beside her future husband. The King gave the wedding-ring to the Cardinal of Bourbon and there in the open, that the crowds of spectators might see, the ceremony took place; and Mary Stuart, Queen of Scotland, became Dauphiness of France.

In the Archbishop's palace a banquet had been prepared for them and immediately after the ceremony they returned there to enjoy it. Because the crown was so heavy the King commanded two of the gentlemen to relieve her of it; and because this might be construed as a symbolic gesture he ordered them to hold it over her head while she ate.

A ball followed and this was opened by Mary with the King as her partner while her husband danced with his mother. the ball went on until four o'clock in the afternoon when the company made its way to the Palais de Justice, Mary being carried there in a litter of cloth of gold. She was so beautiful that the people proclaimed her rapturously. They cheered the King who looked magnificent on his splendidly caparisoned horse; there were no cheers for Queen Catherine, but there never had been for "The Italian Woman" and she had long grown resigned to her unpopularity. The greatest cheers of all were for the handsome Duke of Guise – the hero of Metz, which he had held for France against the might of the Emperor Charles V, and at which he had distinguished himself as one of the greatest generals of his time. With his scarred face and dominating personality *le Balafré* caught the romantic imagination of the people of Paris. And because Mary was his niece and she was the most beautiful girl in France this was a very popular wedding.

A grand entertainment awaited them at the Palais de Justice where there was another banquet to be followed by games and masques. There was a special display by children which was led by young Henry of Guise, the exceedingly handsome son of the Duke (who in his turn would be *le Balafré*). The young Princes Charles and Edward, with other members of the Guise family, rode on hobby-horses; these were pulled across the ballroom by lackeys in dazzling livery and brought to a halt before the bride and bridegroom, where the children sang in their high-pitched voices of the virtues of marriage in general and of this marriage in particular.

The highlight of the evening was the arrival of galleons which appeared to sail over the ballroom floor; they had sails of silver gauze which fluttered as though stirred by a breeze; a cloth had been laid on the floor painted to look like the sea. The same splendid liveried lackeys drew the galleons along; in the first of the ships the King was seated and beside him was an empty chair. When the galleon came to where Mary was sitting it stopped; the King held out his hand to her; she took it and stepped on to the galleon and took her seat beside the King. The idea was that each galleon should contain a prince and this prince should select the lady of his choice to sit beside him. In the next galleon was the Dauphin who chose his mother. It was a certainty that he had been told to do this, for like all her children – except her favourite Edward-Alexander – he was afraid of her, and it was a fear which persisted to the day he died; the Prince of Condé chose the Duchess of Guise and the Duke of Lorraine the Princess Claude; the King of Navarre unconventionally chose his own wife, the valiant

56

Jeanne of Navarre. And the galleons rode over the painted floor cloth no doubt to the wonder of all and the gratification of the Duke of Guise who had organized the pageant.

It must have been rather a wearying day for the royal bridegroom whose health was so delicate; for after the pageant there were songs of praise to the royal pair to be listened to, many of them poems by du Bellay, Ronsard and other distinguished poets.

The Commissioners of Scotland, who had travelled to France to witness the marriage, must have been amazed at all this splendour, as they would never have seen anything like it in Scotland. Mary with her French clothes and French manners would have become a foreigner to them. Their comments would certainly have been critical. Mary's half-brother James was present. It was some ten years since they had met; and while she had grown into a beautiful young girl he had become an ambitious man. It is certain that her mentor, the Cardinal, would have warned her not to mention the documents she had signed and perhaps for the first time she became a little uneasy as to what she had done. This could have made for a certain constraint even if the contrasting atmosphere of the two societies in which she and her brother lived had not set them far apart.

A very unfortunate incident occurred. Before the Scottish delegation reached home they were affected by a mysterious illness. Four out of nine of them died and the others were very ill, Mary's brother James amongst them. Such tragedy was bound to set rumours in action and many people in Scotland suspected that the French had poisoned these gentlemen. Later, when it was discovered that Mary had signed a secret treaty with the French, the belief that the Commissioners had been poisoned grew.

Meanwhile the bride and groom went off to the château of Villers-Cotterets and it seems were delighted to be alone there. Mary, however, who since she had entered her teens had become rather delicate in health, developed mysterious pains and a cough. She ate heartily, perhaps too heartily, and she suffered from occasional fits of fainting.

The Cardinal was very eager for the marriage to be fruitful

57

and appears to have been unable to curb his impatience because they were so young and he feared that the Dauphin was not capable of consummating the marriage, for he arrived at Villers-Cotterets to see how the honeymoon was progressing and promptly cast a shadow over it. Mary loved this uncle passionately, but the Dauphin feared him as much as he feared his mother. One imagines the sly innuendos, the probing that ensued; and the poor Dauphin's embarrassment and resentment because he was not allowed to be alone with his beloved Mary and be happy in a way which was agreeable to them both.

The Cardinal was often angry with the Dauphin and often impatient with him. On one occasion he referred to him as a lily-livered timorous girl masquerading as a man. On another he exclaimed: *"Voilà le plus poltron coeur que fut jamais"*. His contempt must have been great for the boy was destined to be King of France and was in fact to attain that position much earlier than anyone anticipated, but so confident was the Cardinal of his niece's ability to rule her young husband and his own to rule her, that he gave vent to his exasperation.

Another visitor to Villers-Cotterets was the King. He was much more welcome than the Cardinal, at least in the Dauphin's eyes. But he too was concerned by the sickness of Mary and his puny son. As a soldier he believed that physical exercise and discipline with plenty of fresh air was a cure for all ills as far as men were concerned. To the Dauphin's dismay he was ordered to join the camp at Amiens, and to compensate Mary for the loss of her husband, her four Maries were sent to join her at Villers-Cotterets.

The honeymoon was over.

Adieu France

In November 1558 there was great excitement at the Court of France. Mary Tudor, Queen of England, had died and her half-sister Elizabeth had been proclaimed Queen. To the Guises Elizabeth's accession was a usurpation. According to their reckoning the crown of England belonged to their niece Mary Stuart. The conflict which was to last throughout Mary's life had begun.

Francis of Guise wanted to raise an army and take it into England and there wrest the crown from Elizabeth. The King was also a soldier and his vision was clearer since it was not misted by ambition. While agreeing that Mary should bear the title Dauphiness of France, Queen of England, Scotland and the Isles, he would not go to war on such an issue.

The French held that the daughter of Anne Boleyn was illegitimate. Henry VIII had been married to Katherine of Aragon when she was born and his marriage to her mother was no true marriage. Henry's contention that the marriage with Katherine of Aragon was invalid because she had consummated her marriage with his brother Arthur was absurd. Elizabeth was a bastard. Mary Stuart on the other hand was in the direct line of descent from Henry VII, whose daughter Margaret Tudor had married James IV of Scotland. Their son was James V whose daughter was Mary Queen of Scots. Henry VIII had had only two legitimate children – Mary Tudor by Katherine of Aragon and Edward VI by Jane Seymour. Both of these children had ruled England and neither had left heirs of their bodies; the next heir to the succession was therefore Mary of Scotland.

As the King would not consider military action they must

content themselves with displaying Mary's title as Queen of England wherever possible. One can imagine the effect on Elizabeth when she heard that Mary was using the title which she considered to be hers. But at that time it must have seemed of no great importance to Mary who would not understand the enmity being built up against her. She must have visualized spending the rest of her life in her beloved France which was home to her as nowhere else could ever be. Elizabeth of England was far away.

The year 1559 was a fatal one for France. The first event to take place was the marriage of Claude to the Duke of Lorraine which was accompanied by the splendid pageantry necessary to a daughter of the royal house. She was only twelve years old and the marriage would not be consummated until later, but the Guises were eager to have the matter settled. Poor Elizabeth, aged fourteen, was less happy: she was to marry Philip of Spain, for now that Mary Tudor was dead he needed a new wife. A fearful ordeal lay before her and how she must have envied Mary and Claude who could marry and stay at home. For Philip of Spain had the reputation of being something of an ogre and she would have remembered hearing that her father had spent several years in a Spanish prison whither he had been sent as a hostage for his father Francis I.

It was a year of marriages. Margaret, the King's sister, for whom marriage was long overdue, became affianced to the Duke of Savoy. Thus there were to be very special celebrations at the Court of France for there would be two royal weddings. On 21st June Elizabeth was married by proxy – the Duke of Alva standing in for Philip.

The 30th June was the fatal day. What happened came as a shocking surprise to everyone – although Catherine de' Medici who dabbled in the occult was said to have had a premonition of disaster. The King delighted to joust; he was an excellent exponent of the art and found it very difficult to tear himself away from the lists.

A few days before the jousts arranged as part of the celebrations took place, Catherine de' Medici had received an intimation from her astrologer Nostradamus. He had a recurring dream, and recently it had come more frequently and was more vivid. In the dream two lions were fighting. They fought once and rested. One of the lions was young, the other older. They fought a second time and the young lion gouged out the eye of the older lion who died from the wound. As the King's escutcheon was engraved with a lion Nostradamus concluded that this dream referred to him and wrote to Catherine begging her to watch over her husband and not allow him to court danger.

Catherine is said to have possessed that power now known as extra-sensory perception. Astrology in the sixteenth century was regarded as a science and Catherine had brought the Ruggieri brothers with her from Italy and in 1556 had sent for Nostradamus that he might cast the horoscopes of her children. With such respect did she regard the prophecies of these men that she caused a tower to be built for them in Les Halles, and she often went there to consult them. On this June day of the year 1559 she was very uneasy for she was filled with premonitions of disaster which because of the prophecy she associated with her husband.

Crowds had gathered in the rue Saint-Antoine close to the Bastille. When Mary arrived the heralds cried: "Make way for the Dauphine of France and Queen of England, Scotland and the Isles." Catherine and Diane were present, and there was great cheering when the people's hero, *le Balafré*, gave a good account of himself. The Count of Nassau and William of Orange who had come to France in the suite of the Duke of Alva also performed, but the great moment was when the King himself prepared to joust, wearing the black and white colours of his mistress. He had always been particularly skilled and had won great admiration for his performances in the lists, and the people were naturally eager to see him. He broke lances with the Duke of Guise, his sister's bridegroom of Savoy and the Count of Montgomery, a young man who came from Normandy but had Scottish connections. Montgomery was highly skilled in the art of jousting. The King challenged him to break a second lance. By this time Henry was quite clearly showing signs of fatigue and Montgomery, aware of this, begged to be excused, whether because he himself had a premonition, or was aware of the uneasiness of the Queen, or because he feared that the King, being much older than he was and having already taken on some of the most noted jousters at the Court, might be severely vanquished by him, is not known. Whatever the reason, he did beg to be excused. Catherine then asked the King not to joust, but he had never taken much notice of her; and he commanded Montgomery to do his bidding. This command of course Montgomery must obey.

The two opponents rode into the lists; skilfully they broke their lances; but Montgomery accidentally struck the King's helmet, raised his visor and a splinter entered Henry's eye. The King fell forward, blood pouring from his wound.

He was carried to the Hôtel des Tournelles where he lived only ten days – for his brain had been damaged – hovering between great pain and blessed unconsciousness. He died bravely, as was to be expected of this great soldier, and he insisted that Montgomery should in no way be blamed for what had happened. Montgomery was a Protestant and Henry had persecuted Protestants with great harshness; so the young man naturally was suspected. But the King's determination that he should not be blamed and the fact that many people had witnessed Montgomery's reluctance to fight, saved him. It was finally agreed that the King's death was a terrible accident and this was one of the occasions when foul play could not, with reason, be suspected.

Catherine grieved genuinely. There is evidence that this strange woman really loved her husband. Mary wrote to her mother in Scotland. "She is plunged in such grief for the loss of the late King, that I fear her misery will give her a bad illness." Catherine had the walls of her apartment and her bed covered in black and her bedchamber was lighted only by two wax tapers. From that day she adopted the motto *Lachrymae hinc, hinc dolor*, ("Hence the tears, hence the pain"), referring to the lance which had killed Henry. She did, however, break the custom of remaining six weeks in solitude in her apartments. She might be a grief-stricken widow, she was also an ambitious woman. Her sickly son was King of France and Mary, niece of the Guises, was Queen. The power of the

Guises would be greater than it had ever been before and they would have to be watched. But it seemed unlikely that Francis would live long and on his death the crown would pass to his brother Charles who was at that time nine years old; there seems no doubt that she had decided to make this boy her creature; she had it in her power to mould a King of France, to be to him what the Cardinal of Lorraine was planning to be to Francis through Mary. The thought of power to one who had suffered great humiliation must have been exceptionally sweet, and helped to soothe her grief. With what joy she must have contemplated revenge on Diane and made her plans to mould a little King.

She began with Diane. Almost before the King was dead she banished her rival to Anet and demanded the return of the crown jewels and all the costly presents which the King had bestowed on her. It is significant that Catherine appeared to have kept a careful record of these. She determined also to have Chenonceaux, the beautiful château which Henry had given to Diane.

With the tragic death of Henry II Catherine de' Medici had come to power.

People said that there would now be three kings of France: Francis of Valois, who would wear the crown, and Francis of Guise and his brother the Cardinal of Lorraine who would be the true rulers. It may well be that the flat-faced sallow Italian woman promised herself that the situation would not endure for long.

The great nobles of France assembled to pay homage to the new King. His Queen was beside him, his mother behind him; and as they left the chamber Catherine stood aside for Mary to go ahead of her – a significant gesture. She, who had been Queen of France, was now the Queen Mother; Mary Stuart, Queen of Scotland, who called herself Queen of England, was now also Queen of France.

Mary took the crown with reluctance. The carefree days were at an end. To be the petted Dauphine, beloved of all with the poets making verses to her beauty, contemplating a distant future when she would be Queen of France – that was very pleasant. The reality was something less.

Francis was frightened; frightened of his mother, frightened of the Cardinal of Lorraine, frightened of being King. He relied completely on Mary and was never happy unless she was beside him.

The Guises had taken over control – Francis of the Army, the Cardinal of the State. The great desire of their family had been to make itself the royal House of France. Already the reigning monarchs were Valois and Guise. The children born of the marriage would be brought up as true Guises and already the members of their family were in key posts about the Court. There must be children; but how could there be? Francis was a child in physique; his vital organs were not normally formed; he could not beget a child. All his life he had not been expected to live but the Cardinal of Lorraine appears to have been of the opinion that Francis could be bullied into virility.

The Cardinal had vowed to the Duke of Alva that he would rid France of its heretics; and the Huguenots had been persecuted since the death of Henry II even more than they had been during his reign. This was due to the Cardinal. He did not enjoy the popularity of his brother Francis who only had to appear to be cheered. Indeed, with the accession of Francis II, the Cardinal became one of the most hated men in France. A favourite pastime of the age was the making of anagrams on famous names and those which were inspired by the name Charles de Lorraine give a good idea in what odium he was held. One was *Renard lasche le roi* ("Fox, let go of the King") and another *Hardi larron se cèle* ("The bold robber hides"), and these were often shouted at the Cardinal when he appeared in public places. To be referred to as a fox and a thief would certainly have impaired the dignity of that very fastidious gentleman. But of even greater concern was his fear that some harm would befall him. He went in trepidation that there would be an attempt to assassinate him and wore a padded suit beneath his Cardinal's robes in order that he might have some protection from an assassin's knife. He was terrified that wide cloaks might hide some weapon; so he ordered that cloaks should not be worn wide and merely cover the person, so that it would be noticed at once if anything was hidden beneath them. High boots had been worn wide also and these he ordered to be made to fit the leg. Power had brought fear into his life.

Mary must have realized at this time that the man whom she had adored during her childhood was not all he had seemed. The cynical Cardinal is suspected of suggesting Mary get herself with child by a lover. It would not have been difficult. Half the Court was in love with her.

It is a sinister picture that emerges from the Court of France at that time. The Cardinal determined to rule France with his brother; the Queen Mother watching from the shadows. What were Catherine de' Medici's feelings at this time? The picture had changed as certainly for her as for anyone else. She had not yet come into power – the Guises stood between her and that – but in a few steps she could take it. One person stood in her way – a weak and silly boy; her own son. For if Francis died, the power of the Guises would die with him. His brother Charles would be King – a boy not ten years old – and to whom would he turn? He must be made to turn to his mother.

Catherine had not yet really taken a great revenge on Diane. How apprehensively Diane must have waited for the blows to descend; and how Catherine – for she was a vengeful woman – must have laughed. How much more effective to keep Diane waiting to know what ill fortune would befall her. It was at this time that Catherine's true character began to be apparent. She was not the woman to take revenge for revenge's sake; she was too power-conscious for that. Diane was connected through the marriage of her daughter with the Guises and the Guises were all-powerful at the time, but that would not be forever. Catherine contented herself with Chenonceaux – one of the loveliest châteaux in the whole of France.

Diane had loved Chenonceaux dearly, and had often entertained Henry there. Now she had to hand it over to Henry's wife who had always wanted it and had been so humiliated when her wish had been swept aside for Diane's gratification. Diane was given the château of Chaumont in exchange for Chenonceaux. Catherine believed that Chaumont was an unlucky castle.

Mary's health at this time began to give some concern to her watchful relations. She was constantly fainting and suffered from mysterious pains. The latter may have been due to indigestion for she appears to have been rather fond of her food. Moreover, the King's death had been a great sorrow to her; while he had lived she and Francis had been shielded from the exigencies of sovereignity; and, although the Guise uncles had taken control, Mary and her husband were in name at least the Queen and King. Moreover, every slight ailment would cause speculation as to the possibility of pregnancy. Hope would shine in the uncles' eyes; fear in those of the Queen Mother. It was a trying time for Mary, because she had grown out of a childhood where she had been protected from unpleasant truths. She was beginning to realize something of the scheming, ambitious and devious men and women who surrounded her. The halcyon days were coming to an end.

A terrible scene took place at the castle of Amboise which Mary and Francis were forced to witness. A plot to kidnap the King, Queen and members of the royal family had been discovered; the main object was to curb the power of the Guises and set up a Huguenot King on the throne. This King was to be Antoine of Navarre and a new Bourbon dynasty would be founded; but Francis was to be given the opportunity to turn Huguenot. The King of Navarre had been too wise to be actively involved and the rebellion had been led by the Sieur de la Rénaudie. The English Protestants had given support; the English Catholics had got wind of the plot and the Guises were informed of what was about to happen. Consequently the plot failed and the instigators were arrested.

It was the Guises who decided on revenge. Because they knew that their control of the King was unpopular they determined to show in no uncertain manner what happened to those who attempted to oppose it. They staged a brutal display in the courtyard of Amboise, where the Court was at that time; and members of the royal and Guise families were expected to watch the slaughter from a balcony overlooking the courtyard.

The Duke of Guise, the Cardinal and Catherine de' Medici looked on unmoved at the horrific torture and slaughter of the plotters; but Mary was gentle and never cruel, and Francis loathed violence. It must have been a terrible ordeal. Bleeding heads were stuck on the castle battlements; mutilated bodies were tied into sacks and flung into the river which was stained red with the blood of the rebels. Everywhere there was the sight and smell of blood. Gloatingly certain members of the Guise family looked on, but not all of them. The Duchess of Guise wept bitterly, and when asked cynically by Catherine de' Medici why she lamented in such a strange fashion, replied that she could not bear to witness such tragedy and she feared that because of what her family had done to these men a great disaster would fall upon them. The Guises were disgusted by such faintheartedness and the Duchess was reprimanded by her husband.

It was on this occasion that Francis is said to have displayed his kingship for the first time. There was a protest when Mary rose to leave the balcony and she appealed to her husband to spare her an ordeal which she found repugnant. Francis is said to have reminded the Cardinal that he, Francis, was King of France, and commanded him to stand aside so that the King and Queen might leave together. Some historians find this story of Francis's one act of bravery apocryphal, holding that Mary was not even present at the slaughter. But it seems hardly likely that the King and Queen would have been excluded from such a spectacle, and Mary throughout her life could never look unmoved on torture and death.

The carefree days were indeed at an end.

The position of the Dowager Queen of Scotland was becoming more and more untenable. Her unpopularity at home increased; she was after all a foreigner and worse still a Catholic. John Knox was becoming a very prominent fomenter of trouble. He had written his *First Blast of the Trumpet Against the Monstrous Regiment of Women*, which must have amused Elizabeth, but was of course directed against the Dowager Queen and her daughter. Knox fulminated effectively against the "Roman Harlot", his appellation for the Catholic faith. Mary of Guise and the Queen of Scots were Catholic, hence the dissension in Scotland could only react in Elizabeth's favour.

Many Scottish nobles were awaiting the moment to seize power; and the first among these was James Stewart, illegitimate son of James V and Margaret Erskine, who had his eyes on a Regency. William Maitland of Lethington stood firmly behind James Stewart. A party was being assembled, its object ostensibly to drive Catholicism from the land and establish Protestantism, but in truth to set James up as Regent and to cut the power of the absent Queen. Mary would not be forgiven for signing away to France that which it was not in her power to give. Nor would the Queen of England forget that Mary had assumed the title which Elizabeth considered to be her own.

Mary was deeply disturbed when she heard that her mother was dangerously ill, not only because of the affection Mary had always had for her, despite the fact that they had been separated since Mary was not quite six years old and had met only once since, but because of the effect this could have on the Scottish Kingdom.

The Dowager Queen's body and legs were so swollen with dropsy that she could not walk and was in great pain. In June 1560 she died. John Knox was self-righteously and characteristically gloating. He wrote that, "her belly and loathsome legs began to swell and so continued till God did execute his judgement on her."

Mary was heartbroken; she went to her bed and stayed there, and is reported to have collapsed in her grief and sorrow.

Everything was changing. Francis's health had deteriorated since his accession to the throne; his skin was pallid except where there were unhealthy red patches. It was said that he suffered from a number of dreadful ailments; a wasting disease was hinted at, as was leprosy; and there was a rumour that he had a particular loathsome disease which gave him a craving for the blood of freshly killed babies. The rumours multiplied and when he rode through the towns and villages mothers hastily collected their children and hid them away. People shrank from poor Francis, who became more peevish and unhappy. He demanded of the Cardinal why the people hated him and with a rare show of boldness told his tormentor that he wished he would go away for then he would be sure whether the hatred of the people was directed against him, the King, or the Cardinal.

In all his troubles there was only one to whom he could turn; his beloved and beautiful Mary. He must have been repulsive, but there is no evidence that Mary ever shrank from him, and she, the great beauty of the Court, the most admired and desirable girl of the time, never failed to show tenderness for her poor husband.

Shortly before her death, the Dowager Queen of Scotland had sent letters to Mary by a young Scottish nobleman. The messenger, at the time about twenty-four years of age, was, by a strange coincidence, the man who was to have a greater effect on Mary's life than any other. This was James Hepburn, who had become Earl of Bothwell on the death of his father – some four years before this first meeting with Mary.

It is interesting to speculate what these two experienced when they came face to face. Was there some premonition? Surely two people never had a greater effect on each other's lives. Bothwell was to bring more passion, violence, disaster into Mary's drama-packed existence than anyone else. Yet as he stood before her with letters brought from Scotland he no doubt appeared to her as nothing more than a vigorous uncouth Scotsman. And she to him? He was a man who had known many women; he was rough and lecherous. The stories of Mary's great beauty would have reached him, but it is possible that her elegance and delicate beauty were not to his taste. He would no doubt admire a flamboyance to match his own bold sensuality.

Bothwell was a man born to dominate, as strong as his native granite, a wild Borderer accustomed to ravage the land and take what he wanted. His father, Patrick Hepburn, had been called the Fair Earl because he was irresistible to women; and although James could not be called fair, he had a physical attractiveness which was as great as that of his father, who had once planned to marry Mary of Guise and had even gone so far as to divorce his wife – James's mother – in readiness to do so. The Queen had declined his hand and in his fury he had worked against her in the pay of the English. The Bothwells were ambitious men and not too dainty in their methods of satisfying their great urge for power.

69

When his father had divorced his mother, James and his sister Janet had lived with their mother for a while. Without a father's restraining hand they had run wild, until James was sent to his great-uncle Patrick who was Bishop of Moray. The Bishop was a gourmet and a lecher who never let his calling interfere with his pleasures. There had been feasting and orgies in his palace of Spynie, and James, though still a boy, was permitted to join these. The Bishop had numerous progeny and made a practice of legitimizing them several at a swoop. Brought up in this atmosphere James had quickly become what his Bishop uncle called a "True Hepburn".

At an early age he became "handfast" to Janet Beaton, an aunt of Mary Beaton, one of the four Maries. Handfast meant that a couple were betrothed and might live together and, if they found life together pleased them, marry. This was one of the most satisfactory relationships of James's life and he would have married Janet Beaton but for the great disparity in their ages. Even when they ceased to live together they remained friends

During an embassy to Denmark he fell in with a young woman named Anna Throndsen. James was attracted – he was attracted by many women briefly – but Anna wanted more than a short love affair. She hinted that she was an heiress and the thought of a fortune induced James to propose marriage. She became pregnant and then marriage she said was imperative; but meanwhile James had discovered that the fortune of which she boasted did not exist. Anna's family insisted that when he left he must take her with him. He did so but left her in Copenhagen, having no intention of returning there for her.

When he arrived in France with letters from the Dowager Queen to her daughter, he was received by the Cardinal of Lorraine. Sensualists both, there could not have been two men more different than the exquisite and subtle Cardinal and the rough yet direct Borderer. The Cardinal was ageing; Bothwell was in the prime of his youth. They would most certainly have disliked and distrusted each other on sight; and the Cardinal's dislike would have intensified when Bothwell refused to hand over the letters he had brought, declaring that his instructions

70

were to put them into the hands of the Queen of Scots and no other.

And so the first meeting between the Queen of Scotland, and the man who would be her ravisher, her husband, and her evil genius, took place.

Tragedy was approaching fast. Francis had been suffering from a painful abscess in the ear and this had given rise to rumours that one of his servants had poured poison into the ear while he slept.

Aggravated by the cold winds of approaching winter, the abscess grew worse. The Court was at the *bailliage* in Orleans; and whenever the Court travelled, there went too certain furnishings, beds, tapestries and such precious articles considered necessary for gracious living. They were about to leave for Chenonceaux, which had been much in use since the death of Henry II and the decline of Diane. As he was about to mount his horse Francis fainted and there was no alternative but to take him back to bed.

A stream of important people now came hurrying to Orleans – the Cardinal among them. Mary guessed that Francis was very ill indeed and she sought desperately for some means of alleviating his suffering. It is said that she sent for Ambroise Paré, a Huguenot who was undoubtedly the best surgeon in France. Paré told Mary that he could operate on the King's ear as he had a tumour there which was growing quickly and would in due course reach the brain. The operation might well not succeed, but there was a possibility that it would. On the other hand if the King were not operated on, he would most surely die very soon.

Mary decided that the operation must take place but met opposition from Catherine de' Medici. No one can ever be quite sure of what went on in her mind, but Catherine it appears was determined that the operation should not take place. In view of what is known of her character it does not seem unreasonable to assume that she was anxious that Francis should not survive, for his death would mean the end of the Guises's power and that her son Charles would be King. Some historians believe that Catherine deliberately perverted her son Charles, that she played on his unbalanced mind and encouraged his madness, that she brought him up to fear her and yet to rely on her. What is certain is that when Francis died and Charles became King, Catherine was the dictator of French policies; and for a woman who had been forced to see another woman usurp her place, and had been treated as of no account not only by her husband and by his mistress but by all the Court, the promise of power must have been irresistible. Whether she was capable of denying her own son that help which might have saved his life is uncertain, but it seems that at least she delayed it until Paré himself declared that it was too late and he could do nothing to save the King.

On 5th December 1560 Francis died. The Cardinal was with him to the end. One wonders whether that sinister man had a twinge of conscience after all for he told the dying boy to repeat after him: "Lord, pardon my sins and impute not to me, thy servant, the sins committed by my Ministers in my name and authority".

Surely an unnecessary request to an all-seeing, all-knowing Deity; but the strangest thing about it is that the cynical Cardinal should have thought fit to remind God of the child's subservience to men such as himself and ask Him not to blame Francis for the evil deeds which had occurred during his reign.

With the death of her husband Mary was no longer the important person she had been while he lived. Catherine made her aware of this as they left the death-chamber together. It was now Mary's turn to stand aside for Catherine de' Medici.

Custom demanded that a widowed Queen of France should spend forty days shut away from the world, during which time, dressed in white from her coif to her shoes, she should see no one but the immediate members of her own family; she must stay in the darkened chamber lit only by tapers.

The future was grey. There was a new King on the throne. The Guises had lost their power as though by a stroke. That which they had feared had taken place. Francis was dead and had left no heir of his body; Charles, his mother's protégé, was King. The woman who had been of no account was emerging from the shadows; and those who had known power were now stripped of it, while others had risen to take what they had lost.

Mary must have been bewildered. She was eighteen years old and beginning to understand something of the troubled state of affairs. She feared she would be sent back to Scotland. France had become home to her; she could imagine no other. Her mother was dead; the King of France, who had been a father to her, was dead; her husband was dead. She was beginning to understand that her uncles' great concern for her had its roots in their own unbounded ambition. There was, however, her grandmother, Antoinette of Bourbon, the Dowager Duchess of Guise; she offered real affection; yet she, too, was obsessed by preserving the greatness of the family.

After two weeks of mourning Mary's uncles came to see her. They had plans. Catherine de' Medici had taken the position which once was theirs and they were determined to regain what they had lost. The only way in which they could do that was to give Mary a second husband. There had naturally been many offers for such a desirable *parti*. Eric XIV of Sweden and Frederick II of Denmark had offered their hands. The uncles scorned them. The Earl of Arran was another suitor, but Mary did not wish to go to Scotland which she should have expected to do had she taken Arran. One other offer had come from Henry, Lord Darnley; the uncles thought this quite presumptuous. Darnley considered himself royal because his mother Margaret Douglas was the daughter of Margaret Tudor, so that he and Mary had the same grandmother – the daughter of Henry VII. Margaret Tudor, after the death of James IV, had married Archibald, Earl of Angus; their daughter Lady Margaret Douglas had married the Earl of Lennox, and Henry Stuart, Lord Darnley, was their son. Darnley believed that he had a claim not only to the throne of Scotland but to that of England, and therefore saw himself as a very worthy suitor for the hand of Mary Queen of Scots.

But of course none of these suitors was what the uncles had in mind for their important niece. There was only one husband who could bring back the power they had lost through the death of Francis II, and that was Charles IX. That he was mad meant nothing to them. If Mary could marry Charles, eight years her junior though he was and mad into the bargain, and have a son, that son would be quarter Guise and his clever great-uncles would be at hand to direct him. Charles was certainly in love with Mary in his odd manner and the uncles saw no reason why the pair should not marry and bring power back to the Guises. Mary naturally shrank from the prospect.

Another prospect appeared. Philip II had a son who was, of course, heir to the throne of Spain: Don Carlos. If Mary married him, Scotland would come under the jurisdiction of Spain, and Philip was not averse to such a match because Scotland was at present in the grip of Protestantism. An ardent, even fanatical Catholic such as Philip, in whose country the Inquisition flourished as nowhere else, was ready to consider the match so that Scotland might be saved for Rome. Mary would thus one day be Queen of Spain, and with such an influence within their family the Guises would be in a strong position for they would guide the affairs of Spain through their niece and her weak husband, as they would have governed France if Francis had lived.

There was one drawback. Carlos would scarcely be a handsome husband. He was small, wizened and deformed, one shoulder was higher than the other; his speech was thick for he had a strong impediment which made him almost unintelligible. He was sixteen years old. Not the sort of husband a young girl would choose; true, she had loved Francis, but Francis would have seemed handsome compared with Carlos, and Mary had known Francis all her life. Although Carlos was mentally unbalanced, at this time he was not as violently mad as he became later, for shortly afterwards he had an accident which partially paralysed him, and in order to relieve this an intricate operation was performed on his brain. This left him subject to sudden outbursts of passion when he was ready to murder those who displeased him. He was to develop a passion for his young stepmother, Elizabeth, who had recently left France to marry Philip II. His jealous hatred of his father became so unmanageable that, when he threatened to murder Philip, it was necessary to put him under restraint. In his prison the madness of Carlos intensified; he fell ill and died mysteriously.

This lay in the future, but even at the time his name was put forward Carlos was scarcely the bridegroom a young girl would choose if left to herself. However, Mary's uncles' hopes rested either on a mad Carlos of Spain, or on an even madder Charles of France. What after all was a little madness where great dynasties were concerned? Madmen could beget children and any children Mary had by either Carlos or Charles would be quarter Guise; and the great family would move in to rule. They were optimistic. Guises did not sit down and mourn because original plans had gone wrong.

The period of mourning ended. It was no longer possible for Mary to shut herself away. She had her future to consider. She was no longer young enough to plead ignorance of affairs but must face unpleasant facts. Henry Darnley visited her, ostensibly to offer condolences from his mother who was a kinswoman, but in fact to show himself as a prospective husband. He was a handsome boy, though somewhat girlish; he was quite an accomplished musician and he had written some verses for her. He did not have the graces of the French noblemen to whom Mary was accustomed, but she noted there was a charm about him.

Mary accompanied the Court to Fontainebleau and there she was visited by the English ambassador, Sir Nicholas Throckmorton, and the Earl of Bedford. Their manner, like that of others, had changed towards her. The umbrella of France no longer sheltered her; none would be more aware than men such as these of the change in her position. She was nothing now but Queen of a small, impoverished and not very important country. The English demanded the immediate ratification of the Edinburgh Treaty, by which Elizabeth claimed sole right to the throne of England.

It was another mistake of Mary's that she should haughtily decline to ratify the treaty. Henry II had taught her that she was Queen of England and that the red-headed upstart daughter of Anne Boleyn was nothing but a bastard. It had been all very well for Henry to hold such views and impart them to his daughter-in-law, while he and her husband were alive. Now the affairs of France were guided by a sly and subtle woman who saw no advantage to herself in offering help to the haughty girl who had once humiliated her. If it had been politic to save Mary from her eventual fate of banishment, Catherine would have forgotten revenge.

In England Elizabeth heard of the arrogance of the Scottish Queen. There had been such stories of her beauty and charm that Elizabeth, always inordinately vain, was jealous. Mary acquired a bitter enemy.

From Fontainebleau Mary travelled to Rheims to spend a few weeks with her aunt Renée of Guise. On her way she met her half-brother James Stewart who had come to France to persuade her to return to Scotland. James, thirty years old at this time, was an exceedingly ambitious young man, always jealous of the delicate girl who held the position he coveted. He made her aware of the conflict currently raging in Scotland between Catholics and Protestants; James was a Protestant and Mary offered him great benefits if he would turn Catholic; she would seek to procure for him a Cardinal's hat; she could certainly promise him rich estates in France. James, who was clever, understood the state of affairs far better than Mary ever could. His future lay in Scotland. He declined the Cardinal's hat. At the same time he gave the English ambassador, Throckmorton, an account of what had taken place between him and his Queen.

She travelled on to Rheims where Renée, sister of the great Guise brothers, presided over the Abbey of Saint-Pierre-les-Dames as its Abbess. The life there must have seemed very restful. Did she remember the peace of Inchmahome?

The Guise brothers had underestimated the shrewd statescraft of Catherine de' Medici. She was not going to allow her son Charles to marry Mary and return the French scene to what it had been before the death of Francis – with the Guises in control. As for Mary's marriage with Don Carlos, she would not allow that either. It would mean having Guises controlling Spanish policy if Philip were to die and his son Carlos become King. Catherine offered her young daughter Margaret as a bride for Carlos. With her daughter Elizabeth already the wife of Philip and with Margaret married to Carlos, the French influence on Spain would be great. Philip was inclined to view the proposition with interest. Scotland, his spies had discovered was a country in a ferment of religious upheaval. The Protestant influence whipped up by the Calvinist Knox was great. Spain might need an army to subdue it. It was not, Philip decided, after all a very good proposition. And, as further suggestions had come to him through Catherine de' Medici, there was no longer a good reason why Mary Queen of Scots should marry Don Carlos of Spain.

Rejected in Spain, unwanted in France, where could she go? In the documents which she had signed in April 1558 there was a clause saying that if she wished to remain in France she could do so; she had, after all, estates in Touraine and Poitou.

But she knew that this could not be. Had Catherine allowed her to marry Charles, Mary could have resumed her old position at Court. But Charles, though he wanted the marriage, was half her age, a child, and his mother's creature. So Mary must leave her beloved France and go back to her hostile native land.

When Elizabeth heard that Mary was leaving France for Scotland she again demanded that Mary sign the Treaty of Edinburgh in exchange for a safe passage. Again Mary refused, telling Throckmorton that she had come to France although the English had tried to prevent her doing so, and she was prepared to return to Scotland without the help of the English Queen.

Throckmorton reported to Elizabeth that since the death of her husband the Queen of Scotland had taken on a new firmness of purpose which she had appeared to lack before. It was true, and at the same time Mary was learning a great deal about her native land; the more she learned the less inclined she felt to return to it. She was a Catholic and could never be anything else; her brother James and Lord Maitland of Lethington were firmly Protestant and they were the most able statesmen in the land. The Catholics were led by the Earl of Huntly, but she could not believe they were entirely reliable. Huntly had, at the battle of Pinkie Cleugh, been in charge of the rear of the Army; she had heard that he had fled at the first charge and that this action had contributed largely to the defeat; he had been taken prisoner and in London had, for a while, worked with the English. She did believe, however, that she could trust James; he was after all her brother. She knew she would have to be tolerant and that to attempt to force the Catholic faith on Scotland would plunge the country into civil war.

It was an uneasy situation. She delayed her return, looking for an excuse to stay in the land she loved. But Catherine de' Medici was determined she should go. Mary could delay no longer and she sent for James Hepburn, Earl of Bothwell, that he might act as admiral of the fleet of ships which were to take her home.

It was August when she began her journey. Of course there had to be a brilliant cavalcade for the daughter of the House of Guise. Illustrious members of the family accompanied Mary to the coast. In a gilded carriage bearing the arms of Guise and Lorraine rode the brothers, Francis and Charles, who had worked so ambitiously for her and themselves. Mary came next in an equally splendid carriage followed by a resplendent company among whom were her four Maries. Other members of the Guise family were naturally in this party.

Mary looked very beautiful in her white mourning gown of cloth of silver. Her headdress was shaped like a scallop shell and decorated with pearls; she wore a wide necklace like a collar also studded with pearls; the lovely oval of her face would have been set off to perfection by a ruff of point lace.

As she stepped aboard the ship it is said that a sense of great desolation swept over her. Superstitious minds were appalled when precisely at that moment a ship which was coming into the harbour completely turned turtle and everyone in it was thrown into the water and drowned.

Mary was very upset by the tragedy. Foolish she was so often, but never cruel. We are told that when she saw the galley slaves, manacled at their ankles, their bare backs bearing evidence of the lash, she shuddered and gave orders that the lash was not to be used while she was on board.

The ship could not leave immediately as the tide was unfavourable and the wind too high. She was desolate and her Maries took her to her bed which was set up on the poop gallery. But she wanted to see the last of the land she loved.

As the galley sailed out of Calais harbour Mary clung to the rail crying: "*Adieu France. Adieu France. Je pense ne vous revoir jamais plus.*" (Farewell, France, farewell. I believe I shall not see you ever again.)

And sadly she sailed away, with the threat of English hostility on the long journey northwards to the harsh country of which she was Queen but which had no great desire to welcome her. The joyous days of her youth were over. The bitter conflicts were about to rage.

The Chastelard Curtain Raiser

How different was Mary's arrival in Scotland from that first stepping ashore on French soil twelve years before. Then Henry II and her powerful relations had spared no expense in doing her honour. Her Scottish subjects were less lavish. Even the weather was inhospitable for a heavy mist hid the land as the galley came into Leith harbour. Only a few fisherfolk stood watching the boat. No lodgings had been prepared for her and she would have been without one if one of the townsmen, a certain Andrew Lambie, had not stepped forward and offered her a shelter for the night. A room in a humble dwelling for the Queen of Scotland! The Frenchmen were shocked; they had indeed come to a barbarous land. But it was only for one night. On the morrow they would ride into Edinburgh.

By the next day, however, the news of Mary's arrival was spreading, and James Stewart, accompanied by Maitland of Lethington and Châtelherault with his son Arran, came to Leith to greet her. It was discovered that some of the galleys had been lost at sea, including the one carrying the palfrey on which Mary was to have ridden into Edinburgh. A horse had to be provided for her and her retinue were shocked when they saw the old nag which was produced. One member of the entourage was Brantôme, the chronicler whose on-the-spot observations and writings have been of such great interest and worth to biographers through the centuries, and he was able to give details of the journey. Mary was sorry for the poor old horse found for her; and she observed that the horses provided for the rest of the company looked as though they had been taken out of an abattoir to make one last journey – to carry the Queen and her party into Edinburgh.

A few miles from the capital the party ran into a mob of shouting people. They had, it transpired, broken into the nearby prison and rescued a certain James Kellone who had been sentenced to be hanged because he had played frivolous games on a Sunday. Mary was appalled. In France people had been burned to death for their heresy. Her dear "father" Henry II had been a stern Catholic; her uncles had been even more ruthless. But she favoured tolerance. She wanted men and women to live in peace together, to worship as they wished. But this man it seemed had done nothing but dance – or was it sing? – on the sacred Scottish Sabbath. She immediately asserted her rights and her first act as Queen on her own soil was to grant James Kellone a free pardon.

She was cheered by the crowd; but it would have occurred to some of her Scottish subjects that there would be trouble when John Knox heard of her action; and John Knox was a power in the land.

It was dark when she reached Edingurgh. Bonfires were springing up on the surrounding hills to welcome her. People came into the streets to crowd about her. They appeared to be loyal. When at last she came to Holyrood Palace she must have been worn out with emotion as well as fatigue. After a meal she returned to her apartments and the Maries helped her prepare for bed.

They were aroused by a noise which Mary thought very strange. She was told she was listening to the bagpipes. The music they played, she said, was not very cheerful. It sounded like dirges.

They were the hymns of the Kirk.

Scotland appeared to be ruled by the Church, and John Knox was the Church. He was that most unattractive of characters – the self-righteous man who believes that he and only he can be right. Egotistical in the extreme, he saw himself as God's emissary, and everyone who did not fall into line with him as destined for hell-fire. He was uncomfortable, unpleasant and in every way the opposite in character to the Queen of Scots. It was inevitable that they should be in conflict. According to Laing, the nineteenth-century Scottish antiquary who edited

Knox's works, Knox saw himself as having been saved from the "puddle of papistry" about the time of Mary's birth. George Wishart, the ardent Protestant who had died at the stake on the orders of Cardinal Beaton, had been his mentor; and Knox had been present at the assassination of Beaton and been captured by the French when they raided the Cardinal's castle of St Andrews. It was then that he was sent to the galleys – a bitter humiliation and great suffering which he never forgot. When he was released he went to Geneva where Calvin was expounding theories which Knox found to his liking, and he came back to his native land in the middle of the 1550s there to rant against the "Whore of Babylon" (The Roman Catholic faith) and do all he could to bring Protestantism to Scotland.

He was a born reformer, and like many of his kind he preached for the good of the people in general yet was harsh and cruel to them individually. He believed any frivolity to be sinful; and his emphasized dislike of women leads one to suspect that he was far from indifferent to them. He had acted as spiritual adviser to a certain Elizabeth Bowes and married her sixteen-year-old daughter Marjorie, by whom he had two sons. His wife was a mild creature who always bowed to her husband's wishes, recognizing herself as the weaker vessel. He had always been very fond of his mother-in-law who was about his own age and when she, after he married her daughter, left her husband to join Knox and Marjorie, there was a certain amount of scandal concerning his relationship with his mother-in-law. Knox ignored the gossip.

Marjorie died in 1560 and despite his professed contempt for women, he married again – this time the seventeen-year-old daughter of the Protestant Lord Ochiltree – and had three daughters.

The portrait of Knox attributed to Vaensoun, and thought to be the only genuine one of him, shows his long straight nose and sunken eyes. There is great strength in the face, and the obstinacy of the fanatic who *knows* he is God's elect.

It is clear that Knox was fond of female society. The women he could not abide were those who set themselves up in authority over men. There was a Queen below the Border who was such a one, but as she had emerged as an upholder of the Protestant faith and was an ally of Scottish members of it who were determined to keep out the Catholic faith, he had had to revise his views of her. But Mary Stuart was the kind of woman against whom he would work with all the fierce invective at his command. Mary was beautiful, therefore disturbing; she behaved like a Frenchwoman, which in itself was immoral. He soon heard that since her arrival she had turned her apartments at Holyrood House into a "Little France". She had dared grant a pardon to a man who was to have been hanged for desecrating the Sabbath. She had brought with her poets and singers, musicians and dancers. She was introducing wicked papist ways into Protestant Scotland, and trying to draw Scots men and women back into the "puddle of papistry" from which men such as himself had helped to extricate them. Her greatest crime was that she celebrated Mass there in the heart of Edinburgh. That he could not endure.

In St Andrews he preached against the congregation of Satan, recalling to his congregation how God had taken His revenge on the unrighteous. He gleefully reminded them in what could scarcely be called the Christian Spirit that the belly and loathsome legs of Mary of Guise had swollen and she had died in agony when God in His wisdom removed her from this world. As for Mary's husband, the King of France, God had made his ear rot because that ear would not listen to His Truth. What God had been doing when his great friend Knox was sent to the galleys was never explained. So Knox fulminated in his pulpit and did his utmost to stir up public opinion against Mary.

Her brother James and his ally Maitland were not displeased when Mary insisted that she had been brought up in the Catholic faith and could accept no other. They were quite content for Mary to make her Little France in Holyrood Palace. Mary could lead her butterfly existence – ruler in name only – while they would carry on with the serious matter of governing the country.

Surrounded by the four Maries and some of her French friends whom she had kept with her, Mary was tolerably contented. The days when she had been the brightest star in the French Court, pampered, fawned on, admired and so loved had been over before she left. So France, although she loved it dearly, was not the joyous home it had once been. And here in Scotland she was the Queen; she had her friends and she had changed Holyrood so that it was no longer the dour and dull place it had been. She had had tapestries hung on the walls and some of her musical instruments and clothes had arrived from France. There was often music in her apartments. One of her favourites was Pierre Chastelard, a young poet who delighted in making verses praising her beauty. She was gradually making the apartments at Holyrood like a part of the Court of France.

And while Mary sang and danced, Knox was working up feeling against her. It so happened that on the first Sunday in Holyrood Palace a mob of his followers marched on the palace shouting that they would not have the Mass celebrated in their town, that it was Satan's Worship, and that they had come to kill the idolaters. Knox was not with them – it was his custom to incite mobs but not to join them, as if it was necessary for him to preserve himself to do God's work, while it was the duty of others to imperil their lives in this cause. He was always at his most bloodthirsty when ranting from afar.

When she heard the screaming crowds at the gate Mary was incensed. She was the Queen and would not be told how she must act by a fanatical preacher; and when she saw her priest and almoner coming towards her with blood on their faces and heard that the candlesticks had been wrenched from their grasp, she declared that she would hear Mass whatever happened.

Fortunately her brother James was at hand to quell the mob. He was highly respected and known as a good Protestant. He spoke to the people and managed to calm them; and as a result the priests, their heads bandaged, were brought back to officiate. Mary heard Mass in the chapel; but the incident brought home to her that John Knox was not a man to be treated lightly.

Mary was now anxious for her subjects to know that she had no intention of allowing intolerance in religious matters to flourish in her kingdom. She had seen the terrible persecution of Huguenots in France; and she herself had always shrunk from violence. She did not want ugliness brought into her life when there was so much that was beautiful. She wanted to make the lot of her poor subjects easier if possible; she wanted a better life for as many people as possible. She knew that there were many Catholics in Scotland who wished to follow the religion they believed to be the true one. She herself shared their views. But if people wished to learn about the Reformed religion she believed they should be allowed to do so. She wanted tolerance for her subjects.

At this stage she believed her brother James to be in agreement with her. She was too simple politically to grasp the fact that he not only wanted to take her place as ruler of Scotland, but because of his birth believed he had a right to. She was too ready to trust and did not realize that the wily men around her were each and every one interested only in his own advancement.

Yet James realized he must keep Mary's position secure for if she were deposed it might well be that the Stewarts would lose the crown of Scotland, and it could pass to the Tudor below the Border. Thus James's plan at this time – with Maitland close behind him – was to keep Mary occupied with her dances and musicians, let her practise her religion, but keep her on the throne, while James governed in her name.

So when Mary ordered that a proclamation be read at Market Cross to the effect that tolerance would lead the people to a true understanding of religion and only by tolerance could they overcome the schisms which at the moment beset the Church, James gave his approval.

The proclamation was pasted on walls where all might read it, and soon the great topic of conversation in Edinburgh was the opposing views of Knox and the Queen and the conflict this had brought about. The last thing Knox wanted was tolerance. He ranted in his pulpit, referring to Mary as the "Whore of Babylon". He exaggerated rumours of the entertainments which were given in Little France as if they were orgies. But then in his opinion to dance was to do the Devil's work and once a man or woman indulged in such a pastime they were already half-way to hell. He thundered that his

85

followers must fight the Devil – the Devil presumably being the Queen. What Knox wanted was subservience to himself, and he was ready to see bloodshed in Edinburgh in order to gain it. He wanted the "Whore of Babylon" to be either deposed or to come to him meekly confessing the errors of her ways, and send her priests, poets and dancers packing; to bring the dour gloom back into Holyrood House. That Mary would not do and Knox was determined to fight her. When asked his opinion of the Queen, he answered: "If there be not in her a proud mind, a crafty wit and an indurate Heart against God and His Truth my judgement faileth me." As Knox could not conceive that his judgement could ever fail him, he clearly believed that Mary was an enemy of God which meant an enemy of himself.

There appeared to be no alternative but that the Queen should meet this powerful man and that they should attempt to come to some compromise. The meeting was arranged and took place in Mary's apartments at Holyrood House. It availed nothing. How could it? Mary was no match for Knox's fiery eloquence. He was soon preaching to her as he did to his congregations, declaiming that he was God's messenger and the only man in the world who was on such familiar terms with the Deity. In fact he talked as though he and God were one. He was the Messiah who had been sent into the world to free it of idolatry, which was the Catholic faith. God had called him as he had called other prophets before him and nothing would deter him from completing his work. Protestant martyrs were saints; Catholic martyrs were devil's spawn and it was only a matter for rejoicing if their blood was shed. If they were burned at the stake they were merely having a foretaste of the suffering that would be their lot for eternity – and so on.

Mary, amazed at the man's arrogance, asked him if he thought subjects should resist their princes. Knox, remembering no doubt those years in the galleys, was not going to be accused of treason. He answered obliquely in the form of a parable. "A father may be struck by a frenzy," he explained, "in which he would slay his children. If the children arise, join together, take the sword from him and keep him in prison until the frenzy passes from him, do you think the children do harm? Even so is it the Princes who would murder the children of God."

The Queen answered: "I perceive that my subjects shall obey you and not me and will do what they list and not what I command, and I will be subject to them and not they to me."

John Knox realized the need for care because the Queen's brother was present at the interview. Also, as a preacher, when asked a leading question, he could talk round it in an ambiguous fashion. This he did to the boredom of the Queen.

The interview was revealing enough for John Knox to grasp the fact that he could abuse the Queen without placing himself in any real danger.

In spite of John Knox, Mary began to impose her own way of life on Holyrood House. She loved to ride and needed a good deal of exercise to keep healthy. In France she had enjoyed the hunt and during those first months at Holyrood she hunted the deer in, it must be admitted, a rather cruel manner. The deer were herded together and forced into a spot where the hunters would be waiting for them, a custom which was much later followed in Germany and shocked Queen Victoria by its cruelty. Sixteenth-century sensitivity was not so easily disturbed as that of nineteenth-century Victorians; but like so many people today, Mary could witness cruelty to some animals while she was devoted to others. She showed great affection towards her dogs, by which she was always surrounded, and the incongruity of extreme cruelty to one kind of animal and the petting of others passed unnoticed by her. She was a good needlewoman; there are the tapestries worked during the years of captivity to prove this. Most of all she loved dancing and the music that was essential to it. Fine clothes delighted her and she must have startled the people of Edinburgh when she appeared among them in her elegant splendour.

It was her love of music which first brought David Rizzio to her notice. Signor David, as he was called, held a humble post in the suite of the Ambassador from Savoy, the Marquis de Moretta. David had a fine bass voice, and when Mary's choir was short of one his name was suggested to her. From the moment she heard his voice it enchanted her and from then on he became a familiar figure in her apartments. The stage was set early for the drama that was to follow. Bothwell and Rizzio were already on the scene; Darnley had put in an appearance in France but was not yet on the Scottish stage. John Knox was thundering his disapproval of the manner in which life was conducted in the royal apartments. James was biding his time. The tragedy was about to begin.

The affair of Chastelard was a curtain raiser.

The young poet had come to Scotland from France in the suite of the Sieur d'Amville, son of the Constable Anne de Montmorency. D'Amville had for some time before the Queen sailed for Scotland expressed his love for her and Chastelard made it clear that he shared his master's passion for the beautiful Queen. On the journey over he wrote exaggeratedly of the Queen's charms, declaring with more poetry than truth that the galley needed no light, for the Queen's eyes lit up the sea with their beauteous fire. Chastelard's infatuation with the Queen grew rapidly and he must have had the impression that he had a chance of succeeding with her.

There was an evening's masque which might have served to encourage him. Eight of the ladies were to appear masked, in men's clothes, while eight men, also masked, were dressed as women. Mary attracted attention in a white velvet doublet and black satin breeches, a mask of pink silk covering her face. Her "female" partner was the poet Chastelard in a hooped petticoat and ruff. The poet throwing himself wholeheartedly into the masquerade made the most of the occasion and demanded that his dear "husband" kiss him. Mary is said gaily to have complied with his request.

Perhaps Chastelard had listened to the ranting of John Knox, and believed the accusations of the Queen's lax morals. The fact remains that after the masque he concealed himself in Mary's bedroom, clearly with the notion that he could that night become Mary's lover. He was discovered when Mary's attendants were preparing her for her bed.

Mary was furious – no doubt aware that the incident would never be kept secret and would undoubtedly put more ammunition into John Knox's eager hands. She rated Chastelard severely on the spot and the next morning he was ordered to leave Court.

Chastelard was either a foolish or conceited young man or he had a motive other than seduction of the Queen, for when the Court moved to St Andrews, instead of discreetly retiring and thanking his good fortune that nothing was to be made of the incident, he followed Mary and forced his way to her apartments as she was being disrobed for the night, and, before two of the Maries, attempted to make love to her. Mary called for help and the call was answered by her brother James. She was so angry that she ordered her brother to kill the poet. James said that would not be wise, so Chastelard was put under arrest and confined in one of the castle's dungeons.

John Knox was soon sniffing at the scandal. It was unfortunate that another event had recently given him an opportunity to fulminate against the morals of the Court. The Queen's French apothecary had seduced one of her serving women who had become pregnant. The child was born in one of the outhouses of Holyrood and murdered. When its buried body was discovered the culprits were questioned, confessed and were publicly hanged. It was not such an unusual story but Knox made the most of it. These were the servants of Jezebel. Satan was stalking Holyrood House.

Chastelard was brought to trial. His defence was that he had acted foolishly on the first occasion and on the second he had come to the Queen's chamber to ask her for forgiveness. This explanation was not accepted. He was charged with plotting against the Queen's life, James no doubt having decided that for the honour of the Stewarts it would be better for the Queen's life to be in danger than her virtue. Unfortunately Knox had received a report of the masque at Holyrood during which the Queen had actually danced with Chastelard, and would not let such an item pass without a blare of publicity. The Montmorencys were well-known Huguenots, in fact next to the Bourbons they were the leading Huguenots in France. Mary was a Catholic. It is indeed possible that the affair was the result of a Protestant plot to destroy the Queen, or at least destroy her reputation.

There was only one answer for such an offence if the Queen's reputation was to be protected. Mary must on no account show him mercy.

Chastelard laid his head on the block in the market place of St Andrews. The general opinion was that far from conspiring against her, he had been her lover. On the scaffold he quoted Ronsard's "Hymn to Death" although few in the Scottish crowd gathered to witness his dying moments could have understood what he said.

> *Je te salue, heureuse et profitable Mort,*
> *Des extrêmes douleurs médecin et confort!**

Those close to the scaffold declared that his last words were "*O cruelle Dame.*"

It was a meloncholy incident – an unfortunate one too. Knox made the most of it. Another of Satan's minions gone to eternal torment, he gloated.

* *I salute you, happy and profitableDeath,*
Of excessive suffering comforter and healer.

The Love Match

Edinburgh was a charming city with its granite houses and their wooden galleries. Even in Mary's day the High Street was neat and clean with stone-flagged gullies on either side to drain off rain and decaying matter. In the centre of Market Cross stood the great Tron, a weighing machine used for weighing heavy goods; there also were the stocks and the pillories. The streets were alive with young apprentices from tinsmiths in West Bow and the goldsmiths in Elphinstone Court. Dominating the town was the cathedral – and dominating the cathedral of course was John Knox. Stall-holders in the Lawnmarket would have made him and his threats of hell-fire one of the main topics of conversation – that and the scandals of Holyrood House.

Since the return of the Queen the drama of the city had intensified. Highlanders and Lowlanders swaggered through the streets and there was always some quarrel in progress. The Scottish nobles must have seemed to Mary the most quarrelsome people in the world. Personal feuds were constantly in progress; and although many of their differences had their roots in religious doctrines, any little pretext to start a dispute was seized on and magnified. They quarrelled over land, over women, over honours. Nothing was too trivial to start a quarrel. There had been intrigues at the French Court and Mary had been well aware of that, but there they had been conducted in a more subtle manner.

Two men, however, stood firmly together: Maitland and the Queen's half-brother James, tied by their ambition to rule Scotland. They disliked the Earl of Bothwell, the somewhat uncouth Borderer, largely because they suspected he had plans of his own. It was not only a matter of Catholic against Protestant, for ardent Catholics such as the Earls of Erroll and Atholl disliked intensely their leader Huntly who was known as the Cock of the North and clearly believed himself to be Cock of the South as well. The Scots could not resist a quarrel.

An example was the feud between Bothwell and James Hamilton, 3rd Earl of Arran, Châtelherault's son. Arran, who was definitely simple-minded, had been involved in a violent disagreement with Bothwell, and the latter had been so offensive that when the Hamiltons asked that he should be banished from Court, Mary had agreed. Their feuds were bewildering to Mary who longed for peace. In an endeavour to show her tolerance she had appointed both Catholics and Protestants in the government of which her brother James and Maitland – Protestants both – were at the head. Huntly, the chief Catholic in Scotland, was also a member.

Bothwell's dismissal from Court was only temporary and he was soon back, but he was unlikely to forget that it was owing to Arran that he had been banished, and he sought revenge. The affair which followed was typical of the tricks these noblemen played on each other. Being simple-minded Arran was a good butt. The Hamilton clan, however, stood firmly together and, as Arran's enemy, Bothwell was at enmity with the entire clan. The Hamiltons had made a point of spreading scandal of Bothwell and Anna Throndsen.

Bothwell and his friends liked to roam through the streets of Edinburgh, and on meeting any members of the Hamilton clan plague them to such an extent that a fight ensued. But what Bothwell really wanted was to discomfort Arran personally.

This simple young man, who had professed to be so shocked by Bothwell's treatment of Anna Throndsen, himself had a mistress whom he visited nightly. This gave Bothwell an idea. What fun it would be to expose Arran, the puritan, to the world, and how could it be better achieved than to startle him in bed with his mistress?

Bothwell had formed a friendship with Mary's half-brother John – another illegitimate son of her father – who wanted to marry Bothwell's sister Janet. The Bothwell family were not greatly concerned with convention; John found Janet fascinating. Mary's uncle René, Marquis of Elboeuf – one of the Guise brothers who had accompanied her when she left France and was still with her – was also a friend of Bothwell; he and John Stewart liked to join in the mad escapades which Bothwell frequently devised, and they were with him on this occasion.

It was December and bitterly cold, and covering their faces with masks, for Bothwell and his companions were known in Edinburgh for a band of profligates whom decent people must avoid, they made their way to the house in St Mary's Wynd where Arran's mistress Alison Craig lived.

They stormed into the house, knocked down the door of the bedroom, and found Alison Craig cowering beneath a robe with which she had hastily covered her nakedness, and shivering from fright and the cold; the window, through which Arran had just jumped into the street, was wide open. The thought of Arran with what clothes he had managed to snatch up, running through the bitterly cold streets after sporting in a warm bed with his mistress, seemed comic to the revellers; but they turned their attention to the shivering girl and were about to rape her when the Hamiltons came rushing down the Wynd and into the house. The three adventurers were forced to fight their way out to the street; but as the Queen's brother and her uncle were concerned it was considered wiser not to harm them, so the three were allowed to escape. The Hamiltons had now had enough and although they did not consider the Frenchman Elboeuf worthy of their attention, and John Stewart was but a boy, they swore vengeance on the ringleader Bothwell and vowed they would kill him.

Bothwell's Borderers were a wild, unprincipled and undisciplined group, and Elboeuf and Lord John had their followers also. On the other hand, the Hamiltons were one of the richest clans in Scotland and their followers were numerous. The conflict grew and men spoiling for the fight were in the Edinburgh Streets. There could have been riots and bloodshed which could lead to civil war.

This was one of the many occasions when James Stewart showed his mettle. The most reasonable man in Scotland and the shrewdest, he was eager for all to realize how much better it would have been for Scotland if he had been born the heir rather than his sister. As the leading Protestant he asked Huntly, leader of the Catholics, to ride with him through the streets dispersing the rioters and proclaiming that any man who was found on the streets would be arrested and put to death. This strong action averted a very dangerous situation.

James advised his sister that Bothwell must be banished from Court. Elboeuf was a Frenchman, the Queen's uncle, and would soon be going back to his native land. John, her brother, was a youth not yet twenty years old. Bothwell had led these two astray so he was the one who must be punished.

Mary sent for the miscreant. It may be that she was already aware of the powerful fascination he was to exercise over her. Mary was to prove herself a sensual woman but at this time she was clearly unawakened sexually. Certainly it seems likely that her sexual urges wilted after her experiences with Francis; and it needed first Darnley and then Bothwell to loose those floods of passion which must always have been there.

It seems that she was aware of him – but vaguely – for she countenanced his insolence, and although it was necessary to deliver the sentence of banishment she agreed to visit Crichton Castle – the Bothwell estate – for the marriage of Bothwell's sister Janet to John Stewart. She also gave her consent to the marriage, although James was against it and thought that their young brother, as a royal Stewart – albeit an illegitimate one – might have made a better marriage into one of the great Scottish houses.

There appears to have been a very merry celebration at Crichton where 1,800 does and roes were consumed to say nothing of plovers and partridges in their hundreds, and during the revels Lord John distinguished himself as he never seemed to in any other way by leaping higher than anyone else on the greenhaugh below the castle walls.

Bothwell must have been amused. He was in disgrace yet the Queen was visiting his castle where her brother was marrying his sister. Her brother James, the most influential man in Scotland, was there too, though unwillingly. Knowing what we do of Bothwell we can imagine his sardonic observation of the scene. He was ambitious. It might be that even at the time he had begun to make plans.

Bothwell may well have believed that the Queen's lenience was an indication of what he might expect at her hands. To have broken into the house where Arran was sleeping with his mistress might have appeared to be on calmer consideration merely childish and futile. He had to redeem himself if he wanted power in Scotland. He therefore decided on a complete about-face. He would assume friendship with Arran. In order to do this he must first find a mediator and who better than John Knox? It might be supposed that Knox who had been so shocked by Mary's dancing in black satin breeches would have shown some dismay at Bothwell's activities. Robbery, rape and possibly murder it seemed were mild peccadilloes compared with singing, dancing and hearing the Mass. For in spite of his reputation Bothwell was a Protestant and that meant that Knox would look on him with friendliness. Then too Knox was shrewd. Bothwell was a born leader, a man whom it was far better to have as a friend than an enemy.

Knox agreed to bring the two together. He did so and the amazement of the people of Edinburgh must have been great to see these two once deadly enemies walking arm in arm down the Canongate and round Market Square.

This state of affairs was not to last. Arran was more than feeble-minded; he was mad. Shortly after the reconciliation, he sent a warning to the Queen that his father Châtelherault and Bothwell were planning to abduct her and keep her prisoner until she married him, Arran. Whether there was such a plot has not been proved. With what we know of Bothwell it was not impossible, although if he were involved in such a plot it would not be to make Mary Arran's bride but to take her for himself.

One of the Hamilton clan, the Abbot of Kilwinning, arrived at Falkland Palace, where the Court was, with the story that Arran had gone raving mad and that his account of the plot was one of his crazy hallucinations. Châtelheraut had locked his son up but Arran had escaped through the window.

Mary seems to have been unimpressed by the account of

Arran's madness and to have suspected Bothwell. Was it a kind of premonition which made her imagine what might have happened to her had she been Bothwell's captive?

Bothwell was sent for. He swore there was no plot; he demanded to be brought face to face with Arran. He would challenge him to single combat.

It was decided by James that the three movers in the plot – if plot there was – should be punished. Châtelheraut should lose Dumbarton Castle, and Arran and Bothwell should be imprisoned for a spell in Edinburgh Castle.

Matrimony was in the air. James Stewart had taken Lady Agnes Keith to wife, a union which he had long been considering. In his cold calm way he had decided that the marriage would be advantageous.

Mary's very attractive quartette of namesakes were becoming interested in marriage. Maitland, although eighteen years older than Mary Fleming, was casting eyes on her and she seemed eager for his company. Mary Beaton, strangely enough, had an admiration for Thomas Randolph, the English ambassador, which was a somewhat uneasy relationship. Lord Sempill was interested in Mary Livingston. Mary Seton, the most devoted of the Maries, was not involved and would be in fact the only one of the Maries not to marry. A marriage for Mary Stuart herself was a matter of constant speculation.

There had been a great bereavement in the Guise family. The leader of the House, Duke Francis, had been assassinated at Orleans by a fanatic Huguenot, Poltrot de Méray, who had shot him in the back. The news had reached Mary in Scotland and she mourned the man whom she had been taught from childhood to revere. The Cardinal of Lorraine, however, continued assiduous in his planning for her future and was in constant communication. Yet now that she was so many miles away from him she was less likely to be influenced by him; moreover, she was growing up and had a mind of her own. Even so, she was conscious of her royalty and in spite of the reports of Carlos she was more eager to marry into Spain than anywhere else. The Cardinal, however, had come to the conclusion that the match would strengthen Spain and he did not want that. He thought now that Charles, the Archduke of Austria, would be a more suitable match. But a name had been put forward again and now seemed possible. This was Henry Darnley.

James Stewart had long cast covetous eyes on the Earldom of Moray. The rich lands of Strathearn and Cardel were in the hands of the Huntly family and it seemed hardly likely that they would relinquish them, but when James saw an opportunity of laying his hands on them he was determined to seize it.

Trouble had arisen out of one of the street brawls commonplace to Edinburgh. The Gordons and the Ogilvies were in dispute over some property and the Ogilvies had brought a lawsuit against the Gordons. The old Earl of Huntly, the Cock of the North, did not allow suits to be brought against his family. Thus when his son Sir John Gordon came face to face with a member of the Ogilvie family, he drew his sword and attacked him. Gordon was arrested and sent to prison, but soon broke prison and escaped to the North. This gave James Stewart the opportunity he was looking for.

He pointed out to Mary that Elizabeth of England, with whom Mary ardently desired a meeting, would not be pleased to hear that Catholic Gordon was allowed to flout authority, particularly as Protestant Bothwell and Arran were at this time held in captivity. Any favour shown to Catholics would meet with great disfavour below the Border.

Mary would have preferred to free Bothwell and Arran but James would not agree to that. He and Mary rode up to the Highlands with armed men, and a civil war was the result. John Gordon was captured and the old Earl, furious at this intrusion into his domain and knowing that the real purpose was to get the Moray title and the estates which went with it for James Stewart, was so incensed that he had a heart attack and died.

It was defeat for the Highlanders and victory for Mary – or rather James, for he had won what he had long coveted. James Stewart had become Earl of Moray.

David Rizzio was born at Pancalieri, near Turin; his father

97

was a musician and he was brought up to sing and play the lute. At an early age he was sent away from home to work for the Archbishop of Turin, to play to him and sing in the choir; but this was not all. He was required to act as the prelate's secretary. He must have given a good account of himself for from the Archbishop he went to the Court of Savoy; and thus it was that in 1561 he came to Scotland in the suite of the ambassador, the Marquis de Moretta. There is no doubt that he was an excellent musician and that it was this that first brought him to Mary's notice. But because of his abilities as secretary he was doubly useful.

Mary herself had a pleasant singing voice, and she arranged musical parties during the winter evenings at Holyrood House and was anxious to recruit to her service as many talented musicians as possible. Among her servants were three excellent lute players and five violas; and anyone who had any pretensions to a singing voice was welcome. In her servants she often looked for both musical talent and efficiency in whatever task they were chosen for.

Once Rizzio had been brought to her notice Mary took an immediate fancy to him. He was an excellent addition to her choir and band of musicians; and very soon he was given a pos. as valet-de-chambre in her household. There he insinuated himself into a very favoured position, and when Mary's French secretary left, Rizzio stepped easily into the place which had been vacated.

As he was in Mary's service he must be clothed in accordance with his position and Mary provided the necessary garments as she would have done for any servant. Rizzio was by no means popular. For one thing he was an Italian and it was irksome to some that such a post should be given to a foreigner when there were many Scotsmen who would have been happy to fill it. At the time of his appointment Rizzio was in his mid-thirties. He loved fine clothes and on his death his wardrobe was found to be astonishingly well equipped with fine garments. Reports of his appearance are extremely unflattering, but this may have been due again to jealousy. He was said to be a hunchback and well under average height. Buchanan, the contemporary historian, remarks that his elegance was disfigured by his appearance, which statement smacks of envy. The well-known portrait of him shows a far from unprepossessing man – with a trimly bearded face, large fine eyes and well-formed features. It seems likely that the disparaging comments were made by those who resented the favour the Queen showed him.

Rizzio very quickly began to have a certain influence on the Queen. He was accustomed to the intrigues of court and was able to keep her informed and tell her much which she had never guessed at before. He even went so far as to warn her against the Cardinal of Lorraine who was seeking always to advance himself and his family and using Mary for this purpose. He warned her against her brother, Moray, who was equally ambitious. Feeling that Rizzio was opening her eyes to so much which was going on around her, and having no doubt whatsoever of the absolute loyalty of her secretary, Mary grew closer to Rizzio and further from her brother Moray.

Mary was becoming very restive. She needed to be married yet every plan seemed to go astray. Her health began to suffer. Winters in Holyrood were rigorous. She developed a pain in her right side which the doctors could not diagnose. She took to her bed for long periods. John Knox declared that her illness was due to riotous living; she retorted that the chapel in which she had been long on her knees was icily cold and this had chilled her. The real cause of her mysterious maladies seems to have been boredom. Life was dull.

The Queen of England was taking a sly interest in her kinswoman above the Border. She asked pertinent questions of Mary's ambassador, Sir James Melville. Was Mary as beautiful as she was reputed to be? How tall was she? How did she dance? Did she play the lute well? Elizabeth professed a desire to see friendship between the two countries and that was what Mary desired; it had never been her wish to be acclaimed Queen of England. It was something, however, that Elizabeth was not likely to forget.

The Queen of England was a little skittish with the Scottish ambassador, and she made the very surprising suggestion that Robert Dudley was a suitable husband for Mary.

Dudley had some years before been at the centre of a great scandal with which the Queen had doubtless been connected. Elizabeth was probably in love with Dudley – indeed, he was perhaps the only man she truly loved throughout her life, and she might well have married him. Elizabeth's love life is a mystery about which there have been many theories – that she was an hermaphrodite; that she lived her life as a virgin; that she bore a child to Thomas Seymour in her early teens; that she and Dudley had secretly married. The mystery has never been solved. Known facts point to the possibility that she was just not a sensuous woman, though she was a romantic. She did not seek the sexual fulfilment but she greatly enjoyed dallying on the way. She wished to be courted continually but never won. She must always be in command and she feared the domination of a lover. She would not share her power with anyone. But she was fond of the opposite sex. She must constantly have them in attendance on her; they must worship her; and we ultimately have the picture of the ridiculous old woman, bewigged, with blackened teeth, aping the young and attractive woman she once undoubtedly was. But now she was Gloriana; she was the ultimate monarch who would share her throne with no one, not even Robert Dudley, the beloved companion of her youth who had put his life and fortune at her service, and whom she seems to have regarded throughout his life as a husband.

She *could* not marry him. The death of Amy Robsart made that impossible. It is interesting here to draw a comparison between Elizabeth and Mary for by an odd coincidence they both had to face a similar situation. A lover whose partner – in Elizabeth's case a wife, in Mary's a husband – must be eliminated in order to make marriage possible. Both were besmirched by the crime of murder. Either could have been guilty of complicity. And this rocked the thrones of both. Their different methods of dealing with a similar situation gives a revealing indication of their characters.

The facts seem to be that Dudley wished to marry Elizabeth and she was in love with him. Dudley had a wife, Amy Robsart, and when Amy was found at the bottom of a staircase with her neck broken, Dudley was naturally suspected of murder.

Elizabeth was equally under suspicion. De Quadra, the Spanish ambassador, in his letters to his master Philip II, made some damning statements, which if true would appear to incriminate Elizabeth. For instance, Amy was found dead on 8th September 1560, yet De Quadra wrote that on 4th September the Queen herself told him that Lord Robert's wife was dead or nearly so. The Spanish ambassador, reporting court gossip, stated that Lord Robert had talked of divorcing or poisoning his wife. He also stated that the Queen and Dudley were thinking of destroying Lord Robert's wife, and that they had given out that she was ill, but she was not ill at all; she was very well and taking care not to be poisoned. The evidence was to say the least disquieting.

Newly come to the throne at the time, Elizabeth was in dire danger of losing it and wise enough to realize this, for whether Amy's death was due to an accident, suicide or murder made little difference to the Queen's position. There is no definite proof that Amy did not die through one of these causes. It is quite feasible that she had an accident. Yet Dudley had good reason for wishing her out of the way and might well have hired men to kill her. As for suicide, it was said that she suffered from "a malady of the breast"– presumably cancer, which could have caused her great suffering, and knowing that it was incurable she may well have taken her life.

The Queen knew that she must act with the utmost caution, and she did. She gave up all idea of marrying Dudley, because to have done so could have been construed as an admission of guilt. The storm passed over her head. She was secure on the throne which meant more to her than anything else in the world could ever mean.

Mary showed no such political wisdom. She married the murderer and so brought down on herself the terrible years of retribution.

But now, at the stage when Mary was seeking a husband, Elizabeth had already ridden out the storms created by the death of Amy Robsart. She had shown herself to be a shrewd ruler beneath her kittenish manner. She used her femininity, brilliant statesman that she was, with the utmost cunning.

Mary was of tremendous interest to her not only as a political rival but as a woman. Elizabeth was inordinately vain – perhaps because she felt that her physical charms were not all she would wish them to be, and consequently must be perpetually praised. Mary's reputation as a great beauty irked her. It was not only because she was Queen of Scotland and had some claim to the throne of England that Elizabeth wished to humiliate her. So Elizabeth feigned affection for "her cousin of Scotland" to the Scottish ambassador and declared her intention of helping to settle his rather tiresome problem of finding a husband for Mary.

Elizabeth declared that she did not think Henry Darnley a worthy enough match for Mary, and at the same time gave Darnley leave to go to Scotland. He was of a weak character, she knew; he was dissolute and would be an encumbrance rather than a help. So while protesting about such a match, characteristically she did everything she could to further it. Scotland was in a state of ferment, and it was comforting for Elizabeth to contemplate internal strife up there. It meant that Scotland was in no position to attack England and if England should have cause to take an expedition over the Border it would be more likely of success if taken into a disorganized land than into a united one.

So in a mischievous mood she offered Mary Robert Dudley. He was the "most perfect man" she knew and she would magnanimously give him to Mary. Just as she had decided to denigrate Darnley while working for his acceptance, she offered Lord Robert determined that she would not let him go.

James Melville in his *Historic Memoirs* mentions that Elizabeth told him she would have married Dudley herself if she had ever been minded to take a husband; but being determined to end her life in virginity she wished that the Queen, her sister, should marry him. She insisted that before he returned to Scotland Melville should see Lord Robert elevated to an earldom.

We have Melville to thank for the vivid description of that ceremony with the Queen helping him into his robes, he sitting on his knees before her and keeping a great gravity. Elizabeth's gravity was less great for, continues Melville, she could not refrain from putting her hand in his neck to tickle him, smilingly. And this with Melville and the French ambassador looking on!

She then demanded of Melville what he thought of her beautiful Lord Robert – now Earl of Leicester and Baron of Denbigh; and when Melville made the suitable reply she referred to the Scottish preference for Lord Darnley as a suitor to their Queen. "Yet," she said, "ye like better of yon lang lad."

Melville seems to have been on familiar terms with Elizabeth and did not mince his words which her own courtiers were expected to do. When she was reiterating her intention to remain a virgin, he replied to her, "Madam, ye need not tell me that. I know your stately stomach. Ye think, gin ye were married ye would be but *queen* of England and now ye are king and queen baith – ye may not suffer a commander." Which, as Elizabeth's father would have said, was getting the right sow by the ear.

Elizabeth's curiosity about Mary's appearance was so great that she was naïve in her efforts to satisfy it. Accustomed to flattery from her courtiers she tried hard to betray Melville into making comparisons between the Queen of Scots and herself to Mary's detriment. She asked him whether his Queen's hair was better than hers and which of the two was fairer. Melville replied that the fairness of both was not their worst faults; but Elizabeth was not to be put off by such ambiguity and demanded to know which of them he thought the fairer.

"You are the fairest Queen in England," he answered diplomatically," and ours is the fairest in Scotland."

Who was the taller, the Queen wanted to know. There was only one answer to that. Mary was of tall stature.

"Then she is over high," snapped Elizabeth. "For I am neither too high nor too low."

How did Mary play the virginals? Reasonably well for a Queen, was Melville's answer. This was not enough. Elizabeth must know whether she played better than Mary, whether she danced better than Mary. The sense of rivalry was great.

Mary was furious to have been offered Lord Robert and said that she considered it beneath her dignity to marry an

English subject. She was not shrewd enough to see that Elizabeth would never let her have her darling Robert, and what she was trying to do was force her to take the dissolute Darnley. Like many of the schemes of the wily Queen of England, this one came to fruition.

Lord Darnley was undoubtedly handsome. Mary herself was exceptionally tall – perhaps some five feet ten inches – but Darnley was well over six feet. After little Francis, it must have pleased her to have a lover who stood taller than she. His being some four years her junior was something of a drawback, and he was perhaps a trifle effeminate, his features being almost too perfect. His hair was golden, his eyes hazel and his face a beautiful oval which a woman might have envied. His figure was admirable. He was so slender and his legs were particularly well shaped. Elizabeth had referred to him as a "long lad" and Melville as "beardless and lady-faced". There was a hint of petulance, selfishness and sensuality in the beautiful young face. But it was hardly likely that he allowed the less admirable side of his nature to show during his first interview with Mary. His parents had impressed on him the importance of pleasing Mary, though they had no need to. Darnley was very anxious to share the crown of Scotland.

His mother, the Countess of Lennox, wrote to Mary telling her that her son was eager to pay homage to the Queen of Scotland and that he intended to defy the English and slip across the Border. As Elizabeth was very anxious that he should go to Scotland a great deal of defiance was not needed.

Mary took one look at Darnley and fell in love with him. It was inevitable. She, a passionate woman, had been celibate too long. She saw marriage all around her, even for her own Maries. For Mary Livingston there was a son of Lord Sempill; for Mary Fleming, the statesman Maitland. It was surely the Queen's turn.

Darnley danced well, and possessed courtly grace. He set out to charm the Queen knowing full well what was at stake.

Mary's pain in the side disappeared; she was radiant.

Clearly she no longer thought nostalgically of France. She was content to be in Scotland with Darnley.

Moray was against the match, but Mary was growing weary of her sanctimonious brother. Her great desire was to hurry on her marriage with Darnley. Impulsive, reckless, and lacking in judgement, Mary made one mistake after another at this time. She could not see through Darnley's veneer of charm, wheras others were aware of his vain acquisitive nature. Mary could not give him enough; she showered titles and costly gifts on him. She wanted to give him what he desired more than anything: the title of King of Scotland.

She summoned the best tailor in Edinburgh, William Hoppringle, to make him the finest coat and breeches of black velvet and silver lace, taffeta silk or any fine materials that could be found. Johnnie Dabrow the hatter was to make his hats. Fleming Allyard the shoemaker was to make his shoes. Jewellery was bestowed on him. The more gifts he received, the more arrogant Darnley became – although he was careful with the Queen, using his charm upon her, telling her of his devotion and his impatience to be her husband.

At this time there was news of Bothwell. He had escaped from prison and gone into exile, but was growing tired of living abroad and begged the Queen to allow him to return. Mary, not one to bear grudges, was prepared to grant the necessary permission. Moray, however, was against Bothwell's return. It seems that he had already attempted to destroy Bothwell through one of his servants, for a rogue known as Dandie Pringle had taken service with Bothwell and there had been a poison attempt on Bothwell's life which the shrewd adventurer had discovered. When Moray heard that Mary was going to give Bothwell the desired pardon he did all in his power to dissuade her, but Mary was not to be dissuaded. Mary was no longer the passive girl she had been on her arrival in Scotland. She was the Queen and determined to show those around her that she was not to be led.

Bothwell, however, did not get the required permission at this stage. Moray brought his man Dandie Pringle, who had been dismissed from Bothwell's service, to Mary and asked him to repeat a slanderous comment which Bothwell had made in his hearing. This was that when in France Mary had been the mistress of her uncle the Cardinal of Lorraine. The slander had its desired effect. Mary was incensed and the pardon was refused. But not long afterwards Bothwell contrived to come back to Scotland.

Darnley at this time suffered an attack of measles. He was not seriously ill but Mary was distraught and insisted on nursing him herself. The act of the Queen was trumpeted throughout Scotland by Mary's foes as that of a wanton woman. John Knox thundered from his pulpit of the wickedness which went on in Holyrood House; he called on God to take note and arrange for an extra large conflagration for such sinners when they arrived in hell. Elizabeth coyly commented that she was shocked at the thought of such wanton behaviour on the part of the Queen. And all the while Moray was constantly attempting to explain to Mary that marriage with Darnley would be disastrous.

But Mary was in love. She could not see Darnley for what he was – a petulant, selfish boy, and an ambitious one too – even though by now he was not even troubling to hide his ill nature. His servants bore marks of the blows he gave them and once in a fit of anger he is reported as having struck the aged Duke of Châtelherault on the top of his head. Mary could see only his virtues. It is possible that she became his mistress at this stage for he began to behave with such arrogance that it seemed he thought he was already King of Scotland, and now made no attempt to please even the Queen.

The Queen of England now declared herself against the Darnley marriage. Moray and the Protestant nobles were against the marriage; Moray did not wish to see his own influence with Mary replaced by that of the Lennoxes, and he went so far as to prepare his followers to march against the Queen in order to prevent the marriage. The threat of civil war in Scotland was a very desirable state of affairs for the Queen of England. And it had all come about through the "lang lad", the "beardless boy", and Mary Stuart's unreasoning passion for him.

David Rizzio by this time had the Queen's complete confidence. She kept him at her side, to advise her on state affairs. Next to Darnley he was her favourite man.

Rumours were set in motion by the Queen's enemies that the Queen was a wanton woman who had had many lovers, the Cardinal of Lorraine, Chastelard and Rizzio being but a few of them. It was said that she was Darnley's mistress already and that she was insatiable in her sexual desires. John Knox revelled in these rumours, and Moray, who previously had done much to suppress them, no longer did so.

Opposition only increased Mary's determination to marry Darnley as soon as possible, and although a dispensation from the Pope was necessary because of the blood relationship between them, she would not even wait for this.

The ceremony took place on 29th July, between five and six in the morning, Mary, as the widow of the King of France, went to the chapel in Holyrood House wearing a black gown with a black hood attached to it. The Earls of Lennox and Atholl led her to the chapel and shortly afterwards she was joined by Darnley, a dazzling figure glittering with jewels. Mary was radiant, and when it was formally suggested that she cast aside her mourning and put on the raiment of a happy bride which would be a symbol that the old life was over and the new one about to begin, the reluctance she showed, according to the report by Randolph, the English agent in Scotland, was only for form's sake.

Knox recorded that there were four days of balling and banqueting and Darnley, who had been made Earl of Ross and Duke of Albany, was now proclaimed by Mary, King of Scotland. The wedding celebrations were interrupted by Moray's rebellion which forced Mary to lead her armies into battle against her half-brother. By now Mary's tolerance towards those who followed the Reformed religion had won their gratitude and they had no wish to see her replaced by her bastard brother. If many feigned to be shocked by rumours about her scandalous life, it seems certain that since the arrival of the Queen of Scots in Edinburgh, life had been more exciting. So there were many to rally to the Queen.

George Gordon was in prison, but his services were needed to subdue the treacherous Moray. So Mary freed him from prison, and at the Market Cross in Edinburgh the title of Lordship of Gordon was restored to him; a few days later that of Earl of Huntly was also given back to him. He immediately gathered his Highlanders together and the streets of Edinburgh were full of his steel-bonneted men.

Then Mary gave Bothwell permission to return, for she now believed that he would stand beside her, and he lost no time in doing so.

The first rift with Darnley oddly enough came through Bothwell. There was a saying on the Border that Bothwell was worth an army, and the Queen would wisely put him in charge of hers. Darnley, however, showed his resentment. Why should the uncouth Borderer take a post which he had decided should go to his own father? The Earl of Lennox had certainly not distinguished himself by his military genius, but Darnley was anxious to show his family what power he wielded, and that the Queen was so besotted by him that he only had to ask for what he wanted and it would be given to him.

He was right in this. The command went to Lennox. What the emotions of Bothwell were when he heard of the Queen's folly can well be imagined. It is likely that then Darnley took his first step to Kirk o' Field.

Moray in his attempt to seize the crown – for that was at the root of his endeavours – had relied on the help of Elizabeth. He should have known better. Elizabeth had no intention of joining in the fray. Let the Scots fight amongst themselves.

In spite of Lennox the day was won for the Queen and Moray had no alternative but to cross the Border where Elizabeth graciously offered him sanctuary. Elizabeth, however, admonished him for rebelling against his Queen – although she had done all she could to incite him to do so – and offered to intercede with her cousin of Scotland for his return to his country.

The rebellion was over and Mary could now devote herself to her petulant husband.

Bothwell had at this time decided that an alliance with a powerful family would be useful to him. He had hoped that his sister's marriage to the Queen's brother John Stewart would have served his family; but John had died and with him the hopes of favours coming from that quarter. Bothwell decided therefore to wed Jean Gordon, sister of the new Earl of Huntly who had inherited the nickname "Cock of the North" from his father. Jean was in love with Alexander Ogilvie of the Boyne and the thought of an alliance between a proud and dignified Highlander and an uncouth Borderer was repulsive to her. But the Queen's consent was asked to the marriage and she gave it. Only the bride's consent was not asked. In families such as the Huntly's, marriages were made for convenience and Moray's recent rebellion had made them and Bothwell allies.

Mary's attitude to Bothwell was strange. She must already have been aware of his overpowering sensuality which was destined to enslave her. He had slandered her with that horrible implication that she had been the Cardinal's mistress; he had added that she and the Queen of England did not make an honest woman between them. Yet she accepted this as she was to accept so much from him. She asked that the marriage of her attendant Jean Gordon take place in Holyrood House, but Bothwell had no intention of being dictated to by the Queen. It should take place in the Canongate Kirk, he said; and it did.

The wedding was celebrated in Kinloch House with the Queen as principal guest. The new King of Scotland accompanied her; but now that he felt secure in his position his desire to please Mary had disappeared. He sulked and complained. He did not think that the King of Scotland should be asked to attend such a wedding; he did not think that he should be expected to dine in Kinloch House. It was a mansion it was true but he was *royal*. Kings dined in palaces.

That must have been an uneasy occasion for Mary. She could no longer be blind to the character of Darnley. Randolph, Elizabeth's ambassador, wrote to Cecil that Darnley's pride was intolerable and his words not to be borne except where no man dare speak again. It seemed inevitable that she must set one bridegroom against the other, judge them, and begin to compare the lusty brigand with her weak husband.

During the recent rebellion, John Knox had sided with Moray and had suffered a set-back. Now Rizzio suggested to Mary that Darnley should go to St Giles's Cathedral to hear John Knox preach; many of the men who had come to her defence were Protestants and Mary should show her appreciation of this by sending Darnley to the cathedral. This was too much for Knox. Perhaps it was the sight of the arrogant Darnley lolling in his pew, sparkling with jewels, which enraged him. Certainly he was always ready to become enraged about anything concerning the Queen.

He chose a text from the twenty-sixth chapter of Isaiah. "Oh Lord our God, other lords besides Thee have had dominion over us, but by Thee only will we make mention of Thy name." Boys and women, he ranted, were sent to rule over them. He was of course referring to Darnley and the Queen. God had punished Ahab, he reminded his audience, for Ahab had joined with Jezebel in idolatry. He went on in this fashion for two hours, and Darnley, very conscious of his royalty, determined to show his followers that he was indeed the King, and had no need to take insults from a preacher. He called out that he was going hawking and summoned his followers to go with him. Noisily they strode out of the cathedral.

Mary agreed with Darnley that he had done right and ordered Knox not to preach again in Edinburgh when the sovereigns were present. Knox protested and brought up fresh charges against the Queen, but he was as ever a man of discretion where his own safety was concerned; and at that time the steel bonnets of the Highlanders were seen in the camps outside the city and Bothwell's Borderers were close at hand. They had come to protect the Queen from Moray's friends, of whom John Knox was one. On such an occasion the fiery man could be quite docile.

By the autumn of that year Mary knew that she had made a mistake. Darnley's behaviour grew more and more intolerable. It was not enough that high honours had been bestowed on him and the Queen had named him King. He was constantly agitating for the Crown Matrimonial. He wanted everyone to be aware that his power was at least equal to that of the Queen.

Mary was more than a sexually awakened woman; she needed spiritual as well as physical accord. She turned to Rizzio, as she seemed always to be doing now, and naturally the whisperings about them increased.

When Darnley had first arrived at the Court he had befriended Rizzio, knowing his influence with the Queen; but once the marriage was celebrated he showed his contempt for the Italian. Darnley was a fool in that he overestimated his own importance. Even at the height of her infatuation Mary did not forget that she was the Queen by right of inheritance. She was prepared to give him the title of King, but the crown was hers. Darnley had seen the assembling of Highlanders in defence of the Queen; he had ridden beside her at the head of her armies. In his arrogance he believed that they had come to *his* support. After all the issue had been the Queen's marriage and these men would surely have rather a man to lead them than a woman.

Darnley blinded himself to the obvious. The last thing men such as Huntly and Bothwell would do was support Darnley and the Lennox family, for they were not prepared to see another clan equal the importance of their own.

Darnley's success with the Queen had bemused him so that he believed there was no longer any need to woo her. She was won; she was his wife and although she was the Queen, he was the master now. He was frequently intoxicated; he openly discussed his relationship with the Queen and her need for him; he was unfaithful to her. He was becoming a danger to himself because his pride and obstinacy were accompanied by a kind of reckless courage which could lead him and those about him into an intolerable situation.

Randolph wrote to Cecil: "I cannot tell what mislikings of late there hath been between her Grace and her husband; he presses earnestly for the matrimonial crown, which she is loth hastily to grant, but willing to keep somewhat in store until she knows how well he is worthy to enjoy such sovereignty . . ."

It was, therefore, within a few months of her marriage that Mary discovered she had married a very unpleasant young man. By that autumn she was pregnant and had fallen as violently out of love with Darnley as she had fallen in.

Murder at Holyrood House

It was at this stage that Rizzio began to be in acute danger. The situation at Holyrood was becoming tense. Moray was in England desperately trying to get Mary's permission to return. The Protestant lords were jealous of Rizzio's influence; they suspected that he was in touch with Philip of Spain and they had no intention of allowing the Catholic religion to be established in Scotland. Morton, Maitland, Ruthven and Argyll were determined to rid themselves of the Italian. The Queen of England was well aware of what was going on for her ambassador, Randolph, was an excellent spy.

Inevitably Darnley played into the hands of the scheming lords. Mary had no respect for him, particularly after they had attended a dinner party at a house of one of the rich townsmen, and Darnley had behaved with arrogance and total lack of good manners. When he showed to the company that he was the worse for drink, Mary chided him and drew an insolent and obscene rejoinder. It was impossible for the Queen to accept such insults in public; she left the house and Darnley's servants carried him back, for he was quite incapable of walking, to his apartments in Holyrood House.

The Queen confided in David Rizzio. He believed that she could again gather sufficient loyal supporters to stand against Moray and any English he might bring across the Border. Yet David, and his master Philip of Spain, with all good Catholics, would wish to see the two kingdoms as one under a Catholic monarchy and the English bastard Elizabeth driven from her throne.

It is said that Darnley, finding Mary communing with Rizzio, accused them of being lovers. There was a quarrel and it was impossible for the Queen to quarrel with her husband without its becoming common knowledge. Darnley snapped his fingers when the Queen refused him her bed; he swaggered about the town with prostitutes, disgusting the Queen more every day.

The way was clear for the plotters. The instigator was probably Ruthven, though he was slowly dying of a wasting disease and it seems strange that in such circumstances he would become involved in such an undertaking. Yet he had always wanted power, and the fact that he could not have long to live did not deter him. Morton – the treacherous James Douglas – was in touch with the English and doing all in his power to bring about the return of Moray. Maitland had seen himself ousted by Rizzio. It was humiliating that the Queen should show more confidence in an Italian musician than a man who had proved himself a good statesman, who was cultured as few Scotsmen were in the sixteenth century, had suave good manners and had done much good for Scotland at the Court of England. Moreover, he was courting Mary Fleming. Lords Lindsay, Ochiltree, Boyd, Glencairn and Rothes were also involved. They drew up a document which they were all required to sign as they did not trust each other, and there was of course one other signature which was more important than any: that of the Queen's husband. Yet the cleverest of the band – Moray and Maitland – did not put their names to this incriminating document; Moray had the excuse of being out of the country.

The wording of the document was vague. There was no mention that Rizzio was to be murdered; but one clause in the document stated that the life of any who acted in a manner detrimental to Darnley's honour should not be spared. This was pointing straight at Rizzio, and it was tantamount to stating that he was about to be murdered.

Such a conspiracy could not be planned without a certain amount of leakage, and soon there were rumours that something was afoot. It would have seemed not improbable that Mary herself was in danger. For if she died Darnley would have a good chance of becoming King. He was the Queen's husband; he had royal blood; the Queen had bestowed on him the title of King. There was one who would prevent that – the child which Mary carried. She was six months pregnant at this time. It did not, therefore, seem unreasonable to suppose that if a plot was in progress and murder was its object it might be the murder of the Queen which was contemplated. Darnley was disillusioned with his lot; the Queen had showered such honours, gifts and doting affection on him that he had come to believe that he was indispensable to her. He was learning differently; and a man as self-opinionated and arrogant, young and inexperienced as he was could be easily led by wily men.

Rizzio should have been wiser. He knew of the jealousies and hatreds he inspired and the great desire to see him brought low. He was warned by an astrologer that he was in danger from "The Bastard"; he shrugged aside the warning, believing Moray was the one referred to.

And so there arrived the 9th March and the evening of the famous supper party. Darnley's rooms at Holyrood were immediately below those of the Queen and were connected to them by a staircase. Although it was the Lenten season Mary was not observing the fast because of her condition; she was also supping informally because being heavily pregnant it was not easy for her to move about in comfort. She was reclining on a couch as she ate. Her half-sister Jean, Countess of Argyll, and her half-brother, Robert Stewart, were present, so it was something in the nature of an intimate family party. Others included her Master of the Household, the Laird of Creich, her equerry Arthur Erskine, her doctor and of course her secretary David Rizzio. David was rather grandly dressed; his doublet was of fine satin, his hose of russet velvet and over these he wore what was called a nightgown but was the sort of hostess robe which women wear today and was meant for informal evening gatherings. The "nightgown" was made of a rich material and lined with fur.

One of the servants went to the window to draw the curtains as the draught was strong. The door of the supper room opened suddenly and there stood Darnley, and behind him Ruthven. Ruthven presented a startling spectacle as he advanced into the small room. On his head was a steel cap and as his cloak opened it was disclosed that he was wearing armour; reports say that his face was yellow and he looked as though he had risen from the grave which three months later was to claim him; he had the reputation for dabbling in black magic.

"Let it please Your Majesty, that yon David come forth from your privy chamber where he hath been overlong," he said.

Mary demanded to know how Ruthven dared come thus to her private apartments; to which Ruthven replied that he came for David. Mary turned on her husband and asked what hand he had in this outrageous intrusion into her privacy. Darnley was startled. He was not courageous by nature and he must at that moment have realized that he was caught up by ruthless men in an intrigue which he did not fully understand. He stammered a reply and Mary realized that it was not with him she had to deal. Ruthven then began to enumerate the sins of Rizzio and to suggest that the Queen was dishonoured by her intimacy with him. Rizzio, meanwhile realizing fully the acute danger in which he stood, cowered into his seat. Ruthven moved towards him and the Queen's Master of the Household made an attempt to stop him.

"Lay not your hands on me," cried Ruthven. "For I will not be handled."

He took out his dagger and at that the other conspirators dashed into the room. Rizzio clung to the Queen's skirts imploring her to save him but he was dragged away. The Countess of Argyll snatched up the candelabrum as it was about to fall; Darnley put an arm about the Queen as George Douglas took the dagger from Darnley's belt and stabbed the screaming Rizzio. He was dragged from the chamber and each of the conspirators thrust his dagger into the struggling body. The Queen began to call for help but she was seized by Andrew Kerr who whispered savagely that if she were not silent he would cut her into collops.

Mary heard the agony of Rizzio as more than fifty dagger thrusts sent him to his death. She fainted but before she did so she uttered the words: "His death shall cost you dear."

Ironically, Rizzio's mutilated body was laid on a chest which had been his bed when he had first come to Holyrood in a humble position, and was then robbed of its possessions by a porter.

When Mary recovered her senses she found Darnley beside her. The disordered table, the bloodstained room must have sickened her, and she was six months pregnant; but she was able to accuse her husband and demand to know how he had dared take part in such a wicked conspiracy. Darnley stammered that she had betrayed him with the Italian but she silenced him with scorn, for Ruthven was back in the room. He took no notice of the Queen but sat down heavily and demanded wine.

Mary asked if he were drunk and if that was why he now felt ill. She vowed vengeance on him. Her unborn son, she declared, would hear of this night and know which men to hold responsible. She had a powerful family abroad. The King of France and the Pope were her friends. They would not allow her to be treated as she had been without demanding revenge.

She sent one of her servants to find out what had happened to Rizzio and when she heard that he was dead, she wept. She recovered herself almost immediately, however, and said: "Farewell tears. We must now think on revenge."

Others had forced their way into the palace, among them Lord Bothwell. He must have given her new courage for she would know that Bothwell was not in this plot. He dragged Ruthven to his feet and demanded an explanation. Ruthven showed him the paper which the conspirators had signed. "What has been done," he said, "was done in the King's name." Bothwell pocketed the paper and left the room with it. When he had gone and the Earl of Huntly with him, there were shouts from below. The people of Edinburgh hearing the commotion within the palace and seeing men moving about in steel bonnets demanded to see the Queen to be assured that she was safe. Mary ran to the window but was seized by Lord Lindsay who swore that if she let the people know what had happened she would be "cut into collops." Darnley was then ordered to speak to the people and tell them that there was nothing wrong in the palace but a quarrel had broken out among the French servants. They were known to be noisy and quarrelsome and this did sound a likely reason for the commotion.

Mary commanded Darnley not to listen to her enemies and Darnley wavered as before. His vain young mind was beginning to grasp the fact that these violent men were working not so much for him as for themselves. But the men were round him, their daggers red and wet with Rizzio's blood, so he did as he was bid. Mary must have hated him in that moment.

Rizzio was dead; Darnley was a treacherous coward whom she should never have married; she was soon to bear a child and what harm had this night's work done to that?

Mary was helped to bed. She was a prisoner in her palace of Holyrood. But Lady Huntly – whose daughter had recently married Bothwell – was sent to look after Mary and was able to tell her that Bothwell and Huntly had escaped from the palace having discovered that the murderers of Rizzio had planned to kill them too, as well as all those who were loyal to the Queen. They had left only because they were more useful to the Queen alive than dead.

During that night Mary lay sleepless. She was in acute danger and fully aware of it. At this time she showed sagacity of a kind which had she employed it later might have saved her her throne. The child could prove her salvation. If she pretended that she was having a miscarriage everyone would believe her. It was surely to be expected that when a woman six months pregnant was forced to witness bloody murder and suffer threats to herself, she might well miscarry. She knew that if she stayed where she was she would be at her captors' mercy. Therefore she must escape and she would need help to do that. Darnley should help her; she did not trust him, but she would use him.

She sent for Darnley. They could not refuse to allow her to see her husband. He came, no longer the braggart but a very frightened young man. She suppressed her fury with him and made a show of some affection, and forced him to see that his position was as precarious as her own. They had deluded him; they used him because they had wanted it to be believed that the murder of Rizzio was a *crime passionel*. It was no such thing.

It was a political murder. They wanted to bring back the Protestants; they wanted to kill them both and their unborn child. They would perhaps let her live; after all she was the Queen. She had many loyal subjects who would not countenance her murder. But he? Did he think they would make him King? They had reserved that honour for Moray. There was only one thing to do, said Mary. They must escape. He must help her to do this and they would go together. Darnley's terror-stricken mind swayed this way and that, but when he was with Mary he believed her.

Lady Huntly smuggled in a message from Bothwell. If Mary could get away from Holyrood and join him he would have a Lowland force waiting for her. Huntly would be there with his Highlanders. He would have ropes smuggled in; she would be lowered down and horses would be waiting for her.

That was not possible in her condition. Her plan was better. With Darnley's help she would find a way out of this prison.

Now that Rizzio was dead and the Queen in a state of collapse which in her condition might well be fatal, the wily Moray considered it expedient for him to arrive in Scotland. He came at once to the Queen. The fact that she had a child to fight for appeared to give her not only courage but subtlety. She was about to make use of Darnley and would do the same with her brother.

Moray was completely deceived; he believed her still to be the frivolous girl who had arrived in Scotland fresh from France; he did not know that events had sharpened her wits.

He declared himself aghast at what had happened. How she must have laughed inwardly at that. As if she did not know that he was in the plot and that the object of it might well be to see an end of her and place the crown on his head. Two could play the game of deceit. She wept; she called attention to her state. She feared an imminent miscarriage. She had witnessed the murder of a close friend, her own secretary, she knew that she herself had been in acute danger. She needed a midwife without delay. Her door was guarded by soldiers; she complained that she found it most distressing because of her state. She did not want rough soldiers near her at such a time.

Why did they think it necessary to place a guard on her? How could she possibly escape in such a condition! Moray fell into the trap, no doubt because he was anxious to get her to believe that he had not been involved in the plot. She should have the midwife; the stairs should be cleared of soldiers. She embraced him warmly and no doubt marvelled that she could be as false as he was.

The midwife was sent and the soldiers taken from the corridors. The conspirators decided that if Darnley would stay in the Queen's room all night he could give the alarm if she attempted to escape. They had no idea that Mary had so played on Darnley's fears for himself that he had suddenly changed sides.

As soon as the plotters had retired to Douglas House, Mary was ready. She and Darnley left the apartment, went down by way of the backstairs and cut through the burial grounds. Arthur Erskine, her equerry, was waiting with horses. They mounted – Mary behind Erskine – and galloped away. Here again Darnley betrayed his feeble character. As they rode he grew afraid because if they were caught the lords would know that he was no longer with them. As Erskine did not want to gallop because of Mary's condition, Darnley galloped on ahead to save his own life if possible.

It was early morning when they came in sight of Dunbar Castle. News of their coming had gone on ahead of them and a party of riders came out to greet them. At the head of the party rode Lord Bothwell.

awing of Mary in about 1559 by François Clouet.

Mary c. 1565; a portrait done in the eighteenth century, after a contemporary miniature.

e 'Pelican' portrait of Queen Elizabeth c. 1575, attributed to Nicholas Hilliard.

Mary and Francis as king and queen, a miniature from Catherine de' Medici's prayer-book.

Henrie Steuart Duke of
Albanye and Marie
Queen of Scotland
1566

Mary and Darnley, from the Seton Armorial, which was executed for the 5th Lord Seton.

David Rizzio. A nineteenth-century engraving thought to be based on a contemporary portrait.

James Hepburn, 4th Earl of Bothwell – the only known portrait of him.

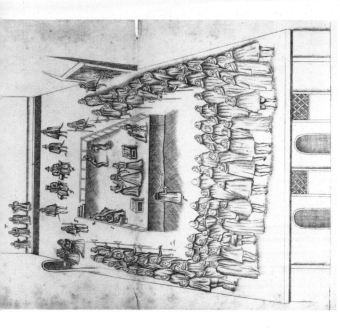

Contemporary sketch of Mary's execution. On the left, she is seen entering, and is then disrobed by her ladies. Shrewsbury is sitting on the platform (1); Paulet is sitting facing the Block (3); and Doctor Fletcher, Dean of Peterborough, is standing (6).

Satirical placard of Mary as a mermaid, or prostitute, and Bothwell as a hare – this was his family crest. It was posted up in Edinburgh in March 1567.

Detail of Mary's white marble monument in Westminster Abbey built by order of James I, and completed in 1612 by Cornelius and William Cure. Within a few years, the tomb was reputed amongst Catholics to produce miracles. Mary's face was probably modelled from the death-mask taken at Fotheringay.

Mary in mourning for her father-in-law in 1559. The 'Deuil Blanc' portrait by Clouet.

Henry Stuart, Lord Darnley, and his younger brother Charles. The portrait was commissioned by the Earl and Countess Lennox from Hans Eworth in 1563, when Darnley was seventeen.

The Rape of the Queen

Mary must at this time have already begun to fall under the spell of Bothwell. Her passion seems inevitable partly because of the weakness of Darnley. Hating and despising the coward she had married, a man who was so different in every way must have been appealing. Moreover, Bothwell was the man of destiny; he always appeared at important moments in her life and always in the role of the strong man, the man of action, the protector. Because she was an extremely feminine woman she was fascinated by those characteristics which Bothwell possessed to such a degree. Power is the essence of masculine appeal to a woman of Mary's nature. Bothwell possessed that power . . . the power to escape from Edinburgh Castle, to defy all her enemies and her too if need be, the ability to protect her while refusing to show her the respect she was accustomed to.

Bothwell's Borderers and Huntly's Highlanders were with her to a man for, hearing that the Queen had escaped from Holyrood and although heavy with child had ridden all through the night, she had become a romantic heroine to them. Men rallied to her banner.

With Bothwell beside her she was able to march into Edinburgh with 8,000 men behind her. This was triumph. The conspirators hurried into hiding. Even Maitland – fearful of being implicated – thought it necessary to go to the Highlands. Moray remained. If he had left it would have been tantamount to a confession that he had been involved. Mary knew that he had, but she realized that they must keep up the pretence that this was not so.

June had come, the month when her child was due to be born. Edinburgh Castle was chosen for his birthplace. The birth pangs were agonizing and of long duration and the Queen suffered greatly. Her son, who would be James VI of Scotland – and James I of England – was born on 19th June 1566, and over his face was a caul which was said to be lucky.

There was great rejoicing in the streets of Edinburgh with carousing in the taverns, and bonfires in many streets. There was also speculation and rumour, inevitable when it was remembered that but three months before the man who, it was said, had been Mary's lover had been brutally murdered, and that the deed had been given all the signs of a *crime passionel* planned by a jealous husband. Many scrutinized the babe, seeking to detect any resemblance in the child to the Queen's Italian secretary. And there were always those who could be relied on to declare that they had found what they had sought.

At royal births which were of great importance there often arose whispered doubts as to the authenticity of the child. The old story of a changeling being smuggled into the royal bed because the royal child had been born dead or had died soon after, had become almost a cliché. It was not possible that it should be forgotten in such dramatic circumstances. On this occasion there was a hint that the Countess of Mar smuggled her child into the bed to be brought up as the royal Prince; but this has been proved to be impossible; and there is no doubt that James VI was at least the son of Mary.

Knowing that these rumours were inevitable, Mary sent for Darnley and with many witnesses declared that the child was Darnley's son. She had recently come through a difficult birth; she had suffered great disturbance and discomfort during the later months of her pregnancy. She wanted everyone present to know that she was aware of her weak condition so that they would believe that when she made such a statement she was speaking the truth.

"My Lord," said the Queen (Herries's *Memoirs*, recorded by Rait), "God has given you and me a son, begotten by none but you. I protest to God, and as I shall answer to Him at the great day of judgment, this is your son and no other man's." She went on to express the hope that he would unite the two kingdoms of England and Scotland.

It seems certain that James was the true son of Darnley, for Mary was a religious woman and would never have made such a solemn declaration when her health was in such a precarious state. All the same, James's parentage was to be doubted throughout his life. It was jokingly said when he attained his reputation for wisdom that he was called the British Solomon because he was the son of David, a remark more witty than truthful. But the dramatic events which had preceded his birth would never be forgotten.

Melville tells how he took the news of the birth to Queen Elizabeth. Lady Boyne (Mary Beaton who had just been married to Ogilvie of the Boyne, the man with whom Jean Gordon, Bothwell's wife, had been in love) brought the news to him; and he left Scotland immediately for the English Court. Four days after setting out he was in England, and he went to Greenwich to see the Queen. "Her Majesty," he wrote, "was in great merriment and dancing after supper." When she heard the news her merriment passed. Elizabeth sat down and with her hand on her cheek made the famous remark: "The Queen of Scotland is lighter of a fair son and I am but a barren stock."

The baby was, of course, of the greatest importance to both countries for since Elizabeth had no heirs, he was in the line of the succession not only to the Scottish but to the English throne.

Darnley's position had been weakened by the birth of his son. He had no chance of being crowned King of Scotland while the boy lived. Knowing the flaccid nature of her husband and his wild unreasoning ambition, Mary had a cause for anxiety; and she was very watchful of ambitious Darnley during those eight months between the birth of James and the death of Darnley.

But at the same time Mary knew a certain amount of contentment. She could enjoy the maternal joys; and there is evidence that at least there was a little happiness at that time of her life. But the ambitious men around her would not leave her alone to live at peace with her child.

Darnley was treated with contempt whichever way he turned. As a statesman he had no hope against Moray and Maitland.

At this time he was alternately pleading and threatening. Moray warned him that any attempt at treachery would receive the punishment it merited. Yet Mary was the one who suffered most. His bouts of drunkenness and his infidelities with the lowest types of women were humiliating. If ever a man courted destruction that man was Darnley.

Mary, always anxious to please those whom she loved, was persuaded at this time to allow Maitland to return to Court. Mary Fleming was in love with the statesman and no doubt put up a good case for him.

The recall of Maitland may well have prodded Bothwell towards action. Since the murder of Rizzio he had risen high in the Queen's favour: he had made plans for her escape from Holyrood, and had been waiting for her at Dunbar; it was Bothwell's aid which had enabled her to march triumphantly back into Edinburgh; Bothwell's star was rising. And if Maitland returned he would certainly do all in his power to undermine that rise, and he would have Mary Fleming to help him. Maitland was in a very enviable position. He was a man of refinement, who had often been sent to Elizabeth as envoy from the Queen of Scotland because his manners were such as might be expected to ingratiate himself with that exacting personage. He was possessed of a subtlety rare at the Scottish Court. It had been a blunder to disappear along with the conspirators at the time of Rizzio's murder unless he was more deeply involved than was apparent. It seems likely he was because Maitland was too subtle a politician to make that sort of blunder had he not been involved.

Bothwell, therefore, sought to consolidate himself. That his manner of making his position firm was through the Queen's passion for him is certain; and that rape took place seems to have been generally accepted. Melville in his *Memoirs* stated that the Queen married Bothwell since he had ravished her and laid with her against her will at Dunbar, but it could well have taken place before. To a man of Bothwell's calibre rape was no novelty. Much of his life had been spent on the Border where frequent raids had taken place. To descend on defence-less villages to pillage and burn and take the women he wanted was merely a way of life. As he was twice as virile as normal men and had never thought it necessary to curb his appetites, it seemed reasonable to suppose that his way of subduing the Queen would have been one in which he had had a great deal of practice.

Considering the return of Maitland and Moray, whose ambitions he well understood, and his assessment of Mary's character, it seems possible that Bothwell saw only one way of making his position secure. Mary was a very desirable woman; she was a Queen; and although Bothwell was very likely not in love with her, forcing her submission in a manner in which he was so well practised would be an exciting endeavour. Marriage with the Queen would be a very desirable state. He had seen foolish Darnley squander his chances. Had Darnley not been a fool, had he kept the Queen in love with him, he would not be in the position he was. Bothwell's method would not be the tender approach which Darnley could have managed; he was by nature the rough Borderer and certainly sensed in Mary's nature that dormant passion which was waiting to be roused, and he would have been aware that he with his forceful ways could arouse it.

She was married to Darnley; he was married to Jean Gordon. Neither of them was free therefore; but marriage with the Queen was Bothwell's ultimate goal. Mary hated her husband; Bothwell did not hate his wife. He appears to have been more intrigued with her than with any other woman. She was clever; she had not wished to marry him and was indifferent to his infidelities; and indifference was a novelty to Bothwell. Women had either desired him passionately or hated him. There were three women who stood out among the armies of others who had submitted to him: Janet Beaton, the Lady of Buccleugh, years older than he was (and aunt to Mary Beaton) who had been his mistress over several years and remained his friend until the end of her life. She was an unusual woman who was married five times and had so many lovers that she was regarded as a high-class courtesan. She was attractive still though in her sixties, and because of her power over the opposite sex was inevitably suspected of practising sorcery. Janet had taught Bothwell a great deal. As far as it was possible for him to love anyone he loved her. He might have married her if the difference in their ages had not been so great. Then there was his wife, who had married him reluctantly and who had brought him a fortune. And then the Queen. The most important of these women to his ambitions was of course Mary and he was forced to act promptly as Maitland was back; Mary must be subjugated.

If it is accepted that rape took place – and this must surely be the case – the question arises of when. Did it take place at Dunbar Castle after the murder of Darnley when Bothwell made clear his desire to marry her? At that time Mary had been to Stirling to visit her little son and was returning to Edinburgh when about six miles from the capital she and her party were intercepted by Bothwell and some 800 men. The strength of this force made it possible for him to demand that Mary accompany him and, as her followers were ready to do battle, to avoid bloodshed Mary agreed to go. Bothwell, having abducted the Queen, made her his prisoner in Dunbar Castle. Sir James Melville was of the Queen's party as were Maitland and Huntly; and it is Melville who has given credence to the story that it was here that, as Bothwell's prisoner, Mary was forced to submit to his embraces.

There are many versions of Mary's submission to Bothwell and several of them are plausible. It is said that she was well aware that Bothwell would be waiting for her at this spot, that there would be an abduction and presumably rape. This would give the Queen an excuse for agreeing to marry her ravisher, which indeed her religious conscience might say was necessary in the circumstances. At this stage Bothwell had, it seemed, certainly been deeply involved in the murder of Darnley; the question was how deeply Mary was involved. Yet that she was the passionate slave of Bothwell is evident and it seems hardly likely that rape would have been necessary at this stage of the affair.

The theory which seems to me more plausible is that the rape took place *before* the murder of Darnley, and that Bothwell planned the murder only when he was sure of his Queen. He intended to marry her, and to do this must first rid himself of his wife – not an insuperable act – but how was he to rid himself of Darnley, scion of a noble and powerful family, who bore the title of King of Scotland? There was only one way of freeing Mary from that marriage, and that was by the death of Darnley. But before he became implicated in such a deed which could cost him his life, it seems reasonable to suppose that he would wish to be sure of the Queen; and being Bothwell it seems that this was the most likely method he would choose.

Probably the rape took place in the Exchequer House. The Queen was spending a few nights there. The christening of her baby son was soon to take place and she wished to check accounts and decide what clothes should be worn. Perhaps she welcomed the opportunity to escape from the Court for a short while. She took with her only one lady-in-waiting and a servant. Next to the Exchequer House was a dwelling occupied by a man who once served Bothwell; and the lady-in-waiting whom Mary had taken with her was Lady Reres who owed her position in Mary's household to her connection with one of those arbiters of power, the Maries. Lady Reres had been Margaret Beaton, and was sister to Janet Beaton; they were, therefore, both Mary Beaton's aunts. Lady Reres had almost certainly been one of Bothwell's mistresses while Janet held sway.

Besides Lady Reres, there was one other servant in the Exchequer House, Bastian, a Frenchman; and next door was David Chambers who had once served Bothwell. Rumour had it that Bothwell had used Chambers's house as a meeting-place with certain women and that Chambers, on occasions, acted as procurer.

Mary would no doubt be taking supper alone in her bed-chamber, revelling in the lack of ceremony which doubtless seemed very desirable from time to time. Bastian, the French-man, could have been easily dealt with; he knew in any case that the Queen favoured Bothwell; Lady Reres could be relied upon to do a favour for an old lover who no doubt still had some attraction for her. (It is surprising how much devotion such a brutal man inspired in his mistresses. One can only assume that this was due to his extreme virility and his prowess as a lover which such women found irresistable and always longed to arouse). It seems reasonable to suppose that by means of these servants so faithful to him, so false to their mistress, Bothwell had entry to the Queen's sleeping chamber.

Mary was already under his spell. What would her reaction be when a practised ravisher broke into her apartments, making suggestions to her, or perhaps not even waiting for that? When Chastelard had been discovered in her bed-chamber she had immediately raised the alarm and she, who disliked violence, had called for her brother to kill the intruder. Yet she had enjoyed a mild flirtation with Chastelard, had allowed him to quote his poetry to her extolling her beauty and the desire she aroused. This was different. Bothwell was no poet, no maker of pretty speeches; he was a man who came right to the heart of the matter without preamble; and the purpose of his visit would have been clear to her.

She would have surely protested; but Bothwell would see beyond the protest. This was a woman who responded to his masculinity, who cried out a feeble No while her body was saying Yes. That experienced handler of female flesh would understand absolutely; there would be no deceiving him.

So, I believe, the rape of the Queen was effected.

It may be asked why, if Bothwell had so behaved, the Queen did not have him imprisoned and sentenced to death. The answer to that is clear. In the first place, even if her dignity had been outraged and she had wished for revenge, she could not have faced the humiliation which would ensue if it were generally known that she had been so treated; she would imagine the rumours this would give rise to, and there would always be enemies to say that she had lured Bothwell to bed and was now making excuses for herself. The other alternative is, I am sure, the true one. The rape was for her an enjoyable experience; she had long been aware of Bothwell; she had given him her favour when he proved himself to be loyal at the time of Rizzio's murder. She was sexually awakened as never before and she was as eager for their physical encounters as he was.

It, therefore, appears highly probable that they became lovers from that date. Mary's nature was against her. Wholeheartedly generous to her friends, she would be lavishly so to a lover. It was unfortunate that her fancy should have settled on such a man. Ambitious, ruthless, sexually insatiable, Bothwell could indulge in such an affair with whole-hearted abandon, and at the same time be calculating how much good would come to him and making up his mind to extract the utmost. Her upbringing in France would have been in complete contrast to his; her refinement and his crudity would have been extremes, but this was an attraction of extremes. Whatever his feelings for her, there can be no doubt of hers for him.

When raiders from over the Border ravaged the land near Jedburgh it was necessary for Bothwell to ride there with his followers to protect his family's property. Shortly after he had left, Mary decided to go to Jedburgh, which is an indication that she wished to be near him. She had a perfectly good excuse for going as an assize was to be held there, but it is something of a coincidence that she should have a desire to attend this particular assize when Bothwell was in the area.

As she neared the town a messenger came to her with the news that Bothwell had been wounded. A certain highwayman, John Elliot, known as John of the Park, had been in the neighbourhood and Bothwell had gone out to get him. He found his prey but in the affray the highwayman, only slightly wounded, escaped after shooting Bothwell through the thigh. Bothwell was put into a cart and taken home to die. He also had wounds in the head and one of his hands.

Mary's relief to discover that he was not dead must have been overwhelming, but she did not immediately go to see him; that would have been to betray herself. She waited until the assize was over and then went to his castle of Hermitage where he lay as though on his deathbed. His life was despaired of.

But Bothwell had the constitution of an ox and recovered; it was Mary who became ill. After visiting Hermitage she collapsed and was taken to the house of Lady Fernyhirst in a litter. This seems further evidence of the fact that she was in love with Bothwell. After having witnessed the murder of Rizzio she had ridden through the night to safety when six months pregnant, and three months later had given birth to a healthy son; but she had seen Bothwell, as she thought, on his deathbed and the result was collapse.

She nearly died. She was plunged into terrible melancholy and was heard to say that she wished she were dead. She was beset by violent vomiting and convulsions, and when this had passed she lay inert, her limbs so cold and she so still that her servants believed she was dying. In the churches prayers were said for the salvation of her soul and all over Scotland people were asking what would happen when the Queen was dead.

Yet, when Bothwell did not die, she began to recover. She summoned her lute player, John Hulme, and her pipe player, John Heron, to soothe her with their talents, and she planned a new dress which should be made in readiness for her when she rose from her bed. It was to be in red silk, taffeta and black velvet, and was to contain twenty, four and three ells of these materials respectively.

Thus there seems evidence of the damning fact that Bothwell and Mary were lovers before the death of Darnley.

The Mystery of Kirk o' Field

Mary's son was christened in the royal chapel of Stirling Castle. The baby was six months old; he had an illustrious set of godparents: the Queen of England, the King of France and the Duke of Savoy. Darnley, with customary lack of foresight protested against the Protestant Queen of England as one of the sponsors, but Mary told him not to be foolish: Elizabeth continued to express her determination not to marry, in which case she could not produce a legitimate heir. Baby James, therefore, stood a good chance of inheriting the crown of England and would by this bring about the greatly desired conclusion – the unity of England and Scotland. The Count of Brienne carried the baby, acting as proxy for Charles of France; and it was an impressive scene, lit as it was by torches.

Elizabeth sent a gold font for the child, and the Countess of Argyll was proxy for the Queen of England. The christening was performed in accordance with the rites of the Catholic Church which made for a little awkwardness when the god-parents were as Catholic as the King of France and as Protestant as the Queen of England. The custom at Catholic christenings was for the priest to spit into the mouth of the child during the ceremony. This Mary very wisely forbade. Mary was proud of her son, and perhaps because of the scandal attaching to his birth and the terrible events which it had so closely followed was very anxious that all homage should be paid to the baby for whom she had such high hopes. Because she had wanted the occasion to be a brilliant one she herself had bought new clothes for all those who attended. There were fireworks, feasting and masques – it was a ceremony worthy of the King who was to be the first to share the thrones of England and Scotland.

There was one notable absentee – Darnley. For what reason it is not exactly known. He was in the castle at the time and remained in his own apartments which was exactly the way to call attention to himself. It could have been construed as an indication that he did not consider the child to be his and that he believed the rumours that James was Rizzio's son; or it may have been that he did not wish it to be seen how little regard the Queen had for him. At all events, he did not attend the christening of the little Prince; and shortly after the christening he left for Glasgow.

Darnley's time was running out.

In Glasgow Darnley became ill. Whether it was smallpox or syphilis from which he suffered there is some doubt, but he was so disfigured by the disease that it was necessary for him to wear a piece of gauze over his face, and the odour of his room is reported as being decidedly obnoxious. It was at this time that the letters which became known as the Casket Letters were said to have been written. If they were actually written by Mary, then she was undoubtedly involved in the murder of Darnley. Who but Mary could have written the poems which betrayed so much? The only person who might have had the education to write so in the French language is Maitland. But it seems unlikely that he would have done this; he was no poet.

It is a question which cannot be solved and on it hangs the question of the guilt or innocence of Mary Stuart.

Even if she had not so urgently desired Bothwell, she would still wish to be rid of Darnley. But now her queenly dignity demanded that she could not continue as Bothwell's mistress, for his manners were so crude that he would not hesitate to treat her as a light of love. She wanted to regularize their union; and there was only one way in which she could do that, by marriage.

Who can say what really happened on that fateful night? It has been a matter for controversy ever since it happened. How far was Mary implicated? How innocent was she? It is something of which we can never be sure.

Darnley's folly is almost incredible. Before his illness he was writing to Philip of Spain hoping to discredit Mary and gain support which would place him on the throne. She was surrounded by Protestants, he complained. Bothwell was her greatest favourite, and as far as he could be said to follow any religion he followed the Protestant one. Moray and Maitland were at her elbows and they were Protestant. But Philip was too wily to strike up any pact with a young man whose foolishness and unreliability were notorious.

Darnley was an encumbrance not only to Mary but to the entire country, and the report that divorce was in the minds of Moray and Maitland as well as Mary seems plausible. Men such as Maitland realized the importance to themselves of bringing back some of the able statesmen who were still in exile after the Rizzio affair; and Mary was offered help in obtaining a divorce from Darnley provided that she recalled Morton and others. This she accepted, provided that the divorce would not weaken the position of her son as heir to the throne.

Moray, according to Huntly and Argyll, discussed the divorce with Mary and used the ominous phrase about "other means" which might be employed, at which he, Moray, would "look through his fingers". This was as near as these men could reasonably come to saying that they were going to be rid of Darnley at all costs. Mary quickly replied that nothing must be done that might tarnish her honour and conscience, at which Maitland assured her that nothing should be done which was not approved by the Parliament. But the fact that Moray was prepared to "look through his fingers" does point to the fact that other methods than those approved by Parliament could be put into action.

It is certain that there was a plot afoot to rid Scotland of Darnley. It was for this reason that he had gone to Glasgow, known as Lennox country, where his family and its followers carried great influence. A band of powerful men were plotting against Darnley's life and the fact that Moray was turning a blind eye (not wanting to take part in such a deed while wanting to reap the utmost benefit from it) suggests that something, not authorized by Parliament, was about to take place. The leading conspirator was certainly the one who had the most to gain, Bothwell, although the others could not have known how much at this stage.

It seems likely that a bond was signed by a group whose intention was to rid Scotland and Mary of Darnley by some unspecified means. Sir James Balfour, the lawyer, doubtless had charge of the bond and was in the plot. He bought gunpowder at a cost of £60 and this was stored in his brother's house at Kirk o' Field. He knew the district well and would have been able to advise the conspirators how best the murder could be carried out. That he was deeply involved seems certain. His name was mentioned on the placards which appeared on the Edinburgh streets denouncing Darnley's murderers; and Bothwell, during the brief spell when he had the authority to reward an accomplice, made him Governor of Edinburgh Castle, an unusual post for a lawyer.

Morton was reputed to have signed the bond after he was allowed to come out of his exile. Others included Argyll, Huntly, Maitland and of course Bothwell, the notable exception being Moray. This bond is not in existence alas; but according to the Queen's secretary, Nau, Bothwell gave it to Mary when they parted for the last time to prove that those nobles who accused Bothwell as the sole murderer of Darnley had all been involved in the crime.

By Christmas Mary had given the necessary pardons to the exiles.

It was at this stage that Darnley was ill of the disfiguring and nauseating disease. Mary was advised to bring him to Edinburgh. One wonders why Darnley left the safety of Glasgow for Edinburgh; there must have been some reason. Mary persuaded him but how did she manage it? She may have feared that in Glasgow he would plot against her, and there had been a strong rumour that he intended to kidnap the little Prince. At all events, there is no doubt that Mary persuaded Darnley to come to Edinburgh, that the house chosen for his convalescence belonged to the Balfour family, and that Sir James Balfour's name was one of those on the bond. It seems a strange choice of a house for a man who bore the title of King of Scotland unless it was intended to be the scene of a murder.

It stood in a quadrangle near the church of St Mary-in-the-Field and was known as the Kirk o' Field. Its advantage was that it was within walking distance of Holyrood House. Hamilton House, which belonged to the Hamilton family, was in the same quadrangle and Darnley's man Nelson, after the murder, stated that although Darnley had finally agreed to come to Kirk o' Field he had not expected to be lodged in the rather humble Balfour dwelling.

One of the reasons given for taking Darnley to this house was that it was built on a slight hill so that it would be more healthy than Holyrood House which was notoriously low-lying. The house had three doors, one leading out to the garden, one into the quadrangle and another which led into the alley. It was a house of two storeys. Darnley's bedroom was immediately above the room which had been prepared for the Queen when she should sleep in the house. A spiral staircase in a turret connected the upper with the lower chamber; there were two small ante-rooms leading to the chambers, and on each of the floors a few cupboard-like rooms known as garde-robes with sliding panels for doors. The house was built over an arched crypt.

Humble it might be but handsome furniture had been brought from Holyrood to give it a royal look. Tapestries were put into Darnley's bedroom with a special bed, given to Darnley by Mary, hung with velvet which was embroidered and trimmed with cloth of gold and silver.

One of the most revealing indications that there was a plot afoot and that many of the nobles were concerned in it was Moray's sudden departure from Edinburgh. Moray was a man with a reputation for honesty and stern devotion to duty to preserve, so he always made sure that when a crime of which he had foreknowledge was to be committed he should not be there to be implicated. Moray left Edinburgh on the plea of his wife's ill health.

The deed had been planned to take place on the night when one of the Queen's servants was getting married. The bride and groom were favourites of the Queen so she would naturally attend their wedding, and because of these celebrations Mary would spend the night at Holyrood House instead of returning to the house at Kirk o' Field. It was Sunday, 9th February. Lent was about to begin and it was for this reason that the date had been chosen for the wedding, so that the Lenten season should impose no restrictions on the celebrations.

The murder of Darnley seems to have been the most ill-planned in the history of crime. The plot must have leaked out, for Robert Stewart, the Queen's bastard brother, heard rumours that a murder was to take place and tried to warn Darnley not to stay in the house at Kirk o' Field, a warning which Darnley did not appear to take seriously.

The wedding was celebrated at noon as planned, but a masque was to be performed that evening, so Mary took supper at the house at Kirk o' Field in the company of her host Balfour, Bothwell, Huntly and Cassillis. While Mary sat with her husband, the nobles diced together. If we can believe the evidence of Bothwell's servant, known as French Paris, who, however, made his statements under torture, gunpowder was at that time being brought into the vaults below the room in which they sat. But whether it had actually been brought in on that evening or had been put there before is uncertain.

In due course Mary said farewell to Darnley and left for Holyrood House. As she passed into the street she met Paris and commented on the fact that his face was blackened, which does suggest that he had been taking the gunpowder into the vaults on that night. Back at Holyrood House she joined the merrymakers and officiated at the bedroom farce which was considered a necessary part of sixteenth-century weddings: to break the benediction cake over the bride's head, to present her with a silver posset cup and throw the stocking. She broke up the proceedings earlier than was expected and retired to bed.

The explosion burst forth and rumbled through the streets of Edinburgh. Many heard it and came running out of their homes. A short time before, Bothwell had been identified running from Kirk o' Field but by this time had managed to reach his bed in Holyrood House. Feigning to have been aroused from his sleep he started up, still wearing his clothes and his face grimy from activities in the house at Kirk o' Field.

"Fie," he cried. "This is treason."

As the chief nobleman, with Huntly, it was his duty to ride out immediately to the scene of the crime. With characteristic bravado he went with his men and his fierce looks challenged any who dared suggest they had seen his recent hurried departure from Kirk o' Field.

The house was blown up but the bodies of Darnley and his valet Taylor lay in the garden. Darnley wore a nightgown and nothing beneath it. He had clearly left his bedchamber in great haste. There was no sign on either body that they had been injured by falling masonry or by gunpowder. Buchanan says there was no fracture or bruise. They had apparently been suffocated, the method suggested being that a damp cloth was placed over the face.

What did happen? Did Darnley and Taylor, hearing strange noises, discover what was happening and manage to escape into the grounds just as the fuses were being lighted? This is the most likely inference; and there in the garden they were doubtless overtaken by those who had planned that they should be blown up in Balfour's house.

The plot had gone awry. The bodies were to have disappeared in the explosion yet there they were, very carefully suffocated. How different it would have been if they could have been strangled in their beds before the explosion. Then their bodies would have disappeared and this grisly evidence lost.

The Queen's Third Husband

The clumsily planned murder must arouse speculation and when it was known that Darnley and Taylor had been found dead, yet untouched by the explosion, all pretence of accident was at an end. Moreover, a shoe belonging to Archibald Douglas was found in the garden near the murdered men. The elaborate planning, the luring of Darnley to the house, the undermining of it with gunpowder – all had been useless because fate had decided to act against the plotters.

Next morning the people were crowding the streets. Placards were fixed to the Tolbooth. "Who is the King's murderer?" asked one. And beneath it was a crude drawing of a man unmistakably Bothwell.

Mary behaved at this stage with the utmost decorum. She appeared stunned by the news. She prepared to go into mourning for forty days and nights and ordered her mourning clothes for her second widowhood.

She went to the castle of Seton for three days and when she returned Edinburgh was in a tumult. A number of placards had appeared, most of them accusing Bothwell; and the Queen's name was being mentioned in connection with him and the crime. Darnley's family, the Lennoxes, demanded that Bothwell be brought to trial. Bothwell reacted in characteristic manner. He rode through the streets of Edinburgh, his followers about him in their steel bonnets, calling on anyone who had something to say against him to do it openly. He would wash his hands in their blood. He would take on any one of them single-handed. His accusers did not accept his challenge yet so great was their clamour that Mary found it necessary to allow Lennox to bring Bothwell to trial before the Parliament.

What followed could scarcely be called a trial. Lennox, the chief prosecutor, was afraid to enter the city because Bothwell had forbidden him to do so with more than six followers. No jury would dare find Bothwell guilty while Edinburgh was filled with his supporters. He had made it clear that any man who defied him would not be allowed to live long, and no man who valued his life was going to support Lennox's cause against that of Bothwell. So the verdict was a foregone conclusion.

There was a strong suspicion by now of Bothwell's relationship with the Queen. Mary had given him the castle of Blackness and many of Darnley's jewels and furs. From the very day after the murder they appeared to act with the most astonishing abandon. Bothwell presumably wanted all to know that he did what he wanted to and would answer to none; but that Mary could have been so besottedly foolish is amazing.

Bothwell rode to the Tolbooth in velvet hose and doublet passemented and trussed with silver. It was not long before the verdict was given. "James, Earl of Bothwell, is acquitted of any art and part of the slaughter of the King." In triumph he galloped along the Canongate offering to meet any who disagreed with the verdict in single combat. No one accepted that challenge, but that did not mean his innocence was accepted.

Bothwell's aim was to be King of Scotland. He had succeeded in removing the King and had been acquitted of his murder – not because he had confounded the case against him but because there was scarcely a noble in Scotland who dared defy him. Moray had found it convenient, as usual, to leave the country. He would return at a more appropriate moment. The Queen was bewitched; there was nothing to stand in his way except his own marriage. He would soon settle that. He would divorce Jean and marry Mary; then when Mary was completely his, Scotland would be also.

He invited the chief of the nobles to Ainslie Tavern and there presented them with a bond to which he said he was going to ask them to affix their signatures. Those who signed this bond promised to side with Bothwell, to defend him against the slander of having been implicated in the murder of the King, to help him maintain any quarrel he might have with those who attacked him and to support him with their bodies, goods and heritage.

Moreover, weighing and considering the time present, and how our Sovereign the Queen's Majesty is now destitute of a husband, in the which solitary state the Commonwealth of the Realm may not permit her Highness to continue and endure, and therefore, in case the former affection and hearty service of the said Earl may move Her Majesty so far to humble herself as preferring one of her native born subjects unto all foreign princes, to take to Husband the said Earl [Bothwell], we and everyone of us undersubscribing, upon our honours and fidelity, obliges us and promises, not only to further, advance and set forward the marriage to be solemnized and completed betwixt her Highness and the said noble Lord . . . but in case any would presume directly or indirectly openly or under whatsoever colour or pretence to hinder, hold back or disturb the said marriage, we shall in that behalf, esteem hold and repute the hinderers adversaries or disturbers thereof as our common enemies and evil willers . . .

Under our hands and seals at Edinburgh this day of April the 19th, in the year of God 1567 years. (Rait, Anderson's *Collections*.)

Bothwell's effrontery must have dumbfounded the lords. They may have been aware of the relationship between him and the Queen, but for a man who had clearly been involved in the murder of her husband and who himself had a wife, his sheer arrogance must have seemed hard to beat. Bothwell had been plying them with liquor so that their minds must have been a little fuddled; and there was Bothwell, the most ruthless man in Scotland, with his warlike followers in Edinburgh, the blood of young Darnley on his hands, and the Queen firmly beside him.

The signatures included Morton, Maitland, Argyll and Huntly. It was surprising that these four should have agreed so readily to Bothwell's demands; it is an indication of how great was his strength and that there was no man in the kingdom who did not go in fear of him.

Little Prince James was at Stirling and thither Mary went to visit him. He was at that time ten months old and in the care of the Earl and Countess of Mar. It was on the way back from Stirling to Edinburgh that the famous "Dunbar abduction" took place. The small company surrounding the Queen were brought to a sudden standstill by the arrival of a band of armed men at the head of which was Bothwell.

It was a typical Bothwell gesture. The Queen was his prisoner, he declared, and taking some of her party with him – including James Melville, Maitland and Huntly – he rode back with the Queen to Dunbar Castle.

Melville, who was present, states that it was at Dunbar that Bothwell had ravished her against her will and that he had boasted that he would marry the Queen whether or not she agreed.

There is no doubt that Mary and Bothwell anticipated their marriage and lived together as if married at Dunbar Castle, but Bothwell's certainty that she would accept him and the fact that he had gained the signatures of the noblemen on his bond surely point to the certainty that they had been lovers before Darnley's death and that the rape took place at the Exchequer House.

Mary had had two weak and ineffectual husbands. Bothwell was a strong man. It seems certain that Bothwell brought her a physical satisfaction which no one else had been able to do. Only his overpowering virility and her need of it could have been the reason for her foolish behaviour.

It seems incredible that a woman in her position could have been so foolish, particularly when she had the example of her wily cousin below the Border which should have been a lesson to her. Had she forgotten that at the time of Amy Robsort's death there had been an ominous rumbling about Elizabeth's throne? Did she not hear the similar threatening sounds close to her own?

The whole world watched in amazement: Philip II following events from the solitude of the Escorial; Catherine de' Medici laughing secretly in the Louvre; and chief of all Elizabeth in her palace at Greenwich.

Mary went from folly to folly. There was but one thing now to be done. Mary was free, so Bothwell must be. Jean must give Bothwell his divorce. The grounds would be consanguinity because a Gordon had married Bothwell's great-great-grandmother. Jean was not going to allow this. She was willing to divorce Bothwell – she had never wanted him – but it was not going to be on those grounds. She brought an action against Bothwell for adultery and cited the blacksmith's daughter Bessie Crawford. This meant that a great deal of undignified evidence was brought forth to show how Bothwell had seduced the blacksmith's daughter and had sexual intercourse with her in the steeple of the abbey at Haddington and in the kitchens of Crichton. The most unpleasant details were brought out, such as how his servant had kept watch while he took the serving-girl into a corner for ten minutes. These details were obviously meant to discountenance Bothwell but he was without shame and his one desire now was to rid himself of his wife so that he would be ready to marry the Queen.

Bessie, Bothwell and the Queen were being freely discussed but that did not prevent the divorce being granted; Bothwell was free.

John Knox was aware of the power of Bothwell, and like Moray, that other good man, had decided it would be convenient to disappear for a while. He obtained permission to visit England and left John Craig to take his place in Edinburgh. Craig expressed his reluctance to take part in the marriage ceremony and even declined to read the banns. Bothwell raged into the cathedral and demanded to see the man who defied him. Craig pointed out that the Church had its law. There were so many points in the case at variance with it.

The Church frowned on adultery, abduction and rape; the divorce between Lord and Lady Bothwell was too sudden; the suspicions that Bothwell and the Queen had been concerned in Darnley's murder needed to be clarified.

Bothwell, who had faced the nobles of Scotland and got his way, who had forced his way into the Queen's apartment and made her realize his strength, was not going to be defied by a preacher. He retaliated in true Bothwell manner. He declared he would have the man hanged outside his own kirk unless he obeyed. Craig, a bold man, replied that only a royal command would make him do what he asked. That must have made

Bothwell laugh. A royal command! The fellow should have it. Bothwell was in command of the Queen.

The question of the rape was a difficult one. Rape was punishable by death and the reason the Queen was marrying so hastily was to regularize her union. Mary was forced to reply that rape could be forgiven if the woman concerned afterwards acquiesced and forgave the man who had forced her. This was what had happened in her case. She made it clear that it was her wish to marry Lord Bothwell. She gave him new titles. He became the Earl of Orkney and Lord of Shetland. The marriage was to take place.

On the morning of the Queen's third wedding day a placard was discovered attached to the doors of Holyrood. "Wantons marry in the Month of May," it read, quoting Ovid. It should have been clear to Mary that she had demeaned herself irrevocably in the eyes of her subjects.

In the chapel at Holyrood Mary married the Earl of Bothwell. She had taken the first step to Fotheringhay.

The world was shocked. One opinion was that the Queen of Scots was mad. She had forgotten her royalty. Philip of Spain could only be contemptuous. No help would come from him for a woman who could forget what she owed to her religion and her rank. Catherine de' Medici declared publicly that she was saddened and shocked by the behaviour of the Queen of Scotland.

The honeymoon was brief. Those Lords who had been bludgeoned into signing Bothwell's bond were not going to respect it. They hated Bothwell because he had become the most powerful man in Scotland; they were waiting for Moray to come back and lead them against him. The Queen's brother with his usual caution was awaiting the right moment to come forward and take over the Regency, for it seemed that after recent events Mary would stand very little chance of keeping her crown.

It was Kircaldy of Grange who gathered together an army against Bothwell. Morton and Argyll were not going to stand out against Kircaldy; Maitland, who would have preferred to remain aloof as Moray had done, was waiting for the opportunity to side with Bothwell's enemies. He was a shrewd politician and he had decided that Mary was unfit to rule such wild and undisciplined men as the Scots. He was ready to side with Moray as soon as Moray returned.

Bothwell left Sir James Balfour to hold Edinburgh Castle and went to Borthwick with Mary, there to make plans for raising an army to fight against the forces which were gathering against them. Bothwell believed his Borderers would join him and they would be ready for any opposing forces. Borthwick, some twelve miles south of the capital, was in a formidable position with its central fortress and windows thirty feet from the ground. But they had not been there many days when, instead of the forces Bothwell was expecting, Lord Home arrived and demanded his surrender. Bothwell scorned this demand, but he realized that he and Mary were besieged in the castle and, although it was guarded, he broke out. His plan was to go to Dunbar and there muster his followers. An ultimatum was sent to the Queen by the rebels: she must abandon Bothwell and return to Edinburgh. There she would be accorded the respect due to the crown. This she scornfully refused to do and was lowered from a window dressed as a boy; a horse was waiting for her and she galloped off to Dunbar and Bothwell.

Mary had no suitable clothes in which to ride out with Bothwell when he had assembled his men together. The only garments which could be found for her were those of a trades-man's wife. So she put on the red petticoat and a black velvet hat, a scarf was found for her, and the sleeves of her bodice were tied with points. But Bothwell was beside her; and he had supporters now. Her hopes must have been high. That was to be the last occasion they would be so, for a long time to come.

They came face to face with the army of the rebel lords at Musselburgh; the Queen and Bothwell camped on Carberry Hill, close to the spot where, when Mary was a child, the battle of Pinkie Cleugh had been fought. But then Scotsmen were fighting the English; on this occasion they were face to face with their own countrymen.

For a whole day the armies remained inactive. The Queen was not anxious to go into combat against her own subjects nor were they to fight against their Queen.

During the afternoon the Protestant Earl of Glencairn accepted the offer of the French ambassador du Croc to mediate, and the latter took a message to the Queen to the effect that if she would dissociate herself from Bothwell whom they wished to bring to trial for the murder of Darnley, they would continue to regard her as their sovereign.

When they heard this, Bothwell fulminated against the traitors who, he said, had signed the bond with him to make good his cause and defend it with their lives and goods, while Mary declared that her husband's cause was hers.

Bothwell boasted to du Croc that he had a bigger following than the enemy but du Croc pointed out that though this might be so he had only himself to command them whereas the other side had Kirkcaldy the finest general in Scotland, with such men as Atholl, Home, Lindsay and Ruthven. This was true and Bothwell could not deny it. Characteristically Bothwell then rode out and challenged Morton to single combat. Morton declined to fight; and while this was going on, those men who had stood behind Bothwell and had heard du Croc's remarks decided that the latter was right and that to remain would be certain death. One by one, they began to slip away to the other side.

Mary was in despair. Those whom she had believed to be her friends were deserting her and soon she and Bothwell would stand alone. She sent for Kirkcaldy and asked what terms he would offer. His reply was that if she would go to Edinburgh with him, Bothwell might go free. If she refused, it would be impossible to hold back his men. In a short time Bothwell would be slain and she their prisoner.

Mary made her decision. She would go back to Edinburgh. She was allowed to say a last goodbye to Bothwell.

As he embraced her, in full view of the armies, he is said to have given her the bond which incriminated those men who were now standing against him and demanding he be tried for a murder in which they had played some part. Yet it is unlikely that Bothwell would have allowed her to go meekly with the enemy. What did he whisper to her during that last embrace? Almost certainly he would have commanded that she make a bold bid to escape. They could mount their horses and gallop off to Dunbar and there gather a force against the rebels. Mary, however, was not able to do this quick turn-about which so many of her subjects seemed to effect with ease. She had given her word to go with the rebels, and she would not break that word. Perhaps she would have feared the consequences to Bothwell if she did. The fact remains that they parted and Mary went to the rebels as their prisoner, in the red petticoat of an Edinburgh tradesman's wife.

She was to learn that not only had she said goodbye to her lover but to freedom.

Mary's return to Edinburgh from Carberry Hill can be compared with that of Louis XVI and Marie-Antoinette from Varennes to Versailles. There she was seated on her jennet, her dishevelled hair hanging about her shoulders, her red petticoat torn and stained, robbed of all the trappings of royalty. She had lost the man for whom she had sacrificed everything worthwhile, her honour and her crown. There is nothing to inflame a ribald mob, long suffering from envy of the rich and powerful, so readily as to see the mighty fallen, and Mary the Queen was indeed brought low. They could shout aloud the calumnies they had only dared whisper before, and could be trusted to make full use of this occasion. "Burn the adulteress! Burn the murderess!" they shouted.

As the party neared Edinburgh two soldiers came close to the Queen and held before her a banner between two pikes; they marched in front of her and on that side of the banner which was turned towards her had been painted a picture of Darnley lying inert, and a small figure beside him represented little Prince James. The boy was kneeling and the words "Judge and revenge my cause, O Lord" were written on the banner. Everything that could humiliate her had been considered. Uncouth Lord Lindsay of the Byres and Lord Ruthven – son of the man who had been in the forefront of Rizzio's murder – were put in charge of her.

In an access of rage she turned to Lindsay and swore that she would have his head for this outrageous treatment, to which he replied with his usual lack of gallantry that she should watch it was not her own that fell.

How she must have suffered during that terrible ride! It was but four weeks since her fateful marriage and already she was separated from the man for whom she had sacrificed everything, the prisoner of men who were determined to strip her of her royalty. Fortunately it was getting dark when the procession reached the capital; but the crowds were thronging the streets, having heard that she was coming. They had thought up a refinement of the torture as an extra turn of the screw. They took her in through Kirk o' Field.

There by the wreck of the house, the procession paused. The banner was brought closer; the people crowded round shouting that the adulteress and murderess should be burned. One pictures the scene: so many faces distorted with rage, in the half-light; an occasional torch lighting up eyes that were gleaming with hatred and envy and desire to see royalty trampled in the dust.

That might have been her last moment had not Lindsay, Morton and Atholl been there to hold back the mob. They had no wish to make a martyr of her; they wanted only to prolong her sufferings. They did not want a murdered Queen, for the victims of murder had a habit of becoming saints. Darnley – that dissolute, vain, arrogant popinjay who had been universally despised – had been gradually climbing to his place among the martyrs since his murder. Kirkcaldy knew that Moray would now be on his way back to Scotland. What they wanted was a captive Queen, a Queen judged unfit to rule, and the strong Regent Moray to rule the country and keep the turbulent nobles in order.

Thus they passed through the mob to the Provost's house; they took her into a room where there was no bed, no means of washing, no change of clothes for her, no food. There was one window in this room and outside that stood the two soldiers with the banner so that whenever she looked out of the window she looked straight at that picture of her murdered husband and her son, praying for justice.

It happened, when looking from her window, that she saw Maitland in the street. Maitland had been her secretary and her friend; he was the husband of Mary Fleming; until Rizzio had grown so high in her favour he had been closer to her than any of her ministers. Maitland would help her, she thought. She called to him. Maitland was cautious – he had no intention of becoming involved. He walked quickly away, pretending not to se her.

What despair must have come to her then! Even those whom she had believed to be her friends had deserted her. Perhaps in that moment of revelation she considered the man who had brought her to this pass. Bothwell! How much did Bothwell really care for her and how much for what she could bring him? Those passionate encounters so wildly exciting to her, what did they mean to him? If she had not been a Queen would she have meant any more to him than Bessie Crawford had?

Life, which had long ago been like an enchanting pageant with herself as the Queen of the Revels, had become harsh and cruel. There was no one who loved her; no one whom she could trust. A terrible melancholy came over her and when she looked out of the window at that fearful banner hysteria broke out. She tore at her bodice so that her shoulders and the upper part of her body were almost bare; she was not in that moment the beautiful Queen but simply a terrified, desperate woman.

All through that night and the next day they kept her in the Provost's house, and then perhaps because they feared for her reason they took her to Holyrood House. This was another ordeal, for she had to walk to her palace by torchlight, with the mob closing in on her and calling her murderess and adulteress, while Morton and Atholl on either side of her walked with drawn swords to protect her. The banner was not forgotten; it was held before her eyes to torture her and inflame the mob.

It must have been a tremendous relief to reach Holyrood for there at least were two faithful ones waiting for her: Mary Seton and Mary Livingston. But the comfort she received from this reunion was brief. Ruthven and Lindsay were taking charge of her; she was not to stay in Holyrood House but to leave at once.

As it grew dark she was brought out of the palace. Horses were waiting and in the company of the two lords whom she disliked most Mary rode into the night. She was not sure of her destination. It was Lochleven, and there in the old castle on an island in the middle of the lake Mary would be the prisoner of the Douglases – Sir William and his mother, Margaret Erskine, who had been James V's mistress and was the mother of Moray.

And so for Mary began the years of captivity.

The Casket Controversy

This seems to be the place to consider that ever recurring theme – the mystery of the Casket Letters.

This notorious collection of documents was believed by some to be the correspondence between Mary and Bothwell. The casket itself was in fact a jewel case which was engraved with the letter F and had doubtless been given to Mary by Francis II her first husband. Mary had in her turn given the casket to Bothwell and he had used it for keeping his private documents. The story is that when Bothwell fled to Borthwick he did not take the casket with him but left it in Edinburgh Castle. After the disastrous happenings at Carberry Hill he sent one of his servants, George Dalgleish, to get the casket and smuggle it out of the country, and bring it to him, after he had already made his escape.

But Dalgleish was arrested, tortured and revealed the hiding place of the casket of letters. So they fell into the hands of Mary's enemies. Balfour appears to have been the man who informed Moray and his friends of the existence of the casket containing letters which Mary had written to Bothwell as well as certain documents incriminating the Queen. That they were important was obvious since Bothwell had sent his servant to smuggle them out of the country.

Sir James Balfour now began to play a big part in the story. He emerges as one of the most unprincipled men of the times – which is saying something. He earned the epithet "the most corrupt man of his age". His family had, according to Knox, "neither fear of God nor love of virtue further than the present commodity persuaded them". Balfour had been undoubtedly involved in Darnley's murder. Seeing Bothwell as the most powerful man in Scotland he had thrown in his lot with him, but Bothwell was to discover that Balfour's friendship only lasted as long as it could bring advancement to himself. It was probably Balfour who had drawn up the bond for Darnley's murder; it was certainly Balfour who provided his brother's house in Kirk o' Field where the murder was committed, who acted for Bothwell in his divorce from Jean Gordon, and who drew up a contract in which Mary consented to marry Bothwell. Such faith had Bothwell in him that he left Balfour to hold Edinburgh Castle and made him governor of it. Balfour was astute enough to realize that after Carberry Hill Bothwell's was a lost cause. Without preamble Balfour immediately made terms with Moray and surrendered the castle. His reward was great. He received the priory of Pittenweem for himself, an annuity for his son from the rents of the priory of St Andrews, and a very important bonus in a pardon for his part in the murder of Darnley.

The ultimate betrayal was the affair of the Casket Letters. If his story of how the casket was found was a true one, Balfour had put something into the hands of Moray and his friends which was of inestimable value to them. Many of them had been involved in the murder of Darnley, the blame for which they wished to throw entirely on the shoulders of Bothwell, and now Mary. How simple it was for them to take from the casket anything that might incriminate themselves and to fabricate documents to involve the Queen. This seems a very likely explanation of what they did.

Morton was given charge of the casket and as Moray's intention at this time was to arrange the abdication of Mary, the accession of her baby son as King of Scotland and to get himself proclaimed Regent, little could have served him better.

James Douglas, Earl of Morton, who played such a big part in Scottish affairs, was one of the leading actors in the casket drama, because if the story of the finding of the casket was untrue, as it may well have been, he could have been the man who invented it; and if any of the documents in the casket were forged, he would have been aware of the fact. It must be said though that when Mary was brought into Edinburgh in such a pitiable condition after the disaster at Carberry Hill, and many of the leading nobles had wished to execute her, it was Morton who had pleaded for her life to be spared. Morton had been deeply involved in the murder of Rizzio; he was in 1581 to be brought to the scaffold for the murder of Darnley; but he was a man of outstanding courage and may have believed that both these murders were necessary to the well-being of Scotland.

In his declaration he states how he was dining with Maitland in Edinburgh Castle, when he was told of the existence of the casket and ordered the arrest of George Dalgleish who, being put to the irons and torments, revealed that he had come to Edinburgh on Bothwell's instructions to bring the box from its hiding-place and smuggle it out of the country. The box was brought forth from a hiding-place under a bed and came into Morton's possession.

Morton called the lords together and on 21st June 1567 in the presence of "the Earls of Atholl, Mar, Glencairn, Lords Home, Sempill, Sanquhar, the Master of Graham and the Secretary [Maitland], the Laird of Tullibardine, the Comptroller and Archibald Douglas, the said box was broken open because we wanted the key and the letters within contained sighted, and immediately thereafter delivered again in my hands and custody."

The principal documents in the casket were eight letters ostensibly written by the Queen. There were in addition twelve sonnets, also said to have been written by her, besides two marriage contracts. The letters and sonnets were chiefly in French and have been translated several times into Scots, English and Latin; and the original documents were soon lost, only the translations remaining.

The letters were undated and so much depends upon the actual time they were written.

The first of the eight letters does, however, bear the inscription "From Glasgow this Saturday morning". In it, she reproaches Bothwell for staying away from her.

It seems that with your absence forgetfulness is joined considering that at your departure you promised to send me news from you. Nevertheless I can learn none. And yet I did yesterday look for that which should make me merrier than

I shall be. I think you do the like for your return, prolonging it more than you have promised.

She then makes what can only be a reference to her baby son:

I bring the man Monday to Craigmiller. He is the merriest that ever you saw and does remember unto me all that he can to make believe that he loves me. To conclude, you would say that he makes love to me, wherein I take so much pleasure . . .

This would appear to be an authentic letter because it is the manner in which a mother would write of her little son, particularly when her visits to him were a treat which did not occur often enough.

It is possible, because of the context, to time Letter II, known as the "Long Casket Letter", and it is this which is the most damning of all the documents. If Mary wrote this letter she was without doubt Bothwell's mistress before the death of Darnley; she was planning his murder with her lover; and she was capable of such conduct as would lose for her the sympathy and respect of all decent people for ever. This famous letter is almost 3,000 words in length, and Mary is reputed to have sat at her husband's bedside while she wrote it and calmly planned his murder with Bothwell. I quote from the English translation.

We are tyed to by false races. The good yere sunder us and God knytt us togither for ever for the most faythfull couple that ever he did knit togither. This is my faith; I will dye for it.

Here she is referring to her marriage to Darnley and Bothwell's to Jean Gordon. She goes on:

I am weary and am asleepe, and yet I cannot forbear scribbling so long as there is any paper. Cursed be this pocky fellow that troublith me thus much, for I had a pleasanter matter to discourse unto you but for him. He is not much the worse, but he is yll arrayd. I thought I should have been killed with his breth, for it is worse than your uncle's breth; and yet I was sett no nearer to him than in a chayr by his bolster and he lyeth at the further side of the bed.

It seems incredible that a woman of Mary's sensibilities could have written so about the husband whom she had once loved and who was the father of her child. It was true that she had fallen out of love with him and that he had become a burden to her; but to write so callously of "a pocky fellow" seems to be out of character. Throughout her life she had never shown any sign of cruelty and was never vicious. Weak she undoubtedly was and led into folly, but to accept the fact that she could have sat by her husband's bedside and written so cold-bloodedly is all but impossible to believe; and for this reason I am inclined to the opinion that the letter – or part of it at any rate – was a forgery.

On the other hand it is likely, if Mary and Bothwell were lovers before Darnley's death, that she would have written to him while keeping weary vigil at the husband's bedside; but as she would feel guilty because of her adultery with Bothwell she would have been more gentle in her attitude towards the foolish boy who was her husband.

Then comes the most damning paragraph in the Casket Letters:

> ... I remit myself wholly to your will and send me word what I shall doo, and whatsoever happen to me, I will obey you. Think also yf you will not fynd some invention, more secret by phisick, for he to take phisick at Craigmiller and the bathes also, and shall not come fourth of a long time.

She goes on to write of a bracelet she is procuring for Bothwell. It has been suggested that a woman planning to murder her husband would not have been concerned with a bracelet; nor would she have written this long epistle when a brief one would have done. One can picture her though, in that unwholesome sick room with the object of her dislike lying in his fetid bed, her contempt, her wretchedness because she was bound to him. She had a certain talent for writing and to such people the pen gives comfort. It seems natural enough that while she sat there she should go on writing as long as there was any paper. That is entirely credible; hence the long screed rather than the few brief words. It could be as though she were talking to Bothwell and the words would come tumbling out. "I should never be weary in wryting to you ..." and "Love me allwais as I shall love you." These are the words of a woman in love.

154

We know that at Jedburgh she was dangerously ill, in fact that she almost died. This was after Bothwell had received his injuries at the hands of the highwayman John Elliot; doubtless the thought that he was dead was a great shock to her, but her collapse seems also in part due to the desperate condition in which she found herself: in love with a man not her husband, a man who himself had a wife. I believe Mary had an active conscience and although she may have been carried away by Bothwell's vehemence she was not capable of callous crudity.

It may even be that if the "phisick" clause was in fact written by her, that she wrote it to soothe her lover, to make him believe that she was ready to go to any lengths to please him. It would not be the first time a woman has done this, and has deceived her lover by pretending to administer poison to an unwanted husband when she has done no such thing.

If, however, one part of these letters is a forgery then the whole is suspect. If unscrupulous men were ready to add to those letters or remove parts of them, then they were capable of removing everything that was found in the casket and re-placing it by documents calculated to suit their purpose.

The third letter is in its original French, and that and Letter IV are love letters. The person to whom she is addressing herself has clearly warned her against writing, for she admits that she has broken her promise. There is no certainty that this was in fact written to Bothwell.

In Letter IV she expresses jealousy; this could have been for Bothwell's wife, Jean Gordon. Jean's indifference to Bothwell would almost certainly have aroused his pique; and it could well have been that even after Bothwell and Mary had become lovers, he was still eager to spend some time with his wife. In this letter Mary warns him that if he does not come back to her, like a turtle-dove deserted by her mate, she may fly out of her cage. Whether this is meant to imply she will die of a broken heart or escape from the bondage of her love is not clear.

The fifth letter deals with Mary's distrust of Margaret Carwood, one of her women, which is extraordinary because at the time of Darnley's murder Mary was attending this woman's marriage to the Frenchman Bastian. The implication here seems to be that the woman was aware of a secret which Mary was afraid she might divulge if dismissed.

The sixth letter betrays the fact that the Dunbar abduction was planned between Mary and Bothwell for the letter was written at Stirling before Bothwell seized her and carried her off "by force". There is a complaint that Bothwell's "false brother-in-law" (Huntly) has criticized the plot and declared that Mary could never marry a married man who had abducted her. If this letter were truly written by Mary it would show clearly that she was implicated in the scheme and was a very willing victim. It is therefore, like Letter II, of great significance. In this letter there is also expressed jealousy of Jean Gordon.

Letters VII and VIII are love letters in the same vein, said to be written from Stirling before the incidents took place at Dunbar.

These eight were the significant letters and if they were written by Mary she must be branded adulteress and murderess.

In addition to the letters there were two marriage contracts – the first is said to have been signed by her at Dunbar soon after her abduction; the second signed immediately after the murder of Darnley and before Bothwell had obtained his divorce. There were also the sonnets. These are suspect, not only because of the sentiments expressed but in the manner of expressing them; and poets of the French Court who had seen her earlier efforts (Ronsard among them) were of the opinion that they could not have been written by Mary Stuart.

On these letters and sonnets hung Mary's guilt or innocence and through the centuries they have been dissected, discussed, argued over; Mary has been vilified and sanctified and no one has been able to say with certainty whether she wrote them or not.

It has seemed to me that parts of what were found in the casket were written by Mary and no other; and that another part is blatant forgery. I believe that the casket was found as Morton tells us and that when it was opened the immense possibilities it could offer were realized by those unscrupulous men. Why should part of the contents not be true and the other part false? It seems plausible that the letters were discovered, improved on, touched up as it were to give the impression which was required.

Moray wanted Mary out of his path. He had always longed for the throne. How easy to touch up the letters, to implicate Mary to such an extent that it was either the scaffold or banishment for her. His object was to force her to relinquish the throne, to have her infant son crowned King – since Moray, illegitimate as he was, could not hope for that honour. But he could be King in all but name.

Who could forge Mary's signature? Maitland of Lethington had been her secretary, and knew her handwriting; her mode of expression, and her character. He was Moray's ally. He was married to Mary Fleming who had been brought up with the Queen. Perhaps Mary Fleming herself had a hand in the forging. Could one of the Queen's four faithful Maries have been guilty of such a thing? Perhaps not. Yet Mary Fleming's loyalty would be first for her husband.

How simple it would be to use the casket; and how much more subtle to have part forgeries rather than the entire batch. Mary was romantic, in love with Bothwell, nauseated by her husband. It is not difficult to believe that she was the willing victim of rape; but we need far more evidence than the letters can give – knowing something of Mary's character – before we can accuse her of murder.

George Buchanan, the historian and scholar who was writing at the time, has had a great influence on the verdict. His powerful literary gifts and his academic leanings made of him a man of considerable stature and he has contributed a great deal to our knowledge of Scottish history.

When Elizabeth summoned a conference to be held at York in October 1568, that the case of the Casket Letters might be studied, Buchanan went with the commission as secretary. It was there that Maitland and Buchanan, who had been her tutor, declared that the letters were in Mary's handwriting; and because of this Elizabeth decided that there must be a fuller investigation and that the commission must come to Westminster. Buchanan accompanied the commission to London.

Yet it is clear that Buchanan had given his allegiance to

Moray, which makes his evidence suspect; and when it is remembered that neither Mary nor her agents were allowed to see the letters one veers to the forgery theory.

Moray, though he achieved his desire to become Regent, did not retain the position for long. He was assassinated in 1570 by Hamilton of Bothwellhaugh in Linlithgow. A year later Buchanan published his *Detection*, which appears to be an attempt to blacken Mary's character. Buchanan's accusers say that he makes use of any trivial incident which could show her in a bad light and that he is indeed guilty of inventing some. She is said to have attempted to persuade Darnley to seduce Moray's wife and so bring about a quarrel between them which could result in the death of one of them or perhaps both; she is of course portrayed as the murderess and adulteress. But if Buchanan had had any hope of making her guilt seem plausible, this breaks down when he accuses her of trying to murder her baby son. This accusation is so absurd and pointless that only those blinded by bigotry could accept it.

Elizabeth sent Mary a copy of *Detection*. Whether to wound her more deeply than she was already or to let her know the kind of calumny which was being circulated about her can only be guessed. Mary's sufferings must have been acute, particularly so because Buchanan was one of her little son's tutors and she must have been in a torment wondering what lies he was telling the boy. Her comment on *Detection* was that it was a defamatory book by an atheist. A year before she had requested that Buchanan be removed from her son's household because she was aware of his impiety.

Although Buchanan was an invaluable on-the-spot recorder of his times, he was fond of drama and liked to provide a good story. He is therefore suspect. He was too fond of the garnish and although this makes entertaining reading, truth is frequently sacrificed for entertainment. He had great gifts but he could be vindictive – and he was against the Queen – and his prejudice was great. He was not, however, always so and could be entirely sympathetic. He delighted in a certain crudity; yet he was cultured and could write with humour at times. His character emerges as one of great contrasts. He was the kind of man to produce a readable history but not a reliable one. It appears that it would be wrong to put great faith in Buchanan's version of the Casket Letters.

Historians give little help. Among them we have those such as Froude who was convinced of her guilt; there are others, for example Agnes Strickland, who are equally convinced of her innocence. Many, like Andrew Lang, can come to no conclusion. There is not enough evidence on any side to make a clearcut decision.

It is necessary to take a dispassionate view and it does seem that very often the religious aspect brings out a certain bias. To discover the true Mary it is necessary to put aside all sentimentalities as well as prejudice; and even though we cannot be sure whether the Casket Letters were in fact written by Mary or by another, we do know a great deal of what happened to her and how she reacted in other situations.

Is too much stress placed on whether or not she was implicated in murder? All characters must be judged against the background of their times. Such store was not set on life in the sixteenth century as it is today. Heads were constantly being cut off in an age when an ill-chosen word could send a man to the gallows. Mary was kindly for her age – it is obvious in so much that is recorded at the time. We know her to be sensitive, generous, kindly. But of course it is possible that being all this she could yet have connived at murder.

In summing up, as was to be expected, there is little light that can be shed on this controversy. But because there is so much to be said for and against, I cling to my version, which is that the letters are part truth and part forgery; and that Mary was a weak and foolish but not a criminal woman, a woman hopelessly in love with a ruthless man, willing to be deceived by him and drawn into drama because of an urgent desire to please him.

The End of Bothwell

When Bothwell left the Queen at Carberry Hill he went to Dunbar. He went reluctantly, aware that in placing herself in the hands of her enemies Mary was giving up the fight. During that passionate farewell, which took place before the assembled armies, he doubtless tried to persuade her to fly with him. In true Bothwell manner he would have found some way of deceiving the generals, and would no doubt have delighted in making an attempt to escape with Mary to Dunbar. But she would have none of it. She believed that in going with her enemies she was saving Bothwell's life. So Bothwell went alone to Dunbar while Mary was taken to Edinburgh to be submitted to the utmost humiliation before being conveyed to Lochleven.

At Dunbar he waited to see what would happen next and when he heard that a secret council had found him chief murderer in the Darnley case he decided that it would be advisable to attempt to get a band of men together to defend himself and his rights. He had married into the Gordon family and although he had divorced Jean Gordon in order to marry Mary the Gordons were loyal friends of the Queen; he decided therefore to go into the Huntly terrain and set about raising an army against Moray and the rebels.

Bothwell obviously had not realized how low he had fallen in the estimation of Scotsmen. The Queen was Moray's prisoner; she was branded adulteress and murderess; her supporters who believed in her innocence blamed Bothwell for putting her in a position in which such slurs could be cast on her. There was little sympathy for him in any quarter. Even his former brother-in-law was reluctant to join with him. Bothwell's cause was too unpopular. As a guest in Huntly's castle, Bothwell clearly became aware that he would receive no help; and as a man in his desperate position must be suspicious of those who would not help, he thought it advisable to slip away from such an uneasy shelter. He went to his kinsman, the Bishop of Moray, with whom he had spent much of his childhood in the lax atmosphere of Castle Spynie. Here he was sure of help and no doubt on the advice of the Bishop he made his plans to leave for Orkney. The Bishop was later accused of helping Bothwell to escape and as a punishment was deprived of his rents.

In the islands of Orkney and Shetland Bothwell characteristically planned to command a naval force which he would put into action against Moray, and tried to attract pirates of any nationality to his flag. This intrepid adventurer was soon intercepting ships, taking their cargoes and pressing their crews into his service. Pirate captains and their crews placed themselves under his command, and in a very short time he was giving Moray and his advisers cause for concern. Kirkcaldy of Grange with several armed vessels at his command sailed north intent on his capture.

Realizing that he was no match for these armed vessels, Bothwell made his escape to Norway, but because his papers were not in order he was taken to Bergen where he was allowed to put up at an inn. He was treated well but like the Queen he was extraordinarily unlucky, for surely it was the most amazing ill fortune that Anna Throndsen, his one-time mistress whom he had deserted some years before in Copenhagen, should have, on the death of her father, taken up residence in Bergen. Realizing that her old lover was close by she threatened to bring a case against him. With typical adroitness he managed to persuade her that she would do better to drop the case because if she did he would not only grant her an annuity to be paid in Scotland but give her one of his ships. This she accepted and withdrew her case.

From Bergen in September 1567, Bothwell was sent to Copenhagen and while he was there Moray demanded of Frederick II that he be surrendered as he was wanted to answer a charge of murder. Bothwell swore that he had been acquitted of the murder and offered the Danish King the

Orkney and Shetland Isles in return for his help. Frederick was tempted but was aware that Bothwell had no power to bestow these islands on him; however, he longed to possess them and was prepared to wait a while in case events turned in Bothwell's favour. During his stay in Copenhagen Bothwell wrote an account of his adventures under the title of *Les Affaires du Conte de Boduel*, in which he attempted to justify himself without success, for Frederick sent him to Malmö in Sweden where he thought there would be greater security, and Bothwell occupied the north wing in the castle there.

Bothwell's luck was out. He chafed against his confinement. His hopes dwindled when he heard that a proposal had been put forward for a marriage between Mary and the Duke of Norfolk, and Mary herself had appointed Lord Boyd to explore the possibility of her getting a divorce. A convention to consider this proposal was held in Perth in July 1569 and by September of the following year the Pope himself passed sentence of divorce on the grounds that Mary had been raped before her marriage.

It was then obvious to the King of Denmark that Bothwell would be in no position to put the coveted islands into his possession and his attitude changed towards his reluctant guest. Bothwell's position worsened still further when it became clear that the Queen's hopes of regaining her crown were unlikely to be realized.

By June 1573 the King had come to the conclusion that Bothwell was of no use to him. He therefore had him removed to Zealand and put into the prison at Dragsholm where he was completely cut off from life. There could not have been a worse punishment for such a man of action. As the years passed his despair must have been terrible. He had previously enjoyed the best of health; he had possessed unrivalled vitality and he had lived his life out of doors. Added to his physical discomfort was the knowledge that at any moment he might be taken to his execution but perhaps this, in the circumstances, could only be a blessed relief.

For five years he lived in shocking surroundings. It is said that he was chained to a pillar and could not stand up straight or sit down, and that he was obliged to maintain this position, living in his own filth; and since his food was passed to him through a grating, he had no converse with any human being. It is small wonder that he is said, in desperation, to have flung himself against the walls of his prison. That he went insane seems evident. Claims to the truth of this are made by Buchanan, Sir James Melville and De Thou, who were all contemporaries.

He is said to have written a confession before he died in which he cleared Mary of guilt in the murder of Darnley, but like most such documents its authenticity is suspect. There was another confession which was supposed to have been written at Malmö in 1575 but as he appears to have left Malmö in 1573, again its genuineness is doubted.

So ended Bothwell's bid to dominate the Queen and Scotland. The picture of him dashing his head against the prison walls in desperation is as melancholy as that of the Queen destined to spend twenty more years in draughty English castles – a pathetic end to history's most passionate, reckless and controversial love affair.

Escape from Lochleven

Lochleven – a castle in the middle of a loch – was the ideal prison from the jailers' point of view. It was impossible for the captive to escape without crossing the water, and the castle buildings occupied most of the island. It had been built in the fourteenth century and was the property of Sir William Douglas.

Moray had chosen this castle to be Mary's prison because his mother, Margaret Erskine, had married Robert Douglas, who had died at the battle of Pinkie Cleugh in 1547; their eldest son was William, now the castellan of Lochleven. Moray could thus be sure that every effort would be made to prevent the Queen of Scots from escaping.

Margaret Douglas was an unusual woman; when she was the mistress of James V she had borne him six children (the eldest being Moray); and when she had married Robert Douglas of Lochleven she had presented him with seven. As well as William, another of her Douglas sons was living in the castle at the time of Mary's arrival: George, Margaret's youngest, was handsome and romantic, and it was inevitable that he should be deeply impressed by the plight of a young and fascinating Queen in distress.

Moray gave as his reason for sending her to Lochleven the necessity to preserve her life. Many hostile nobles were demanding her execution for her complicity in the murder of her husband. His real reason was to force her to sign her abdication while she was there.

How desperate Mary must have felt to find herself in that gloomy vaulted chamber on her island prison! Perhaps she was reminded of Inchmahome which had once provided a refuge for her. But the constant surveillance, the tramp of guards outside the castle walls, the hideous memories of the night in the Provost's house, the parting with Bothwell, all this would remind her of the difference between Lochleven and Inchmahome.

One wonders about the relationship between the two women – Margaret Douglas and Mary Stuart. Margaret would scarcely be human if she had not felt resentful because her own brilliant first-born (whom she must have considered so worthy to wear the crown) had to stand aside for this foolish, reckless woman who was now suspected of complicity in the murder of her second husband.

It is not suggested that Mary was ill-treated at Lochleven; she was, in the first period of her stay there, allowed the freedom of the island; she was not confined to one room, but could wander in the grounds, the only restriction being that she could not leave the island. In the past she had visited Lochleven frequently; she had used it as a lodging during hunting expeditions, and because she had come so often she had had tapestry of her own choosing brought to the castle and a bed of her own installed.

The Douglases were respectful to their Queen – and slightly apologetic that they must be her jailers. She had her own suite of rooms, ladies to wait on her, a cook and an apothecary. Nevertheless the Queen remained in a state of collapse for two weeks. Mary was undoubtedly pregnant at this time and determined to cling to Bothwell; she had begged Maitland not to separate her from him "with whom she had hoped to live and die with the greatest contentment on earth". She did not know then of the discovery of the Casket Letters and the case which was being built up against her.

Although there was a strong desire among many of the nobles – chief among them Ruthven and Lindsay – to bring Mary to the block, there was a hesitation among the more serious-minded on account of her royalty and right to the throne. They did wish, however, to separate her from Bothwell and the first decision they tried to force on her was an agreement to the divorce. They were most eager to accuse and execute Bothwell and let him take the blame for a murder at which quite a number of them had connived. Mary, however, was firm in her intention not to divorce Bothwell. She declared that she would rather sacrifice her kingdom than do so and the reason she gave was that she was pregnant with Bothwell's child.

It seems inevitable after Mary's terrible experiences that she should suffer a miscarriage, but there are conflicting views as to whether she actually did. There is no doubt that she was pregnant. She had said in July that she was seven months pregnant, which would have meant that she conceived in January when Darnley was still alive; in which case she and Bothwell were already lovers. But mystery surrounds what actually happened in Lochleven concerning this child or children.

The general opinion is that she gave birth to stillborn twins. Her secretary, Claude Nau, who was writing with her authority, states that there were "*deux enfants*". But there is another version in Castelnau's Memoirs that the child was a daughter, and that Mary did not give birth at the time she was believed to: later this girl was said to have been smuggled out of Lochleven and sent to France where Mary's French relations placed her in the convent of Soissons where she was educated, and eventually became a nun. Although this story has been accepted as truth by several historians, it seems improbable that Mary could have concealed the birth of a child in such a place as Lochleven; and not only that, smuggled it across the lake to the mainland and so to France. But such feats have been performed. Mary had friends on the island and on the mainland; and in view of her own adventures and attempts to escape, it is just possible that the story could be true.

In any event, an ultimatum was presented to her while she lay weak from her ordeal. Three courses were laid before her; she might divorce Bothwell, submit to a trial at which the Casket Letters would provide a substantial part of the evidence (she had by this time been informed of their discovery), or abdicate in favour of her son. She chose the last; but it is typical of Mary's affairs that in the end she submitted to all three.

She was ill when Ruthven, Lindsay and Robert Melville

came to Lochleven with the abdication papers. The enormity of what was demanded occurred to her; she would be passing over her heritage to a son who was little more than a baby and that meant of course that she was placing Scotland in the hands of ambitious men. She refused to sign.

The crude Lindsay, whom she had always hated, threatened to cut her throat if she did not sign; Melville, however, used subtler methods; he took from the scabbard of his sword a letter which appeared to be written by Nicholas Throckmorton, the English ambassador, in which there was a protest against Mary's imprisonment and Elizabeth's advice to her that she sign the Abdication and save her life; along with the suggestion that she repudiate this later when she was no longer in danger, on the plea that she had signed under duress. Looking at the brutal face of Lindsay, Mary would have realized that if she did not sign he would carry out his threat to murder her. So on 24th July Mary Queen of Scots gave away her kingdom, at the same time signing an act which nominated as Regent her bastard brother the Earl of Moray.

In December of that year an act of Parliament was passed which made it clear that the action taken against her was due to her own conduct. It was stated that she was "privie art and part of the actual device and deed of the murder of the King". Her hasty marriage with the murderer-in-chief was proof of this, it was stated, as were the letters discovered in the silver casket.

Surely at this stage watching events carefully from Greenwich, Elizabeth must have shivered a little to recall the past and how she, at the time of the death of Amy Robsart, might have jeopardized her throne as certainly as Mary had. Elizabeth might lack the fascination of the Queen of Scots but in its place she had gifts of far greater value to a woman and a queen.

Mary's fascination was no myth. Even in the gloomy fortress of Lochleven, even after the ill health she suffered, the debilitating effects of the miscarriage of twins or the concealed birth of a daughter (whichever the case might be), even while she was suffering from some vague malady which turned her yellow and gave her a crop of sores, with her body swelling so that her servants suspected poison, yet she exerted that fatal fascination.

Lord Ruthven fell victim to it. He was the son of the man who had played such a big part in the murder of Rizzio and had risen from his sick-bed to lead the conspirators. Ruthven had up to this time been among the Queen's enemies – he had stood against her at Carberry Hill, and he and Lindsay had been in charge of her on the ride from Edinburgh to Lochleven. It was he with Lindsay and Melville who had come to force her to sign the abdication document; but he became enamoured of the fascinating Queen. Before long he was offering to help her escape, implying that in return for which service he hoped she would become his mistress. Mary scornfully rejected his advances; and his feelings being realized by those about him, he was immediately sent away from her.

There was one other at that time who was prepared to offer Mary a different kind of devotion. This was the young and handsome George Douglas whose attitude towards the Queen was all that a romantic woman in distress could ask. George was that "verray parfit gentil knight" who sought only to serve.

On 24th July 1567, James – one year and one month old – became James VI of Scotland, and was crowned at Stirling on the 29th of that month. He was then given into the care of the Earl and Countess of Mar. From the windows of her chamber in the castle of Lochleven, Mary would have seen the bonfires and no doubt heard the sound of music and revelry coming from the mainland. It would have been a sad moment to realize that the people were rejoicing in her abdication and the passing of her crown to an infant who could not know what it meant.

Moray came to visit her. He was not yet proclaimed Regent: that was some days off; but he was ever one to hide his true motives and Mary was too sentimental to see through him. He was her brother and as such she expected loyalty from him; she would not accept his true character, until it was impossible not to recognize him for the ambitious self-seeking man he was. He did not come alone – Morton and Atholl were with him. He was uncommunicative; she did, however, ask him to take supper with her. He was somewhat ungracious in his manner towards her, no doubt owing to his guilty conscience: he might have realized that if she did not see through him at this time she very soon must. He failed to observe the courtesy of giving her her napkin which since he was so much below her in rank he should have done. She reminded him of this. Little appears to have come from this meeting. She knew that John Knox was back in Edinburgh and that he could be relied on to work up feeling against her. Perhaps Moray told her this: he would certainly have reminded her, in typical Moray fashion, that it was largely for her own good that she was in Lochleven. Certain powerful nobles were clamouring for her execution with that of Bothwell; and the women of Edinburgh were "furious and impudent" against her. Moray built up a picture of terrible dangers and certain assassination if she moved from the refuge in which he had placed her.

He left giving her no more satisfaction than that. On 22nd August he was declared Regent.

It is pleasant to know that Sir Robert Melville was human enough to understand Mary's feminine needs. It must have been a day of rejoicing when the box of good things arrived on Sir Robert's orders. There were lengths of Holland material which she and her attendants could make into dresses; there was taffeta for the same purpose and gold, silver and coloured silk thread to be used for embroidery; there were boots and stockings, chignons of false hair and wigs. One imagines the exclamations of delight as she and her women, Marie Courcelles and Jane Kennedy, unpacked the treasure-chest.

Another happy incident occurred. Mary Seton – the most faithful of her four Maries – arrived at Lochleven.

Mary's health improved, and she began to think of escape; and there was her devoted knight, George Douglas, seeking only to serve her. There is no doubt that she found opportunities to talk to George. They would pass each other in the grounds when it was natural to pause and exchange a few words. He would naturally have made clear to her his determination to serve her and how better could he do that than by planning her escape?

George was too young and chivalrous to hide his feelings.

Many were aware of them, including surely his mother. Why did she not warn Moray of what was going on? One must remember that she was also George's mother. Moray was the most powerful man in Scotland: her maternal pride in him would have been great; but George had his way to make. Could it have been that she hoped that the friendship the Queen obviously felt for her gallant young admirer might ripen into a warmer feeling? Mary had married Bothwell, a commoner. Why should she not marry George Douglas? Lady Douglas was clearly devoted to her son Moray, but this younger and charming legitimate son was doubtless as dear to her as the dour illegitimate one – son of the late King though he was, so that she turned a blind eye to what was going on.

There was another member of the Douglas household who was to play his part in Mary's affairs. This was a young boy of some fourteen or sixteen years of age; he was said to be an orphaned cousin of Sir William or perhaps one of his natural children; in any case Willie, known as the "Wee Douglas", lived with the family to whom he acted as a kind of page. He was cheeky and amusing and on familiar terms with them all. He too, in his way, became enamoured of Mary.

George and Willie naturally smuggled letters ashore to the Queen's supporters. The most loyal and important of these was Lord Seton, who was on the mainland close to Lochleven. Sir William, aware of this, and realizing George's feelings for the Queen, decided that a closer guard must be kept on their prisoner. He came to the conclusion that her ground-floor apartment was too easily accessible, and ordered that a new lodging should be found for her. She was, therefore, given new quarters on the third floor of the square keep. It was a sign that although some inhabitants of the castle might be willing to help her, Sir William was too loyal to his half-brother – or too much afraid of him – to overlook any detail which might aid her escape.

George, determined to rescue his lady and win her undying gratitude, was not deterred. He brought great comfort to her with news from beyond the island. Lord Seton was ready, waiting for the moment she could get away. The Hamiltons,

Huntly and Argyll let it be known through George that they would rally to her banner once she was free. She might hear that they were seeking an agreement with Moray, but that would be a ruse to deceive. The Catholics of the North were ready to follow her once she was in a position to lead them. George Douglas was invaluable – coming and going as he pleased.

The hope of rescue, the excitement, the recovery from illness, must have made Mary very attractive at that stage. She was young, only twenty-five years old – a beautiful Queen in distress; it was no wonder that the romantic young George Douglas, impatient with delay, made wild plans. They knew that escape must be effected before the winter came; it would be impossible for Mary to ride through a blizzard. The difficulty would be in getting across the lake, but boats came and went, and the largest were those which carried coal and stores to the castle. George's plan was that instead of such commodities the largest boat should be filled with some fifty or sixty of Mary's supporters, fully armed, who should come over as though they were a consignment of coal, and when the boat touched the island, leap out, attack the castle, and carry off the Queen.

Perhaps this plan was too obvious; perhaps George in his zeal had been seen assessing the possibilities the boat could be put to; in any event William Drysdale, who was in command of the garrison, decided that the boat could provide an easy means of escape and that it should be very specially secured so that none could release it except those who had special implements to do so.

The boat secured, Mary more closely confined in her tower, the autumn passing, there was little to be done but wait for the spring. Through the darkening days Mary held her little court in the tower; fortunately she had her silks and canvases, by the grace of Melville, and her dear Mary Seton and faithful women with whom to work and talk of escape.

There was George ever ready to serve her and the quaint "Little Douglas" showing her a kind of unceremonious loyalty which would be amusing in one so young. There were dances – in which no doubt she partnered George – and there were card games; in addition to her attendant women she had other female companions in old Lady Douglas, young Lady Douglas – wife of Sir William – and their daughter and niece, girls in their early teens to whom the Queen quickly became a romantic heroine.

The news that came to Mary was disquieting. She was by this time aware of the discovery of the casket and guessed to what use its contents would be put; she had at last realized that Moray bore no affection for her whatsoever and intended to keep her prisoner so that he could rule in peace.

Her spirits must have been low that December; she had been six months a prisoner. One can imagine the dreary desolation of Lochleven in winter; the wind howling about the castle walls; the draughts and discomfort; the leaden skies, the frosty roof-tops of the little town of Kinross, so near and yet out of reach. It would be impossible to sit long over needlework during the dark short days, but the chief depression would be due to the fact that there could be no hope of escape until spring.

To the castle that December came Moray and with him were two men whom Mary had learned to distrust perhaps more than any others – Morton and Sir James Balfour. The sight of Balfour appeared to infuriate her. She doubtless remembered how he had feigned to be Bothwell's friend, and how Bothwell had made the great mistake of leaving Edinburgh Castle in his hands.

It was another occasion when Mary betrayed her impulsive behaviour. Instead of calmly receiving the visitors and playing their game of cynical subterfuge, she burst forth in a tirade which bordered on the hysterical and told them all exactly what she thought of them and their so-called loyalty. She was deceived no longer. She knew them for what they were. Particularly did she castigate her brother. He was the one who had hurt her most because from him she had expected some affection. She upbraided him for his conduct towards her; she accused him of working against her; she poured such scorn on him that he shrank from her and was glad to escape from her presence.

Moray consulted with his friends and the members of his family whom he could trust to serve him. It was obvious that George was enamoured of the Queen and ready to do anything she asked him. Moray decided that George must be banished from the castle.

All through that long winter she must have planned and hoped. Although George was forbidden to enter the castle he was not far off. Willie was taking messages back and forth and Mary would have known that on the mainland George was in touch with her friends and was busy making plans.

Before George had left Lochleven Mary had given him a pearl ear-ring and this was to be used as a signal. When he had completed plans for her escape he was to send the ear-ring back to her so that she would know it was time to be ready.

George's schemes were those of a not very practical but very romantic young lover. Young Willie was more practical and indeed was to play a major part in the escape. It was a great handicap to George that he was not allowed on the island but he remained in constant touch with the Queen. One of his plans was that a large box should be sent to Mary containing clothes and papers. When this arrived she was to unpack it and a few days later hide in it; it was then to be conveyed back to the mainland. This provided so many difficulties that it was at length abandoned as impracticable.

Young Willie had a better idea. Once a week a party of laundresses came to the island to collect the washing; they arrived by boat and left for the cottages in the afternoon with the soiled linen in great baskets. Why should Mary not dress up in the clothes of one of the laundresses and in the midst of the party be rowed to the mainland? There George Douglas and Lord Seton with some of their trusted followers would be waiting for her with swift horses; and they could gallop away to safety.

It seemed a good plan. One of the tallest laundresses was persuaded to give the Queen her clothes; Mary put on the coarse gown and muffler which was necessary, for the March winds were piercingly cold, and carrying a big basket of soiled linen, which in itself was a useful disguise, staggered across the courtyard in the midst of the other washerwomen. She passed the sentries at the gates of the castle with the greatest ease and got into the waiting boat.

Alas for Mary's fatal charms and her persistent bad luck. She was very slender and tall so that she stood out among the others. Not even a great basket of soiled linen could disguise her natural grace and as she stepped into the boat she displayed a very elegant ankle.

One of the boatmen was overcome by a desire to see more of the provocative figure who held the muffler round her face so firmly. He noticed what white hands she had, what long tapering fingers. How did a laundress manage to keep her hands so beautifully? Naturally he was intrigued, and wanted to see what her face was like. Playfully he tried to peep behind the muffler. The head was turned sharply away; the boatman seized the muffler and pulled it aside. One can imagine his dismay when he found himself looking into the well-known face of the Queen. She might command him to row to the mainland; but he had his own safety to consider. What would happen to him if it were known that he had helped the Queen of Scots to escape? The boat was turned and rowed back to the island.

The affair was naturally reported to Sir William, who must have been horrified to realize how very nearly the plan had succeeded. He wondered what his half-brother Moray would say – and do – if he was careless enough to let his captive slip out of his hands. There would be great trouble. Moray had never been a man whom it was wise to cross and now that he was Regent he wielded great power indeed.

Sir William increased security. Mary must be watched day and night. He began to look round for those who might be working for her. Young Willie had been a close friend of George, and when it was noticed that Willie had been gambling with the soldiers and had had gold pieces in his possession, Willie was under suspicion. He was closely questioned by Sir William and although no doubt the cheeky youngster gave a good account of himself it became clear that he had had a hand in the laundress affair and he was sent away to join

George on the mainland. This must have been a very depressing state of affairs for Mary, with George and Willie both gone.

George was aware that with Willie out of the castle they could not get very far, so he decided that he must get Willie back somehow. He wrote to his mother telling her that he had decided that there was no future for him in Scotland and that he was going to try his fortune in France. Lady Douglas had no wish to lose her son. Perhaps she believed that if fortune turned against her son Moray, and Mary regained the throne, George might rise to greatness through the Queen. The result was that George was allowed to call at the castle to say good-bye to his mother who tried to persuade him not to go. He replied that he was determined and asked his brother not to be too hard on Young Willie. It was tue that Willie had carried messages for the Queen, but he had done so at George's request, and George asked Sir William to forgive Willie and take him back into the castle. Willie served a useful purpose: he looked after the boats and stood behind Sir William at table and waited on him; and Willie could scarcely look after himself when George went to France.

It is indeed possible that Willie was one of Sir William's bastards, for he seems to have had a certain fondness for him; the fact is that Willie was allowed to return to the castle. George Douglas did not of course go to France, and had no intention of doing so until he had freed his Queen. A month passed after the laundress attempt. During this time Mary wrote despairing letters to Queen Elizabeth and to Catherine de' Medici. She appealed to them both to have pity on her and not to abandon her in her terrible calamity. What effect this pleading had on the two cynical recipients of the letters can be imagined.

May had arrived; and the time had come for another attempt. A heartening incident occurred. One of the boatmen brought a pearl ear-ring to the island. His story was that before George Douglas had left for France he had asked the boatman to deliver the ear-ring to one of the Queen's maids. A boatman had tried to sell it to George saying he had found it on the island, and George had recognized it as belonging to the Queen. Mary knew what this meant. On the mainland they were prepared for her escape. The moment of action had come.

Willie had worked out the plan of escape to the smallest detail. It was the 2nd May and he asked Sir William's permission to organize a celebration; Sir William gave his consent and Willie set about organizing the event which was to be so important to his plans. He bestowed on himself the title of Abbot of Unreason, this title like that of Lord Misrule giving him special powers for the day. If he signed that he wished one of the company to follow him that person must do so. He arranged a feast with plenty of potent wine and saw that Sir William partook freely of this; then he entertained the company with his antics so that, we hear, they shook with merriment. During the ceremonies Willie made use of his prerogative by signing to the Queen to follow him, and she, falling in with the spirit of the occasion, did so, knowing full well that it was the prelude to escape.

In the afternoon Mary retired to her apartment to rest; as she lay on her bed she heard one of the servants remarking to Lady Douglas that she had seen Lord Seton riding close to the lake accompanied by a party of horsemen; she added that it was rumoured that George Douglas had taken a lodging in Kinross and had not gone to France at all. How sickened Mary must have felt as she heard this maid chatting away! It must have seemed to her then that she was going to be victim once more of her habitual ill luck. With such rumours going around she guessed that security would be doubled.

She rose from her bed and went to take a walk in the grounds. Lady Douglas, quite clearly on her guard, was there to accompany her. As they walked close to the water they saw a party of horsemen ride by, and Mary commented that it must be Lord Seton returning from the assize to which he had gone earlier in the day.

It was seven o'clock when Sir William joined them – clearly rather uneasy – and suggested that as it was time for dinner, he would conduct the Queen to her apartment. It was unfortunate that he should glance from the window just at the precise moment when Willie was pegging all the boats to the shore, with the exception of one which had been selected for the escape. The object was to prevent their being used to follow the escaping boat quickly. Sir William shouted a demand to know what the boy was doing, and Mary went to the window, looked out and must have felt faint with anxiety because it appeared that Willie had been discovered. It could not have needed a great effort to feign sickness. She declared that she was feeling suddenly ill and asked Sir William to bring her wine immediately. He hurried away to do this. Meanwhile Willie completed his task and disappeared.

Sir William could not have had any real suspicion for he seemed to have forgotten the incident, so concerned was he for the Queen's health. She took supper in her apartment, Sir William waiting on her, and when the meal was over – which was very soon as she was feeling too excited to eat, which Sir William put down to her recent attack of faintness – he went below to the hall to take supper with the rest of the household.

Left alone, Mary put on a red kirtle belonging to one of her women and sat at the window waiting for the signal, with her faithful maid, Jane Kennedy.

Since the Queen of Scots had been entrusted to his care, Sir William had never let out of his keeping the bunch of keys on which the security of the castle depended. Even at mealtimes it was his custom to set them on the table beside him so that he could have them under his gaze while he ate.

Willie had to take those keys; they had to be in his possession long enough for him to unlock the outer gate of the castle, usher the Queen through it and lock it again so that no one could get out to pursue them.

Sir William was a little fuddled from the revelries. This was Willie's great chance. Sir William's plate was empty; he was awaiting the next course; the keys laid on the table beside him. Willie let a napkin drop over them as he picked up the plate; when he picked up the napkin he took the keys with it, and calmly walked out of the hall. Everything depended in the next five minutes. If Sir William glanced down and missed the keys that would be the end of the escape of Mary Stuart and it would very likely have been the end of Willie Douglas.

Willie walked out of the hall and out of the castle; he signed to Jane Kennedy who was at the window waiting. Willie made his way to the gate; the Queen in her red serving-woman's kirtle appeared with Jane; they swiftly walked across the courtyard. Several servants were there, and although they looked curiously at the Queen they did nothing to stop her. Willie opened the gate and they passed through. Willie locked the gate behind them and threw the keys into the mouth of a cannon. The boat left unpegged was waiting. The Queen and Jane got into it and Willie rowed them swiftly across the lake; George Douglas was the first to help her ashore.

She was free. For nearly eleven months she had been a prisoner. At last it must have seemed that luck was on her side. She mounted the horse which was ready for her and rode with all speed to where a few miles away Lord Seton and his band of men were waiting for her.

Disaster at Langside

Across the Firth of Forth by ferry went Mary and when she alighted it was to find Lord Claud Hamilton waiting to pay his homage and, what was even more encouraging, with him was a party of men ready to fight for her. Lord Seton suggested that the Queen needed to rest and that she would allow him to conduct her to his castle of West Niddry. How full of hope she must have been on that night – free at last, men rallying to her cause which was to bring about the downfall of her traitorous half-brother and reinstate herself on the throne. During the night Lord Livingston arrived with more men.

West Niddry was meant only to be a temporary resting-place and at dawn Mary left for Hamilton Castle. Sir Robert Melville arrived soon after she did. One wonders what his feelings were since he had been one of those who had brought the Deed of Abdication to her and had been present when she signed it. It was characteristic of Mary to bear no rancour. It did not occur to her to wonder whether a man who could change sides so rapidly might be a worthy friend. Melville was now on her side and had advice to offer her; she had signed the Abdication under duress, he pointed out, indeed he could bear witness that she had been threatened with death if she did not sign; she could therefore repudiate the document. Mary took this advice, called a council and declared that because she had been forced to sign the Abdication she no longer considered it binding.

Her council consisted of Lords Livingston and Seton, Lord Claud Hamilton, Lord Herries, Sir Robert Melville and George Douglas. They all agreed that Moray was stronger than they were, in addition to which he had in his possession the arsenals of Edinburgh, Stirling and Dunbar. Mary then suggested that they should ask help from Charles IX of France. The council approved of the idea and the faithful John Beaton was despatched to France. Lord Seton thought they should prepare for battle without delay. Mary, again characteristically, shrank from going into battle against her own brother. She wished him to relinquish his Regency, and to acknowledge that the Abdication was over; she wanted to be his friend. Against the advice of her advisers she wrote to him.

Moray's rage at her escape can be imagined. He must have guessed that she would appeal to France for help and he knew the Catholics might be ready enough to give it. He himself would be obliged to rely on Elizabeth – an uneasy ally. Moray was shrewd; he saw immediately that the sooner there was a conflict of arms the better for him.

So a battle there must be. Men had been rallying to Mary's banner and she had a force of 6,000. Moray had under 4,000. Moray of course had the good generals, such as Kirkcaldy, which was of great importance, but with good luck Mary might have won the day. Poor Mary. When did she ever have good luck?

Trouble began within the ranks of her followers. Foolishly she had given the command of her army to the Earl of Argyll – not because he was a military genius, but because he was the husband of one of her father's bastard daughters, Jean Stewart, of whom Mary was particularly fond. Lord Claud Hamilton was incensed. He believed he had more right to the command. Bad feeling from within was like a canker, particularly as they had to contend with that military wizard Kirkcaldy. Rain began to fall heavily. This slowed up Huntly's progress from the North. Kirkcaldy saw that the sooner the battle took place the greater hope of success he would have. He knew what was happening in the ranks of Mary's army. It was a simple matter to send over his spies in the form of men who declared themselves to be rallying to her cause. When information reached him that Mary had decided to march to Dumbarton where Lord Fleming with a band of men were waiting for her, Kirkcaldy decided that he would intercept the Queen on the way. He would then be in a position to choose his battle-field.

Mary and her army set out for Dumbarton and rested at the residence of her kinsman Sir John Stewart at Castlemilk. The next morning on looking from her window she could see Kirkcaldy's men amassing, but she was confident at that time of her strength and had high hopes of victory.

There was more petty jealousy between her men. Arthur Hamilton and John Stewart, minor scions of illustrious houses, quarrelled over which of them should take supremecy over the other. Mary – foolishly again – gave Stewart the superior post because he was a Stewart and a distant connection of her family. This bestowing of a post for the wrong reason was unfortunate and certain to make bad blood.

Imagine Kirkcaldy's glee. In the first place he was the finest general in Scotland and knew it. He had little but contempt for Argyll as his opponent. Superiority in numbers counted for little under bad generalship. Moreover, he had been allowed to choose the battle ground, which was always an advantage. He had already chosen Langside, a little village not far from Govan Moor. The battle should take place before Huntly had been able to join the Queen and the timing, like the place, should be of Kirkcaldy's choosing. He would make use of hackbutters – snipers – who would be posted at various points of vantage to account for a number of the Queen's men as they marched along.

What were Mary's feelings as she rode along with Lord Livingston on one side of her, George Douglas on the other, and Young Willie bringing up the rear carrying a two-handed sword almost as high as he was? Surely she must have recalled the disaster of Carberry Hill. Did she think of the stalwart Bothwell who had then meant so much to her that she had jeopardized her crown for his sake? Was she aware of the dissension within her ranks? Did she wonder how many of her men were going to desert to the other side before the day was over as they had on that other disastrous occasion?

Moray had crossed the Clyde and Morton was in charge of the vanguard. It seemed to Lord Claud Hamilton that the time had come to attack. He believed, erroneously that he was well protected by the artillery on Clancart Hill and he led his men on to the road, not realizing that, hidden along the route, were the hackbutters whom Kirkcaldy had placed in strategic positions. The hail of fire as they advanced was devastating; and when at last the remains of Hamilton's men battled their way to the end of the road, they found themselves face to face with the pikemen who were waiting for them.

Kirkcaldy ordered the pikemen to push forward and there followed the heaviest fighting of the battle. The pikemen were a solid wall through which the opposing army could not pass.

It seemed as though the issue would be decided at this point but Hamilton's men were determined, and realizing his initial mistake, Lord Claud had made up his mind to stand firm. He might have done so, and the result of the battle could have been in Mary's favour, but trouble came from another quarter.

Argyll, in command of the main body of troops, suddenly fell from his horse. It was said that he either fainted or had an epileptic fit, and that the sight of their commander in such a state completely demoralized the men. They were in immediate confusion; they did not know which way to turn or what was expected of them, and Hamilton, finding himself unsupported, retreated before the onslaught of Moray's pikemen. The army was in confusion and the battle lost, and Mary's loyal supporters Lord Seton and Sir James Hamilton were taken prisoners.

It will be remembered that Argyll was Moray's brother-in-law and it was naturally suggested that the fit or faint, coming at such a time which was crucial to the outcome of the battle, had been pre-arranged and was an act of enormous treachery.

Mary, watching the progress of the battle, must have been overcome with depression. It was the recurring pattern. She could not win. The fates were against her.

The battle of Langside had been fought, and won by Moray – with Kirkcaldy to help him. And the Queen once more must fly for freedom and perhaps her life.

With Lord Herries and a small party, Mary left the battle-field while there was still time. She would have been fully aware that Moray's intention would be to imprison her once more and this time in such a manner that escape would be a hundred times more difficult than it had been from Lochleven. Dumbarton, on the West coast, was the obvious port to make for. There would certainly be seaworthy vessels which could carry the Queen to France, where her powerful maternal relatives would be ready to help her, even if Catherine de' Medici was not. But to reach Dumbarton they must cross the Clyde; and to arrive at the river bank they must pass through Lennox country. Mary could hope for little help from Lennox, the father of Darnley whose murder had sparked off the unhappy situation in which she now found herself, and to attempt to cross the Lennox estates would be as dangerous as going back to Langside. Since they could not do this, Herries suggested that they go to Galloway and Wigtown, which they did, riding hard through the night until they reached Terregles Castle. It was unsafe to rest anywhere for long. News was brought to them that Moray was sending out several search parties.

Travel-stained and weary Mary pursued her journey; the roads were rough; it was necessary to snatch a few hours of sleep on the ground and at length they came to Kenmure, the home of the Laird of Lochinvar. He was as chivalrous as his namesake in the ballad and would have offered her the best of hospitality but he had news that Moray's men were in the neighbourhood and it would be unsafe for her to tarry. So they rode on.

There is rather a charming story concerning the Queen at this juncture. The little party of fugitives had reached a bridge across the Dee which they decided to cross and then destroy to prevent pursuit. While they did so the Queen with Willie Douglas walked a little way and came to a cottage. Smoke puffed from the chimney which indicated that something was cooking, so she and Willie knocked. The old woman who opened the door was horrified at their travel-stained condition and their obvious weariness. She insisted that they come and sit at her table. There was little to eat but oatmeal and sour milk, but she insisted on sharing it.

The emotional Mary was immediately touched by this gesture, and explaining to the bewildered woman that she was the Queen promised her that the cottage which she rented should be hers. As the cottage was on Lord Herries's estate this could be arranged. The generous gesture is characteristic of Mary. She was flying for her freedom, possibly her life; she had been given a little oatmeal and sour milk; and she must reward the giver with her cottage.

After this pretty little adventure they came to Dundrennan Abbey.

At the Abbey Mary called together a council consisting of Herries, Fleming, Livingston, Boyd, George Douglas and the Laird of Lochinvar, who had joined with them, to review the situation. Dundrennan was well fortified. Huntly was on the march and had been delayed by the rains, or the result of Langside might have been different. The majority of the counsellors, however, believed that Mary's best hope of regaining her throne would be through her French relatives. She should go to France, where she would persuade her family, the powerful Guises, to give her the help she needed. She would then find many Catholic Scotsmen willing to rally to her banner. It seemed very likely that she would get the help she needed – Catholic France would wish to see a Catholic Scotland.

Mary must have known that this was the wise course to take, yet she turned from it. Was it because she, who had been the petted darling, could not bear to return as a suppliant to the land in which she had known such triumphs? Was it true that now she was older and wiser she did not trust her uncle the Cardinal of Lorraine? Did she remember too vividly the flat expressionless face of her French mother-in-law? Whatever the reason, she could not face a return to France; she was gazing across the Solway Firth to England.

Those seated round the table must have been astounded when she suggested going to England to throw herself on the mercy of Elizabeth and attempt to come to some understanding with that Queen. Elizabeth, who had received Moray, given him asylum in her realm and had engaged in a confidential correspondence with him, was not to be trusted. The English were the enemies of the Scots and had been through many generations. And Mary proposed to throw herself on the mercy of the English!

Mary would not be dissuaded. She saw her cousin Elizabeth

as a woman just like herself. She herself would have great pity for a Queen who had suffered so, and would wish to help her with every means within her power. Mary believed that she would be invited to Hampton or Greenwich and there meet the Queen of England, and that together, two women knit by royalty and blood, they would find the solution to Mary's troubles.

Mary was determined. And since her loyal friends could not dissuade her, the only alternative they had was to go with her. Lord Herries sent a message to Sir Richard Lowther, the Deputy Governor of Carlisle, asking him for a safe-conduct for the Queen and her friends.

Mary then sat down to write to Elizabeth. In the letter she condemned fiercely those in whom she had confided and raised to the highest honours and who had now taken up arms against her. She was now forced out of her kingdom and next to God had no hope but in the goodness of Elizabeth. "I beseech you therefore, my dearest sister, that I may be conducted to your presence, that I may acquaint you with my affairs . . ."

Poor Mary! Little did she know her dearest sister.

George Douglas could find only a fishing boat. The Queen declared this would suffice and on 15th May – a Sunday afternoon, fourteen days after she had escaped from the castle of Lochleven – the Queen of Scotland set sail from the Bay of the Abbey of Burn-foot on the Solway Firth and came to England.

Elizabeth's Prisoner

The arrival in England may have reminded Mary of her coming to Scotland less than ten years previously. Then the people of Leith had come out to watch in amazement the arrival of their Queen but there had been no one of rank to greet her. Now she stepped ashore from a fishing boat, no doubt dishevelled, her clothes travel-stained, her hair disordered, to a not dissimilar situation. But at least then she had been a Queen coming home, to a doubtful welcome it was true, but still to her kingdom; now she was a fugitive throwing herself on the mercy of strangers.

Sir Henry Curwen, the local squire, hearing of her arrival, in due course came out to meet her and to welcome her to his mansion, Workington Hall. Lady Curwen provided clothes for the Queen – always a consideration as far as Mary was concerned – and during her first night in England Mary's spirits must have been high for she appears to have had no premonition of what was to come.

Soon after her arrival the Earl of Northumberland came to Workington Hall. Mary was delighted. Northumberland was a Catholic and she was certain that he would be her friend. She did not know that he had already had instructions from Elizabeth that Mary was to be closely guarded, to be a prisoner in fact, although she was not yet to be made aware of this. The guards, it was explained, were to protect her. He took her to Cockermouth Hall, the home of a rich merchant, Henry Fletcher. There she wrote once more to Elizabeth, pleading to be sent for as soon as possible, signing herself "Your very faithful and affectionate good sister and cousin and escaped prisoner Mary R."

While she was at Cockermouth several members of noble

186

families visited her; among these was Lady Scrope, sister of the Duke of Norfolk, and Mary was informed that Carlisle Castle was to be put at her disposal. Lady Scrope would conduct her there and wait on her.

Some members of the party thought it ominous. To reach Carlisle Castle they must travel north whereas Elizabeth was in the south. Mary, however, was undisturbed; she had the utmost faith in her good "sister"; and as she passed under the old portcullis into the red stone castle which had been rebuilt by William Rufus (it had been in ruins for 200 years after being destroyed by marauding Danes), she appears to have felt no misgivings.

Mary was probably visited at Carlisle by the Duke of Norfolk, and this visit would have done much to lift her spirits. Mary was always deeply affected by men; she needed love as Elizabeth needed admiration. Her attitude suggests that Bothwell was becoming a memory, and perhaps not a very happy one. He had won her hand in marriage with the burning intensity of his passion and the response she had been forced to give to it; it was inevitably transient. Without him there to kindle it it died quickly.

Norfolk was some six years her senior; he was one of the richest men in England, and the leading peer of the realm. He was, moreover, a widower. He had recently married for the third time Elizabeth, the daughter of Sir Francis Leybourne of Cunswick Hall in Cumberland, who had been at the time of the marriage the widow of Lord Dacre, and there were a son and three daughters of this marriage. Norfolk was in the North at this time because his stepson Lord Dacre had died when falling from his vaulting horse, and as there was a great deal of property involved the Duke's idea was to marry his three step-daughters to three of his sons by previous marriage, so that the Dacre property should not go out of the family.

No doubt hearing of the legendary charm and beauty of the Scottish Queen, he wanted to see her. Whether he did actually call on her is uncertain, but it seems likely that he did and that the meeting had a salutary effect on them both; could it have been that Norfolk's desire to marry Mary came during that first meeting?

If Mary was optimistic, her friends were not. Carlisle was as much a prison as Lochleven. They knew that the guards who surrounded the castle were not so much for Mary's protection as to prevent her escape. Elizabeth's fear was that the Catholics of the North might rally to her and an attempt might be made to set her on the English throne.

Elizabeth sent Sir Francis Knollys and Lord Scrope to Carlisle. They had received instructions from Elizabeth's devoted minister, Sir William Cecil. The Queen of Scots was to be closely guarded; her letters must be intercepted; she must on no account receive help from the French; they must report her words and actions; Elizabeth wished her to be kept a prisoner in such a manner that the Queen of Scots was unaware of the fact.

Mary was delighted to receive Elizabeth's emissaries. She betrayed her belief that they had come with invitations from the Queen of England for her to travel south. She was undoubtedly feeling quite happy at that time for Mary Seton and Marie Courcelles had arrived in England to join her.

Her hopes were soon deflated. No sooner had she exchanged greetings with Knollys and Scrope than they reminded her that she had come into England under suspicion. The reason Elizabeth gave for not sending immediately for her dear sister of Scotland was typical of her. Her emissaries pointed out to Mary that her second husband had died in very mysterious circumstances and that Mary had almost immediately married again. The Queen of England had her reputation to consider. She was a virgin (how she liked to stress that – it might have been said that the lady did protest too much) and as such could not receive at her Court one who – she doubted not unjustly – was under suspicion. Because of this reputation of hers it would be necessary for Mary to be *proved* innocent before Elizabeth could receive her.

Mary at last began to realize that all was not as she had hoped. This was strengthened by the arrival of a box which Elizabeth had sent to her sister, and which when opened was seen to contain rusty velvet garments, underclothes in need of mending and shabby boots. Was the coy virgin implying: "You came as a beggar so must expect to be treated as such"?

It appears that Sir Francis Knollys was a little fascinated by Mary and when he saw her dismay at the contents of the box he remarked that the Queen had intended them for her maids.

Even if Mary would not accept the true state of affairs, Herries and Fleming did. They suggested to her that Herries should go to Elizabeth and try to discover what she was prepared to do for the Queen, and that Fleming should travel to France to put Mary's case before her Guise relations. Any action was better than none, and Mary agreed to this.

Elizabeth was certainly not going to allow Fleming to go to France. What she dreaded most was that Mary might receive aid from that country, and if she did the French would not stop at regaining the Scottish throne for her. Had they not once bestowed on Mary the title of Queen of England? The mission of the two lords was doomed from the start.

Although Mary had been disappointed by Elizabeth's box, she did receive some of her clothes from Scotland which Moray was gracious enough to send; she then asked for others to be sent to her, and because of the desire to please her on the part of Sir Francis Knollys this was done.

At this time Henry Middlemore, in whose care Elizabeth had entrusted letters to Moray, called at Carlisle on his way to Scotland. When she heard that a messenger from the English Court had arrived Mary's hopes must have soared; but Middlemore's demeanour towards her, which was far from respectful, would have made her despair. He gave her the news that Elizabeth believed she would be happier in other surroundings and suggested that she move from Carlisle to Tutbury. The fact was that Elizabeth would be happier with Mary in Staffordshire rather than close to the Scottish border. Mary poured out her feelings in an impassioned appeal to Elizabeth referring to herself as her sister and natural cousin. She was also writing to France for help; she could not have hoped for much from Catherine de' Medici, but Charles IX had at one time shown great affection for her.

She did not know that in Scotland Moray was arranging for translations of the Casket Letters which he intended to use to prove Mary guilty of adultery and murder. He was employing George Buchanan to compile the *Book of Articles*, the object of which was to blacken her character and to prove that she was unworthy of her crown. When the translations of the letters were completed Moray sent them to England that Elizabeth might realize what a weapon they would prove if they could be used against his sister.

In ignorance of the forces which were working against her, Mary waited for succour. She was indeed a prisoner. Whenever she moved from the castle walls she was watched, and Lord Scrope slept in the room next to hers.

Elizabeth had decided that Bolton Castle would be a better refuge for Mary than Tutbury. Mary told Sir Francis Knollys that she did not wish to go because she preferred not to be too far away from her native land. Sir Francis could only imply that it was the wish of Elizabeth that she go and since she was in England she would be obliged to obey its Queen.

George Douglas was in constant attendance and Mary could never forget all he had done for her. It was typical of Mary that she put George's welfare before her need of him. She insisted he go to France where he might make his fortune. There was little chance of his doing anything if he were confined to Carlisle, Bolton or Tutbury. When she told George that she needed him to tell the true story to her relations the Guises and do all in his power to raise arms and men who would come to Scotland and fight her cause, George was prevailed upon to leave. Soon after his departure Mary heard that she was to leave for Bolton Castle. Mary declared she would not leave Carlisle; Elizabeth's reply was to send a litter and horses to convey her there, and Mary knew that she would have to obey.

Bolton Castle was in Wensleydale. Sir Francis Knollys was right when he remarked that it was "the highest walled castle I ever did see". Mary's apartments were close to the north-eastern tower. Several of her followers had returned to Scotland. There was no point in their sharing her prison. She must have realized by this time that was what Elizabeth was offering her, and she would conclude that men such as Lord Claud Hamilton could be more use working for her cause in Scotland than remaining with her in England. Too, Lord

Fleming had not been allowed to go to France and had returned to Mary. But George Douglas had not been refused permission, which was an indication that Elizabeth did not think much of his chances of raising an army for Mary. Fleming was another matter. Herries she kept at her Court.

Mary's hostess at the castle was Lady Scrope, sister of the Duke of Norfolk, She was pregnant, and Mary who herself was acquainted with that state, would have felt a fellow-feeling for her hostess. Moreover, they both enjoyed needlework (there is plenty of evidence of Mary's passion for this kind of work) and doubtless chatted amicably about the virtues of Norfolk over their canvases.

Despite the fact that Mary was aware that she was the prisoner of the Queen of England, her hopes were still relatively high. Letters from George Douglas were being smuggled in to her; the Cardinal of Lorraine and the King of France assured her of their support. Moray was unpopular, and Huntly and Argyll were awaiting the moment to strike. Herries came back from the English Court and was able to report that Elizabeth had said that if Mary would have her case tried by her order, not as her judge but as her cousin and friend, she would do all possible to have her reinstated. She would send for those people who had made accusations against Mary and demand to know why they had deposed Mary.

There were certain conditions. Mary must renounce all claims to the throne of England. That was not difficult. Mary had never wanted the crown of England and would never have thought she had any right to it if her father-in-law the King of France had not insisted that she had. She must not plan with France; she must break her alliance with that country and become the friend of England. The last demand was the most difficult: she must forbid the Mass to be celebrated in Scotland and receive the Common Prayer as was the custom in England.

Mary was tolerant. She wanted to follow her own religion and let others do the same. Herries pointed out to her that there would be no objection to people's celebrating the Mass in private.

Queen Elizabeth did not wish to pass judgement on her sister of Scotland, Herries explained. She only wished the case to be heard so that the innocence of Mary could be proved. Herries was deceived by the shrewd Queen of England who knew that the Casket Letters were going to damn Mary's case utterly. This was another of Mary's tragic mistakes. She turned from the help France would have given her; she ordered that her faithful supporters in Scotland should disband their armies. She turned from her friends to her enemy. She put her trust in Elizabeth.

How Herries must have despised himself when rumours of the use to which the letters were to be put came to Bolton. Both he and Mary would have realized then that Elizabeth had known that the letters implicating Mary were to be produced. The fact that they had been successfully hoodwinked would have been altogether humiliating.

It was not surprising that when, during the month of August, Mary heard that plans were in motion to bring about her release, she entered into them with enthusiasm.

Few people were to be in on the secret. Willie Douglas, always adept at this kind of adventure, would be invaluable, of course. Mary was to be let down through the window by means of knotted sheets. Mary Seton was to follow her, and Jane and Marie Courcelles would make sure that the sheets were safe. Horses would be waiting for them and when they reached them they would gallop away to the Border to the Laird of Fernyhirst who would place his castle at their disposal, and from there the Queen could once again gather her armies together.

All went well at the beginning. Mary escaped by means of the knotted sheets. With the usual ill luck, after the Queen had safely reached the ground, Mary Seton, about to follow her, fell heavily and knocked over a piece of furniture. The jailers, lightly sleeping, rushed in and saw what was happening. Mary's escape route was immediately cut off and as she mounted her horse prepared to gallop off to the Border, she came face to face with Lord Scrope who told her that he was obliged to conduct her back to the castle.

Although little was said about the Queen's nocturnal escapade, the guards were doubled. The spot where Lord

Scrope had come face to face with her on that night was known as The Queen's Gap.

It was during her stay at Bolton that Mary became interested in the Protestant faith. This was largely owing to the efforts of Lady Scrope and Sir Francis Knollys – Protestants both. Mary was at heart a Catholic, but the study of the Reformed religion provided an interesting occupation during the long days. Moray was naturally alarmed when he heard what was happening. Mary's Catholicism had been one of the main reasons for her rejection by so many Scotsmen. He saw his case crumbling if she became a Protestant. He retaliated by attacking her supporters in Scotland, depriving them of their lands. But his great hope was in the conference to be held in York. Norfolk was one of the Commissioners Elizabeth had set up, a fact which pleased Mary when she heard because she believed she could expect favourable treatment from him. Maitland had persuaded Moray to hold the letters back for a while; he was apparently not at all certain what effect they would have on his own position if they were circulated. Moray did, however, show them to Norfolk. The sight of them appeared to increase Norfolk's desire to marry the Queen and it occurred to Maitland that if she could be divorced – for the divorce from Bothwell had not yet been secured – and marry Norfolk, she would remain in England and leave Scotland clear for her son and those ministers who in fact ruled the country. But if Mary were proved to be a murderess, which the disclosure of the letters might result in, Norfolk could not marry her, even though she were a Queen. No doubt Moray was disappointed; he appeared to have been venomous in his attitude to his sister; but he was too much of a statesman not to see Maitland's point.

In early October 1568, the Commissioners representing Mary, Elizabeth and Moray came to York. For Elizabeth, with Norfolk, came the Earl of Sussex and Sir Ralph Sadler; among those to represent Mary were the Bishop of Ross and Lords Boyd, Herries and Livingston; Moray's friends were Morton, Lindsay and the Bishop of Orkney.

Moray was anxious for Norfolk's opinion as to what effect the Casket Letters would have on Elizabeth, and Norfolk, uncertain how to act, wrote to his mistress asking for instructions.

Elizabeth decided that since the Conference was achieving very little in York, it should be transferred to Westminster. This was a more serious occasion. Among Elizabeth's Commissioners there were William Cecil and the Earl of Leicester. And here Moray produced his accusations against his half-sister. He declared that the Earl of Bothwell was the chief murderer of Darnley, who had been the Queen's lawful husband, and that she had had foreknowledge of the murder and had gone so far as to marry the murderer-in-chief, Bothwell. He produced a written accusation which was signed by himself, Morton, Lindsay, the Bishop of Orkney and the Abbot of Dunfermline.

Elizabeth considered the accusation and did not appear to realize that she was unfair in allowing Mary's chief accuser, Moray, to be present and state his case while Mary was not permitted to attend but was confined in Bolton Castle. Mary's Commissioners pointed this out, but Elizabeth had no intention of allowing Mary to come to London. She greatly feared the sympathy which she could arouse, and that the secret Catholics in the realm might rally to the aid of the Scottish Queen. She declared that Mary could answer the accusations to her own Commisioners who could then put her answers before the Conference, or she could simply answer them herself. If she wished to do neither, Elizabeth would send her own Commissioners to Bolton and Mary could speak to them.

Mary now realized that she could not hope for justice. She, a Queen, was commanded to answer accusations, in itself humiliating. She had heard that writings had been produced and that these were damaging to herself but she was not allowed to see them. It was quite clear that there could be no justice for her and she recalled her Commissioners. Elizabeth was not displeased. The Scottish Queen's character had been blackened; Elizabeth had an excuse to hold her rival captive. As for Moray, he could return to Scotland and retain his office of Regent.

Elizabeth, however, was aware of Norfolk's ambitions and she sent for him and told him bluntly that she did not approve of her leading peer's planning marriage with a rival Queen. She posed a few artful questions to him in an outwardly artless manner but Norfolk knew his sovereign well enough to recognize the deadly intention behind them.

"Your Majesty," he told her, "that woman shall never be my wife who has been your competitor and whose husband cannot sleep in security on his pillow."

Mary celebrated her twenty-sixth birthday at Bolton. The dancing and lute playing doubtless reminded her of other occasions at Holyrood House when poor David and tragic Chastelard had danced with her. It was to be one of the last festive evenings at Bolton. Queen Elizabeth had heard of her growing friendship with Sir Francis Knollys. This fascinating cousin of hers seemed perpetually to attract men. She was certainly not going to make a slave of Knollys. In a letter to Mary's jailers of Bolton Castle she told them that she was displeased with the leniency they had shown to the Queen of Scots and consequently she was removing her from their care. Mary was to leave for Tutbury Castle and the Earl and Countess of Shrewsbury were to be put in charge of her.

It was February before the weather permitted the party to leave Bolton. Mary had to be carried in a litter; the progress was necessarily very slow on account of the frozen roads. And so she came to Tutbury.

Tutbury Castle, now a ruin, is said to have once been the residence of the Saxon Lords of Mercia and is named after the god Thor or Thoth who was worshipped at this spot. The castle stood on the red sandstone hill overlooking Hanbury and Needwood, and from the high towers it would have been possible to see the Derbyshire Peak district. Close by is the ancient town of Tutbury. The castle was ideally situated for defence. To Mary, as she crossed the drawbridge and was carried under the portcullis, it must have seemed a formidable prison.

She was taken to apartments on the south-east side of the castle which consisted of two large rooms, an upper and a lower. The lower room had only two small windows although the two in the upper chamber were large and pointed; from these she had a magnificent view of the countryside. But her spirits must have sunk because there could be no doubt that Tutbury was one of the bleakest residences in the country.

Elizabeth seems to have taken a delight in Mary's discomfort. She was jealous of Mary's obvious and overwhelming power to attract people – and in particular the opposite sex. She seemed determined therefore that Mary should not marry; that she should spend her time in prison where she would not find it so easy to flaunt her charms; that she should suffer hardship; that she should not forget that she was Elizabeth's prisoner.

Elizabeth would no doubt have congratulated herself on the outcome of the Conference. The letters had been produced; Mary was branded as an adulteress and murderess; and although it could be said that nothing had been proved or disproved, the smear was there. The big question mark was hovering over Mary. Meanwhile Mary could be kept in captivity and Elizabeth had the pious excuse that for her own honour's sake she could not see her until her name was cleared.

It was at Tutbury that that forceful personality Elizabeth Talbot, Countess of Shrewsbury, came into Mary's life. Bess was one of those women who are determined to get their own way, who sweep all obstacles from their paths and are sure that their views of what should and should not be done are always right from every point of view.

She has been known throughout history as Bess of Hardwick. She was born in 1518 so was some twenty-four years older than the Queen; Shrewsbury was her fourth husband and at the time Mary came to Tutbury their marriage was not a year old, but that was long enough for Shrewsbury to have learned who was master of the household. At fourteen Bess had married Robert Barlow, who died shortly after the marriage leaving his wife a very rich woman. Her next husband was Sir William Cavendish who bought Chatsworth, died in the process of rebuilding it and left it to Bess to finish. Her third husband was Sir William St Loe. He owned "divers fair lordships in Gloucester which in articles of marriage she took care should be settled on her and her heirs in default of issue by him." He died too as the others had done leaving everything to

196

Bess to the exclusion of the children he had by a previous marriage.

Bess appeared to have no difficulty in finding rich men and persuading them to marry her and thereafter be guided by her. The next was George Talbot, Earl of Shrewsbury, her junior by some ten years. Elizabeth trusted him as she did few; he was rich, he owned several great houses in the middle of the kingdom and appeared to be an ideal custodian for the captive Queen of Scots.

How Mary's spirits must have sunk when she arrived at Tutbury and saw those cold draughty rooms with the damp seeping through the walls. There was something even more to be deplored. She was immediately aware of an offensive smell which came from the privies just below her apartments. Tutbury was to prove the most unhealthily obnoxious of all her prisons and one which did more to impair her health than any other.

Shrewsbury himself would have made a good impression; he was a kindly man and deeply conscious of his guest's royalty, and eager to make her as comfortable as he could in this medieval fortress to which Elizabeth had condemned her. And what of forceful Bess? There could not have been two women of more different natures, but during the early part of their acquaintance they appear to have got along comfortably together.

Mary was very quickly ill; she had one of her mysterious fevers and experienced the first signs of the stiffening of her limbs, that rheumatism which was later to plague her and which was a result of living in cold and draughty surroundings.

It was while she was at Tutbury that Willie Douglas returned. She had sent him away a short while before when they were at Bolton with the idea that he should go to France and join George Douglas there. In her generous way, she wanted to reward Willie for what he had done for her and she knew there was little hope for him to make a career waiting on her in captivity. Willie had gone to London, acquired a passport and was preparing to leave for France when he was set on, knocked unconscious and awakened to find himself in a cellar. He was thrown into prison and kept there in vile conditions; and then, presumably because it was realized that he was of little importance, he was released and he found his way back to the Queen.

The Earl was indeed a kindly man. Knowing how Mary was suffering, he had asked Elizabeth if comforts might be supplied to her and Elizabeth granted this request. Consequently tapestries were sent and as these were lined with canvas, when hung on the walls they did keep out some of the draughts, although nothing could prevent that foul smell seeping into the apartments. Four feather beds were also sent.

It was the Earl who asked Elizabeth's permission to remove the Queen of Scots to Wingfield Manor – another of his homes – as the rigours of Tutbury were affecting her health. This request the Queen granted. It is doubtful whether Bess had a hand in these arrangements. The Queen of Scots had a reputation for being one of the most fascinating women of her age, irresistible to the opposite sex; the Earl was going to great lengths to add to her comfort. What if he had done so without first consulting his dominating wife? It would be natural that she would be piqued and suspicious. Was it at this time that the first seeds of jealousy were sown? Moreover, if Shrewsbury was taking decisions without consulting her, he would have to learn that this was something her husbands were never allowed to do.

The fact is that Mary left for Wingfield Manor.

Wingfield must have delighted her after the horrors of Tutbury. Small by comparison with the castles which had housed her in England, it had been built on the orders of Ralph, Lord Cromwell, and to remind all that he was Treasurer of England the decorations over the gateway were of bags and purses. It was built round two square courtyards on a hill and had panoramic views of beautiful country including the valley of Ashover. Mary's apartments were in the tower.

The move, however, had come too late to save Mary from the effects of those cold weeks in Tutbury; she was so ill that her attendants despaired of her life. But she recovered in due course and her recovery may well have been helped by the excitement of fresh intrigue. Always in her mind there must have been, as there had during the period she spent at Lochleven, the hope of escape. Through the long days of convalescence of which a great part of the daylight was spent in working on her tapestry, the conversation must have been continually on this absorbing subject.

It was while she was at Wingfield that Norfolk loomed up again in her life. The Duke of Norfolk was one of the most powerful English lords; he was personable, young and would in fact be a worthy husband; and Mary needed a husband.

She and Norfolk communicated with each other. When she was short of money he sent her some and a promise of more. When Leslie, the Bishop of Ross, called at Wingfield to see the Queen he was able to tell her that many powerful Englishmen were in favour of her marriage with Norfolk. Strangely enough the Earl of Leicester was one of them, obviously without the knowledge of Elizabeth. Leslie's explanation was that Cecil was determined to keep a Protestant ruler on the throne and gave his support to Moray, and Leicester, being jealous of Cecil's favour with the Queen, was eager to flout him. Mary's hopes were high; she built up an idealized picture of Norfolk and Leslie was able to assure her that there would be no difficulty whatsoever in getting the marriage with Bothwell annulled.

The Assassination of Moray

At this juncture Shrewsbury had a slight stroke and was confined to his bed, and Leonard Dacre made his appearance. Dacre was a man with a grievance against life. He was the second son of Lord Dacre of Gisland; moreover, he was a hunchback. His elder brother had died leaving a son, George, and three daughters. The son was that boy who had died when leaping over his vaulting horse and Leonard believed that the family estates should therefore have passed to him. But his brother's widow had married the Duke of Norfolk who was busying himself arranging marriages between the three Dacre girls and his own sons to keep the Dacre fortune in his family. Leonard was determined to have his revenge on Norfolk. He wrote letters of sympathy to Mary and when he called at Wingfield asked permission to see her. He was able to tell her of his close association with the Catholic Party of the North of which his cousin, the Earl of Northumberland, and his neighbour, the Earl of Westmorland, were members. They were in deep sympathy with Mary's cause.

Mary's days had become considerably enlivened. There was intrigue all around. A contract was drawn up between her and the Duke of Norfolk and they wrote affectionate letters to each other. With Shrewsbury confined to his bed there were greater opportunities for sending and receiving letters than previously, and the conspirators naturally made the most of their good fortune.

Dacre was aware of Norfolk's schemes and determined to thwart them. His idea was that Mary should be affianced to Don John of Austria who should come to England and fight her cause; when victorious they would dethrone the Protestant

Elizabeth – whom they considered to be a bastard – and set up Mary on the throne of England as well as that of Scotland.

Dacre planned that Mary should escape from Wingfield. It appeared at first that events were working in her favour. Bess had thrown herself with her usual energy into the task of looking after her husband and she decided that now that he was recovering a little he needed the waters of Buxton to help him regain his health. She wrote to Elizabeth asking for permission to leave Wingfield and take him there. Elizabeth delayed answering. Bess was not the woman to allow anyone to stand in her way – not even the Queen of England; if she could not get Elizabeth's permission she would go without it.

Dacre and Mary were aware of what was going on. They knew that ere long Bess would go to Buxton. Someone else would be sent to guard her but before that person arrived Mary was going to do her best to escape from Wingfield. The plan was that Mary should wear Mary Seton's clothes and Mary Seton the Queen's; they should keep themselves aloof and talk together, and Mary Seton should be addressed as "Your Majesty". Jane Kennedy and Mary Seton could walk into the manor, Jane talking as to the Queen all the time while Mary walked out of the Manor to where horses would be waiting. It was reminiscent of Lochleven.

It was a good plan and circumstances were set fair. But Mary's attempts to regain her throne seemed always doomed to failure; indeed it must be admitted that she invited it. She declared that since she was affianced to Norfolk she must first ask his advice and get his approval before she agreed to Dacre's scheme.

Bess and Shrewsbury left for Buxton without Elizabeth's consent; the moment to leave was at hand. Mary stood a very fair chance of escaping from captivity but Norfolk's reply had come. On no account must she fall in with Dacre's schemes, he wrote, knowing very well that Dacre wanted her married to Don John. Mary had lost another chance.

When Elizabeth heard that the Shrewsburys had left Wingfield Manor she was outwardly incensed; but it seemed certain that knowing why Bess had gone – and Bess and she being of not unsimilar natures – she secretly sympathized with her. But it must not be seen that she allowed anyone to flout her. She ordered the Shrewsburys to return, not to Wingfield Manor but to Tutbury, whither the Queen of Scots was also to be sent.

Meanwhile, Leicester, eager to lose no advantage, had tried to curry favour with both Mary and Elizabeth at the same time, and had supported Norfolk in his plans to marry Mary. Realizing his mistake, he became alarmed. He feigned illness and asked Elizabeth to visit him, knowing that if she saw him in his sick-bed she would be more inclined to be lenient. When she was at his bedside he confessed, naming with others Pembroke and Arundel as his confederates. Elizabeth forgave him, but not the others who were involved. She sent for all those men whose names Leicester had given her. Norfolk, realizing what had happened, imitated Leicester in feigning illness. Elizabeth's reply was that sick or not he was to present himself to her without delay. As he left Kenninghall, where he was staying at that time, he was arrested and sent to the Tower.

Mary's brief hope of rescue was over, and moreover she was back at noisome Tutbury and in place of the Shrewsburys as her guardians she was given the Earl of Huntingdon. Henry Hastings, 3rd Earl of Huntingdon, was descended on his mother's side from Edward IV's brother the Duke of Clarence, and he believed that after Elizabeth he was the next heir to the throne. He would have every reason to wish Mary out of the way because it was hardly likely that he would be accepted as Elizabeth's successor while Mary lived.

Huntingdon was a harsh jailer. It was not easy to get letters smuggled in. What Mary's fears must have been in that most hated of her prisons can well be imagined as she brooded on what had happened to royalty in the past. She must constantly be on the alert for poison; she must be careful not to be alone where she might be thrown from a window or flung downstairs. Fortunately for her she had the faithful Mary Seton with her and Willie Douglas as well. Intrigue intensified in such an atmosphere. Northumberland and Westmorland were ready and waiting, determined to find some means of getting her out of Tutbury.

Norfolk wrote that on no account must she listen to them. It was obvious to Mary's friends that his great concern was not for her well-being, but once more she was duped by her emotions. She was in love with her image of Norfolk.

When one of Mary's maids became pregnant and needed a midwife, this woman on her visits to the castle carried letters to and fro. A plan was considered by which Mary should change into the midwife's clothes and walk out of the castle. This was absurd because Mary was outstandingly tall and it would have been realized at once that she was not the dumpy little midwife. The Countess of Northumberland, who was nearly as tall as Mary, then offered to visit the castle, change clothes with Mary and let her walk out in her place; but before this plan could materialize it occurred to Huntingdon that the midwife was coming more frequently than warranted; she was searched; fortunately at the time she was carrying no letters, but Huntingdon continued to suspect her and announced that he would be present when she discussed the condition of the pregnant woman with the Queen. It then became clear that the midwife project could not be put into action.

Soon after this event Elizabeth decided to forgive the Shrewsburys and ordered Huntingdon to leave Tutbury. The Shrewsburys were to be in sole command again. Huntingdon had no sooner set out from Tutbury when he was ordered back, for the northern earls of Northumberland and Westmorland were in revolt; their aim was to bring back the Catholic faith to England and release Mary, and they had the support of Pope Pius V. The Queen of Scots must be put in a safer prison, further south, and was to be taken without delay to Coventry.

Escorted by Huntingdon, the Shrewsburys and her own loyal band of servants which included Mary Seton, Willie Douglas, the faithful Marie Courcelles and Jane Kennedy, Mary spent the first night of the journey at Huntingdon's castle at Ashby-de-la-Zouch. The move had been so sudden that a safe fortress had not been designated as her final destination and in Coventry it was necessary to put up at the Black Bull Inn. An inn of course was no place to lodge a Queen and in due course an old house called St Mary's Hall was found for her. Mary spent her twenty-seventh birthday in this house, and stayed there until the insurrection was put down in a manner satisfactory to Elizabeth. In January 1570 she was back in Tutbury.

During that January the Regent Moray was assassinated. He was shot in the streets of Linlithgow by James Hamilton of Bothwellhaugh. The reason for the assassination had been a matter of some controversy and a romantic story sprang up which may have had some truth in it. According to this, Alison, wife of James Hamilton, was in childbed when Moray's men arrived at Woodhouselee, the house which she had inherited; they told her that the house had been confiscated and was no longer her property, and she must leave at once. She was forced to get up from her bed and taking her child with her go out into the snow, where she was frozen to death, according to one version. Another, in the *Historie of James Sext*, states that after being violently expelled from her house she "conceived sic madness of spreit as was almost incredible". Sir Walter Scott in his ballad "Cadyow Castle" tells of the sheeted phantom who haunted Woodhouselee for generations to come. The facts suggest that Bothwellhaugh may well have had a private grievance against Moray but it appears that he was not without supporters, and these were the adherents of the Queen.

The assassin took up his stand at the window of a house owned by the Archbishop of St Andrews; it was only four doors away from that in which Moray had spent the night. John Hamilton, the Abbot of Arbroath, had given Bothwellhaugh his own carbine and had arranged for a fleet horse to be waiting at the back of the house to carry Bothwellhaugh away once the deed was done. He did in fact escape. Moray's body was taken to Edinburgh and buried in the south aisle in St Giles's Cathedral; John Knox preached a sermon in which he moved 3,000 people to tears for the loss of such a good and godly governor.

The assassination of Moray had its effect on Mary. In Elizabeth's eyes she would now be doubly dangerous, for the English Queen would be uncertain as to what effect the death of Mary's half-brother and bitter enemy was going to have in

Scotland. She seized Mary's ambassador in England, Leslie, Bishop of Ross, and put him in the Tower. She was right to be wary. The Highlanders were on the march; the North of England was once more in revolt; and Kirkcaldy of Grange, the best general in Scotland, had changed sides. He had felt for some time that it would be possible to come to terms with Mary, but had preserved a state of neutrality; then, deeply shocked by the assassination of Moray, when Lennox was chosen as the new Regent he refused to be present at the election.

Elizabeth acted promptly. The guard at Tutbury was doubled. Not only did she subdue her own rebellious subjects but she also sent a punitive expedition into Scotland. The Earl of Lennox was a candidate Elizabeth favoured for she knew, as Darnley's father, he was an enemy of his daughter-in-law the Queen of Scots.

The rigours of Tutbury were becoming harder to endure, perhaps because Mary was growing older and all her plans seemed to go wrong. Her marriage to Bothwell was dissolved that year on the ground of rape. She wrote pathetically to Norfolk signing herself, "Your own faithful to death Queen of Scots, my Norfolk". Norfolk was wise enough not to reply.

At last the horrible winter was over and with the spring the household moved to Chatsworth. To leave Tutbury must always have been a pleasing prospect; and to go from that gloomy, draughty, evil-smelling place to beautiful Chatsworth could only result in a lifting of the spirits. The original manor belonged to the crown and had been in the custody of a certain William of Peveril who, when he received a grant of property from the Conqueror, built for himself a mansion known as The Castle of the Peak. The property then passed to a family appropriately named Leech as one head of it was doctor or "leech" to Edward III. In the sixteenth century the estate was sold to a family named Ayard who in their turn sold it to the Cavendishes.

Sir William Cavendish, with the help or perhaps one should say under the guidance of his formidable wife, built the original Chatsworth, a quadrangular building with turrets. It was a beautiful mansion, but Mary would be immediately aware of the difficulties of escape from it, hemmed in as it was by the mountains of the Peak district and the moors.

Meanwhile Elizabeth had offered Norfolk his freedom if he would sign an undertaking to renounce forever all thought of marriage with the Queen of Scots. This he agreed to do and he was set free.

Elizabeth then sent Cecil to visit Mary to explain to her that she, Elizabeth, would help restore Mary to her throne if Mary would send her little son James to England as a hostage. Mary declined this offer.

And while Mary was at Chatsworth yet another escape was planned and came to a failure. This was fabricated by two sons of the Earl of Derby, Thomas and Edward Stanley, and Sir Thomas Gerard and two neighbouring landowners named Rolleston and Hall. The idea was to let her down by a rope from her window and get her across country to Harwich. However, the son of Rolleston betrayed the conspirators, they were arrested, and Mary was moved to Sheffield.

The Ridolfi Plot

Roberto di Ridolfi was a Florentine, clearly a lover of intrigue. He was a banker by profession and had come to England when Mary Tudor had married Philip II of Spain. Although he was an ardent Catholic, since he was a financial wizard he was employed by influential men of the Queen's govermnent, including Cecil. He became absorbed in English politics and was naturally in sympathy with the Catholic factions. He was involved in the rising of Northumberland and Westmorland.

He was suspected and examined at this time by Sir Francis Walsingham himself. His house and business premises were searched but his financial dealings had been conducted on a strictly business level and nothing could be proved against him. In fact his business acumen impressed the Queen and her ministers to such an extent that they believed it could be used to their advantage.

This was a great asset to Ridolfi in his schemes, and during the year 1570 Mary's ambassador, Leslie, and the Florentine put their heads together and a new plot was conceived.

Mary was told of it by Leslie. Elizabeth was to be overthrown by foreign armies, and Mary was to be freed and set on the throne of England. To put such a plan into action foreign aid was necessary and those who would be willing to supply it were the Pope, Philip II and the Duke of Alva.

By March 1571 documents were drawn up. Norfolk was required to sign a statement first that he was a Catholic, and secondly that he would place himself at the head of the army which Philip II would send to remove Elizabeth from the throne. It was small wonder that Norfolk hesitated to sign such a document, but carried away by his vanity and arrogance he eventually did; it was to prove his death-warrant.

Ridolfi left London with the documents, his first call being Brussels where he consulted with Alva; there he summoned Charles Baillie, an enthusiastic supporter of Mary and Catholicism, and commissioned him to take letters to Norfolk and Leslie.

Sir Francis Walsingham had the most effective spy system in Europe, which he is said to have financed from his own pocket, a fact which made him very popular with Elizabeth. Through his spies he learned something of the Catholic project and Charles Baillie was arrested when he arrived at Dover. In the Marshalsea prison Baillie was submitted to fearful torture; he held out bravely but finally the torment was too much for him; he broke down and confessed, implicating Norfolk, Ridolfi, Leslie and Mary.

Ridolfi remained abroad. Pius gave him senatorial rank and he lived for another forty years.

Norfolk was brought to trial for high treason on 16th January 1572. Elizabeth was always averse to bloodshed in her name, and Norfolk was the premier peer. She followed her favourite shilly-shallying tactics. Parliament was petitioning for the execution of Mary, who was involved in the plot; but Elizabeth hesitated once more. There can be no doubt that she could not rest securely on her throne while Mary lived, but Mary was a Queen and Elizabeth was wise enough to know that it is not a good practice lightly to execute royalty. One would never be sure whose the next head would be.

Norfolk, however, was doomed. He had been found guilty of high treason and must die. It was not until 2nd June that he was taken out to Tower Hill and executed. He declared on the scaffold that he was never a papist since he knew what religion meant. He was some thirty-six years old when he died.

Mary was grief-stricken for "Her Norfolk". She knew that Elizabeth's ministers were clamouring for her death. Elizabeth would give no answer to them. All the same restrictions at Sheffield were intensified. It was decided that a certain danger lay in her having so many attendants, and some of them were sent away. Willie Douglas was among these.

This was that fatal year 1572, and England was not the only country in which there was conflict between Catholic and Protestant. In France there was about to befall the most horrible massacre of all time. It took place on the night of 24th August 1572, the Eve of St Bartholomew.

Suddenly in the early morning, the stillness of the Paris streets was broken by the ringing of the tocsins throughout the city; this was the pre-arranged signal for the Catholics to rise against the Huguenots. There was such sickening slaughter in Paris that night as had never been known before. The terror spread throughout France.

There are conflicting opinions as to the number who died in France during those days and nights of terrible massacre. Edith Sichel points out the discrepancies in reports. In Orleans 2,000 were said to have suffered, but the minister, Touissant, names only 700. The total given varies from 5,000 to 20,000.

When news reached Sheffield of the atrocities which had been committed on that night and which continued for days, Mary was horrified. That this carnage should have occurred in her beloved country where she had spent her happiest years made her take to her bed in anguish. The stories which were told were hair-raising: the cruel murder of that good man Admiral de Coligny, the slaughter in the streets, the rivers running with blood. And the leader-in-chief of this massacre was the Duke of Guise, kinsman of the Queen of Scots.

Horror ran through the Protestant world. The fact that Mary had recently been involved in a plot to bring back Catholicism to England was remembered. She was a Catholic; she wanted to bring the Catholic religion to England. People were talking of Bloody Mary's reign when the fires of Smithfield had sickened them, of the Spanish Inquisition and the tortures that were inflicted in its name. And a member of Mary's family had led this terrible new massacre during which people had been slaughtered for no other reason than that they were Protestants.

The Protestants of England united to make sure that Catholicism was never allowed in England; and the best way to ensure that was to put the head of the Scottish Queen where in their opinion it belonged – on the block. There was a new cry in the streets: "To the block with the Fair Devil of Scotland." She was fair, they conceded that. She bewitched men with her charms. Norfolk had died because of her; she had had three husbands; two were dead, the third as good as dead. She was a devil, they said – the Fair Devil of Scotland.

Mary waited in Sheffield Castle for death. She must have been certain at that time that it could not be long delayed. At the end of that fateful year she reached her thirtieth birthday.

It was characteristic of Elizabeth that realizing Mary's fortunes were at their lowest she should decide to be lenient. Mary's health was deteriorating rapidly in the draughty, damp castles in which she had been lodged, and Elizabeth gave her permission for Mary to go to Chatsworth; and even extended her leniency to allow her prisoner, if well guarded, to take the waters at Buxton.

Away from the damp and the draughts Mary's health improved; and she was allowed a little freedom; she could even ride a little – always surrounded by guards; and we hear that she explored the caves in the neighbourhood, being fascinated by the stalactites and stalagmites. One of the groups of stalactites is called Queen Mary's Pillar after her and is said to have been so named by the faithful Mary Seton.

Before the winter settled in the party was sent back to draughty Sheffield. It was at Sheffield that Mary became a godmother to little Bessie Peirrepoint. Bessie was the granddaughter of Bess, the Countess of Shrewsbury, and no doubt that ambitious lady felt that it was a good idea to have a Queen as her grand-daughter's godmother – even a captive one. The little girl became a favourite with the Queen, slept in her bed and spent much of the day with her. She gave great comfort to Mary who was happiest when she had someone on whom to shower her affection.

The years passed in a wearying procession from Sheffield to Chatsworth, to Buxton back to Chatsworth, back to Sheffield; and with the passing of the winters Mary grew a little more despairing; her pains increased, there were a few grey hairs and she was relying more on wigs and hair-pieces to augment her once luxuriant hair.

In 1574 came the news of two deaths in France – that of her uncle, the Cardinal of Lorraine, who had so influenced her in the past, and that of Charles IX of France who had been mad but had always had a fondness for her. Mary must have felt that she had lost two more friends although it was so long since she had seen them.

It was in October of that year that the Countess entertained Charles Stuart, the younger brother of Darnley. Bess's daughter Elizabeth Cavendish and young Charles Stuart were taken with each other, and because of the young man's royal connections, Bess decided that no obstacle should be put in the way of their marriage. Queen Elizabeth was furious at the presumption of the woman. She had forgiven her for taking her husband to Buxton without permission but this was different. Both the Countess of Shrewsbury and Lennox who had arranged the match were sent to the Tower. In three months' time the dominating Bess was free and the following year a child of the marriage was born; she was Arabella Stuart, who was destined to a tragic life on account of her royal connections.

Poor Arabella was born to trouble for she was next to her young cousin James – later James I – in the line of succession to the English throne. Moreover, the fact that she had been born in England would incline the favour of some towards her. Mary, who loved children, was enchanted by the baby Arabella and made her her special protégée. She gave the child presents and made plans for her future. Alas, when a quarrel between the Shrewsburys broke out involving the Queen, this brought an end to that pleasant relationship. When James came to the throne he treated Arabella with kindness and even gave her a pension; but when she was betrothed to William Seymour – the Suffolk heir and therefore of royal connection through Henry VIII's sister Mary – she and Seymour were made to swear that they would not marry without the King's consent. They broke their word and married secretly and when this was discovered were sent to the Tower. Arabella eventually escaped and set out for France but was captured in the Straits of Dover and brought back to the Tower. Seymour reached France in safety, but Arabella spent the rest of her life in the Tower.

So if Bess had brought glory to the family she brought little happiness.

Mary Seton at last fell in love. The object of her devotion was Andrew Beaton – younger brother of the Archbishop. The Queen, although it would have been heartbreaking to part with this most trusted of all her friends, was not the woman to stand between the happiness of two people who so clearly loved each other as these two did. They were mature people, and the atmosphere of the castle prisons had had the same effect on Mary Seton's health as on the Queen's, who decided that her faithful friend must marry Andrew Beaton.

Mary Seton could not bring herself to leave her mistress; she made excuses declaring that her family would never consent to her marrying a younger son. The Queen declared that she would immediately bestow a title on Andrew. Mary Seton was adamant. She had vowed to stay with the Queen and would not break her vow. The vow must be broken, declared the Queen; she would send Andrew to his brother in Paris and get a dispensation so that Mary could feel free from a vow she had made years ago. She would take no refusal and in due course Andrew set out for Paris. Mary Seton was persuaded that she must marry; she blossomed and the Queen gave herself the pleasure of planning her friend's trousseau.

Alas for poor Mary Seton. Her lover died of a fever on his way back to England and there was no wedding for the last and most faithful of the Maries. It was some years later when they were back in the dreaded Tutbury that the Queen insisted on Mary Seton's departure. Mary Seton was becoming crippled with rheumatism, even as the Queen was; but although Mary the Queen was forced to bear such ills, there was no need for Mary Seton to do so.

This time Mary did not ask her friend what she would like to do. She wrote to her aunt Renée who was the Abbess of a convent in Rheims, and asked her if Mary Seton might join her. Mary could not bear to see her dearest friend growing more crippled, more prematurely aged every day.

Mary Seton protested but this was an order she must obey. So the Queen lost a faithful friend.

The Babington Conspiracy

As the years passed Mary's hopes faded. She realized that Elizabeth had no intention of releasing her. The plans for her liberation went constantly wrong. Yet even though crippled with rheumatism, she still retained that powerful fascination.

In the year 1574 her secretary Raullet had died, and before his own death her uncle the Cardinal of Lorraine suggested she employ Claude de la Boisselière Nau, who had worked for him and been under the protection of the House of Guise. Nau arrived at Sheffield in the spring of 1575. His duties were shared with another named Gilbert Curle and both these men were to play a part in the tragedy which followed.

Meanwhile trouble was brewing in the Shrewsbury ménage. Bess had subdued three husbands and had had little trouble with them; but George, Earl of Shrewsbury, was not to be browbeaten. He had formed a liaison with a beautiful servant-girl in his household, Eleanor Britton. Whether it was owing to this or not is uncertain, but in view of what we know of the character of Bess of Hardwick, we can guess that the trouble arose out of financial disagreement. Bess had had a family before she married Shrewsbury; she was determined to govern them all. It was essential to her that she had her own way. Because Shrewsbury would not fall in with her wishes she set about harming him in every conceivable way.

Bess started the scandal that Mary and Shrewsbury had been lovers. The stories were seized on with eagerness. Rumours multiplied and it was said that Mary had borne the Earl two children.

When Mary heard these rumours she was furious. She wrote to Elizabeth and told her that Lady Shrewsbury had slandered Elizabeth herself. Whether the letter ever reached Elizabeth is not known, but in view of the circumstances, the Shrewsburys could no longer be Mary's jailers.

The relationship between the Earl and the Countess deteriorated. They quarrelled incessantly about their properties and parted. Shrewsbury's relief to be rid of his wife and the custodianship of the Queen of Scots was great. The Spanish ambassador wrote to Philip of Spain that Shrewsbury thanked Elizabeth profusely. He was rid of two devils – his wife and the Queen of Scots.

Elizabeth sent Sir Ralph Sadler to take the Shrewsburys' place. He was nearly seventy years old and did not relish the task of jailer to the Queen of Scots. He had proved himself to be a good servant of the Queen and Walsingham; he had played his part in the troubles which centred round the Queen of Scots, and had often been Elizabeth's emissary on important occasions – for example he had been sent to Mary "to expostulate with her by way of accusation" after the execution of Norfolk. He had been a member of the commission which had sat in judgement on the Casket Letters and had previously been the guardian of Mary when the Shrewsburys were absent.

No sooner had he taken on the task, than he was writing to Walsingham to apply a good helping hand to try to relieve him because of his age and the cold weather. Elizabeth was a long time considering this request. The stage was set for the final act.

The conspiracy known as the Babington Plot was about to begin.

The plot could be said to have been contrived with Sir Francis Walsingham as the *agent provocateur*. Sir Francis was an ardent Protestant who began his career by becoming a student at Gray's Inn. When Mary Queen I ascended the throne he thought it advisable to leave the country and he remained abroad until Elizabeth's accession. He had not wasted his time. During his exile he had learned several foreign languages, had studied the customs of other countries, learned a great deal about their spy systems and when he returned possessed all the qualifications to make him a diplomat. He entered Parliament and was employed in secret intelligence when he came to the notice of the Queen and was soon admitted to her service.

His frankness angered her now and then, but her shrewd assessment of his character was that he was one of the most valuable servants she possessed and he became her chief secretary. He had the most efficient spy service in the world and this was put at the Queen's disposal. At one time he had fifty-three agents spread throughout various countries whose duty was to bring him information. He would stop at little to gain this. He was fond of repeating: "Knowledge is never too dear". Elizabeth bestowed a knighthood on him in 1577 as a sign of her approval of his conduct.

Walsingham was aware of the many plots which had been concocted around Mary Stuart. As a stern Protestant he was determined that Protestantism should be maintained in England and he believed that while Mary Stuart lived, Protestant England, and therefore Elizabeth herself, were in danger. Mary had been incriminated more than once. She should, he felt, have been brought to the scaffold at the time of the Ridolfi affair; but Elizabeth was reluctant to be the one who signed her kinswoman's death-warrant. If, however, Elizabeth were presented with proof that Mary had been involved in a plot to assassinate her, she could not refuse to sign the warrant for her execution.

Believing this state of affairs had to be brought about to save Elizabeth and Protestant England, Walsingham determined to do it. He called in Gilbert Gifford. Gifford came of a well-known Roman Catholic family and had been trained for the priesthood. He was one of Walsingham's spies, and a useful one, for since he had been a Catholic priest Catholics believed he could be trusted with their secrets.

Walsingham intimated that the object of Gifford's mission was to incriminate the Queen of Scots in a plot to assassinate Elizabeth and get herself placed on the throne. That should not be very difficult. Such plots were being continually fabricated. Gifford was aware of what was expected of him.

There was known to both Walsingham and Gifford a certain Thomas Morgan, a Welshman, who had a few years before attempted to raise a rebellion in favour of the Queen of Scots and against Elizabeth. For his part in it he was imprisoned by the French in the Bastille; but he was allowed to receive visitors there and was clearly not treated as an ordinary prisoner. Elizabeth had attempted to have him brought to England but the French would not give him up. It was clear that he was a man whom the French might try to use at some future date.

The plan suggested by Gifford and Walsingham was that Gifford, in his role of ardent Catholic, should go to Morgan and tell him that he was in a position to smuggle letters to the Queen of Scots. The letters written by Morgan and those Mary wrote in reply would of course pass into Walsingham's hands.

Mary had been removed from Tutbury to Chartley. Life must have become very wearying. There had been an unhappy incident at Tutbury. A certain Humphrey Briggs had reported to Sir Ralph Sadler that his master and his master's secretary, named Rowland Kitchyn, had been hearing Mass in a secret room set apart for the purpose. It turned out that Briggs had been dismissed and this was his way of revenging himself. Sir Ralph was old; he wanted nothing so much as to be freed from the burden Elizabeth had placed upon him. The life Mary endured in the draughty castles was scarcely one of comfort and Sir Ralph complained that it was ruining his health. He wanted to escape to peace. But the fact that the tiresome Briggs had reported his master and the secretary to him meant that he could not afford to ignore the matter. He sent for Kitchyn to come to the castle and answer questions. Kitchyn admitted that he was a Catholic and heard Mass; he was therefore suspected – as all Catholics must be – of plotting to free the Queen of Scots; and the fact that he lived in the near vicinity meant that his case could not be ignored.

Sir Ralph decided that he must attend the Tutbury Chapel and as Kitchyn refused each day he was dragged across the courtyard below Mary's window to the chapel and dragged back. Mary would no doubt have seen this and have heard rumours of what was happening.

It seems likely that fearing to be put to the torture during which he might be forced to lie about his master – or even tell the truth and incriminate him in some way – Kitchyn strangled himself in his cell. In any event his body was hung from the turret which faced Mary's window, no doubt as a warning to her. This was what happened to those who were suspected of plotting against Elizabeth. But nothing was proved against Kitchyn except that he was a Catholic. Mary may have wondered whether they were planning to kill her for the same reason.

She was very uneasy; there was trouble in her domestic circle because her secretary Nau had fallen in love with Bessie Pierrepoint, at this time an imperious young lady of sixteen; and of course the grand-daughter of the Shrewsburys would never be allowed to marry a secretary. Mary, who was romantic and emotional, would be sympathetic to the lovers while her sense of rank would make her realize the impossibility of the marriage.

Life must have alternated between dreary boredom and horrifying incident, with the ever-present discomfort which was continually affecting her health. Then Elizabeth decided to listen to Sir Ralph's pleadings; he might retire from his unwelcome task, and in his place she would send Sir Amyas Paulet.

When Mary heard she must have been doubly depressed. She had no affection for Sir Ralph Sadler but she was well aware that she could have a more stern guardian. Paulet was known to be puritanical and a fervent hater of Catholics. Elizabeth gave orders that security was to be tighter. The affair of Rowland Kitchyn, although nothing had been discovered to show that there was a plot to rescue Mary, had its effect. Whenever suspicions were aroused that some people might be working to rescue Mary, there was always a tightening of restrictions. Paulet arrived with a list of instructions: Mary's correspondence was to be minutely examined; she was to be watched more closely; she must not be allowed to keep the state of a Queen.

Paulet professed his determination to prevent the Queen from entering into traitorous acts, and confided to Walsingham that if there was an attempt to rescue her which he believed might be successful he would kill her rather than allow her to escape.

Paulet had not been long at Tutbury when Mary became ill, as she always did after a sojourn at Tutbury, and Elizabeth agreed that she might be moved to Chartley. Chartley – like every other place – was a blessed relief after Tutbury. It was built on a hill rising from a green fertile plain and it overlooked some of the most beautiful scenery in the county of Stafford. The keep was circular and the loopholes were made so that arrows could be shot into the ditch horizontally or from under the towers. Mary arrived there on Christmas-day.

It was soon after her arrival at Chartley that Mary heard that a priest, Gilbert Gifford, whose home was not far from the Chartley estate, had called asking for an audience with her. To her surprise, Paulet, after appearing to give a great deal of consideration to the matter, allowed the interview to take place. It is almost certain that Paulet knew that Gifford was one of Walsingham's spies.

Gifford told the Queen that he was in touch with friends of hers on the Continent and he was going to attempt to get letters in to her and get hers smuggled out. Mary would naturally have been excited. The prospect of escape must constantly have been in her mind; the hope of achieving it must have been the reason why she could keep reasonably well and sane in what seemed her interminable captivity.

She would certainly have pointed out that it would be more difficult than ever for her to enter into a correspondence now that Sir Amyas Paulet was her guardian.

But Gifford had an idea. He had sounded a local brewer and this man had promised – for a consideration – to conceal a box in one of the barrels. This would contain letters from Mary's friends; Mary could place her letters in the box and put it into an empty barrel. The brewer would take these barrels away and pass on the letters. It seemed a clever and novel plan and Mary agreed.

Through Thomas Morgan, Gifford was put into touch with John Savage, a man who had long been marked down as a possible assassin of Queen Elizabeth. Fiercely Catholic he was a born fanatic. He was a soldier who had been in service with the Duke of Parma in the Low Countries and was able to tell Gifford that he was already in touch with a priest named John Ballard who was involved in a plot which had been organized by an Anthony Babington.

Thus the conspirators were linked.

Anthony Babington was in his mid-twenties – handsome, adventurous and wealthy enough to pay for his fancies. His was an old family which could trace its lineage back to the Normans. He was born in Dethick in Derbyshire in the year 1561, and at the age of eighteen married Margery Draycot, like himself a secret Catholic. When he was very young, he had been sent to Sheffield Castle and for a short time acted as page to the Queen of Scots. Like so many men – young and old – he had fallen victim to her charm; and it was natural that he should wish to play the chivalrous deliverer.

He studied law but soon found that somewhat irksome, and as he was rich and charming, he was welcomed in fashionable circles.

In due course he travelled abroad and there met Thomas Morgan, and no doubt listened to plans to liberate Mary with which he would be in entire agreement. Catholics abroad decided that he was the man to lead a rebellion against the Protestant Queen of England in the cause of Mary Stuart. And this was what he was doing when Gifford linked up with him. He was working closely with John Ballard, a Roman Catholic priest who believed that many Catholics in England would be ready to rise to Mary's cause once the call to arms was given.

The conspirators met almost every night through June 1586, sometimes in St Giles's Fields, sometimes in city taverns; they were Edward Abington, Anthony Babington, John Ballard, Robert Barnewell, Jerome Bellamy, John Charnock, Henry Donn, Robert Gage, Edward Jones, Thomas Salisbury, John Savage, John Travers and Chidiock Tichbourne.

Babington, a somewhat vain young man, was very anxious for Mary to know that he was the leader; he insisted that she write to him personally. The letters he wrote to her were damning. In one written on 12th July he explained the methods which would be employed for the assassination of Elizabeth and delivering Mary. Alas for Mary. She wrote an approval of the plot and asked for more details.

In spite of the fact that a vain young man was the leader of this plot, it was treated very seriously in Catholic circles abroad and Philip of Spain became interested. As soon as Elizabeth was assassinated the ships in the Thames were to be seized; and Walsingham and Cecil were to be killed or captured. The Spanish ambassador in Paris, Don Bernardino de Mendoza, wrote to Philip that the Babington Plot was the most serious of all those as yet attempted and that all depended on the successful murder of Elizabeth.

All this damning information was being fed to Walsingham through Gifford. He had enough to accuse everyone concerned – and that included the Queen of Scots – and try them for treason.

In August Ballard was arrested as he left the gathering of conspirators; but for a while no hint was given that anything was known of the rest of the band. Fully aware of what was happening, Paulet told Mary that Elizabeth was concerned for her health and had decided that Mary should have two weeks in which to hunt a little. She would of course be closely guarded during the hunt. Mary was delighted and unsuspectingly left with her retinue for the house of Sir Walter Ashton in Tixall. While she was away her apartments and coffers were thoroughly searched for incriminating documents, and her letters were taken away to London. When she returned to Chartley she quickly became aware of what had happened and why Elizabeth had granted her this concession.

When Ballard was arrested Walsingham had, as mentioned, given no indication that he knew others were involved in the plot. Babington had for some time been trying to get a passport to travel in Europe so he would be prepared should it be necessary for him to leave the country hurriedly. His fears proved to have firm foundation. Walsingham, knowing exactly who was involved, ordered men in his service to invite Babington to supper, to make him drink too much and see if they could trap him into admitting something. Babington, however, was wary; he pretended to drink but remained perfectly sober. It was Walsinghan's servants who drank too much, thus enabling Babington to make a brief examination of Walsingham's study, and there on a desk he saw a note with his name on it. He knew then that he was in acute danger. He left his house in the Barbican and went to hide in the densest part of St John's Wood. He cut his hair, stained his skin with walnut juice and went to the house of one of the other conspirators, Jerome Bellamy, and asked for shelter. What he did not know was how fully informed Walsingham was, and that this was the worst possible place in which he could have gone to hide. He was arrested there; and the rest of the band were soon in custody.

They were all found guilty. There was ample proof against them and they were sentenced to the horrible death of hanging, drawing and quartering. This was one of the most barbarous deaths of all, and Babington was forced to witness Ballard's execution before he endured his own.

His suffering was cruel. He was cut down from the gallows while still alive and the executioner's knife ripped up his body while he was still conscious. He was heard to murmur: *"Parce mihi Domine Jesu"* as the knife entered his body.

The other conspirators who were to die the next day were fortunate, for Elizabeth, hearing of the terrible sufferings of Ballard and Babington, ordered that the remainder of the traitors should not suffer the last and most cruel part of their sentences until they were dead. So they were cut down only after life had left them.

That was the end of the Babington Plot, the last of many by which Mary's supporters had planned to free her.

On 25th September Mary left Chartley for the last of her prison castles – Fotheringhay.

Fotheringhay

In the Great Chamber in Fotheringhay Castle the trial of Mary Queen of Scots was held. At the upper end of the room a throne had been placed and above it were emblazoned the arms of England; this chair was for Queen Elizabeth, who of course did not attend. Facing this throne but at a good distance was a red velvet chair which had been set there for the prisoner. Between them were forms for the Counsel and for four judges. There were chairs facing the throne for the Commissioners. Among those present were Cecil, Walsingham, Shrewsbury, Sir Ralph Sadler and the Queen's friend, Christopher Hatton. There was no one to represent Mary. A barrier had been placed across the room and the space on the other side of this was reserved for spectators.

At nine o'clock, on Wednesday 15th October 1586, the proceedings opened with the entrance of Mary. She wore the costume with which she is always associated, flowing black velvet and the white headdress shaped rather like a shell.

She was dismayed when she realized that the throne had not been placed there for her use. "I am the Queen by right of birth, and my place should be there," she said. It was difficult for her to understand that it was possible for a queen to be on trial. The danger of her situation must then have been brought home to her for she turned to Melville and remarked that there were so many counsellors there and not one of them for her.

The trial was opened by the Lord Chancellor who said that the Queen of England had discovered that Mary had been involved in a plot to destroy her and her realm, and that it was for this reason Elizabeth had commanded there should be an enquiry.

To this Mary answered that she had come to England to ask Elizabeth's aid and not as a subject. She was an independant sovereign and therefore answerable to none but God. At the same time she stressed that she was not guilty of the crime of which she was accused.

Sir Thomas Gawdy, Elizabeth's judge, then rose to his feet and detailed the facts of the Babington Plot to which Mary replied that she knew nothing of the conspirators. However, Sir Thomas's answer was that he had copies of the correspondence which had passed between Mary and the six gentlemen involved.

Mary disputed the authenticity of the copies and demanded to see them, but this was not permitted. She gave her answers skilfully and with shrewdness. She knew by now she was fighting for her life.

When she discovered that her secretaries Curle and Nau had given evidence against her, she was greatly upset and insisted that they must have been tortured to have done so.

She was accused by Lord Burghley of having assumed the name and arms of England when she was in France, to which Mary replied that she had done so on the command of her father-in-law, Henry II of France; but Burghley reminded her that she had continued to lay claim to the English throne after her departure from France. To this she replied with dignity that she had never given up her rights and had no intention of doing so.

She then accused Walsingham of deliberately setting out to trap her. With tears in her eyes she declared that she would rather die a hundred times than see Catholics suffer for her sake. Walsingham retorted that no faithful subject of the Queen had been put to death on account of religion, though some had for maintaining the authority of the Pope against the Queen's. Mary answered that she had heard contrary to this.

Walsingham said firmly that he harboured no malice against the Queen of Scots. He was, he continued, Secretary of State to his revered mistress, Elizabeth, and he was determined at all costs to work for her safety and that of his country. He kept a close watch over conspirators because it was his duty to do so.

The following day Mary was allowed to address the Court.

She complained bitterly of the humiliation she had suffered in being brought to this state. She was ready to answer questions on one point only – the alleged plot against Elizabeth – but she had been pestered with questions which were outside the matter. She declared that her letters had been garbled and intentions read into them which were not there. She admitted that she was weary of her imprisonment and had longed to escape from it. She had written to foreign princes, and being a true Catholic her religion was of the greatest importance to her. But she would not admit that she had desired the death of Elizabeth.

At length the proceedings were over and she left the Court as she had come in, on the arm of Melville.

Walsingham then declared that he would lay the findings before Queen Elizabeth. The Queen of Scots was guilty, he said, but they could not pass sentence on her. That must be a matter for their Queen.

And Elizabeth procrastinated. She must have thought of all the Catholics in her realm who in their hearts supported the Queen of Scotland. Her feminine instinct told her that much as she longed to be rid of Mary, her death – and particularly by her, Elizabeth's order – might do more harm than good. Moreover, she did not wish to have the blood of Mary of Scotland on her hands.

In the Star Chamber at Westminster Mary's case was opened once more on 25th October. On this occasion the two secretaries appeared in Court and Nau, ashamed because he had given evidence against the Queen – or rather had admitted writing the damning letters for her – spoke in her favour. But nothing could save her. She was found guilty.

Into the winter of 1586-7 Mary waited for execution. She was ready for death and must have welcomed it. She was forty-four years old now, so crippled with rheumatism that she could hardly walk. She had come a long way from the gay, light-hearted girl who had danced with the King of France at her first wedding.

Elizabeth took a long time before she could bring herself to sign the death-warrant. All her ministers urged her that the deed must be done. Leicester attempted to persuade her; Walsingham had contrived for this one end, and Elizabeth herself knew that only Mary's death could bring her the security she must have. She *wanted* Mary dead but she did not want to have the responsibility of her death; and the law demanded that she sign the death-warrant. Before doing so she did her best to persuade Sir Amyas Paulet to murder the Queen and so save herself from the blame of her death. Paulet the puritan, was horrified. "God forbid," he wrote, "that I should make so foul a shipwreck of my conscience or leave so great a blot to my poor posterity, to shed blood without law or warrant."

There was nothing Elizabeth could do but sign the warrant.

And so to the last scene in the hall of Fotheringhay.

On the night before, after she had retired to bed, there was a knock on her door and a deputation consisting of Shrewsbury, the Earl of Kent, Robert Beale and Sir Drue Drury came into her room.

Shrewsbury said: "Madam, I would have greatly desired that another than I should announce to you such sad intelligence as that which I now bring on the part of the Queen of England ... It is to admonish you to prepare yourself for the sentence of death pronounced against you."

Mary replied: "I am thankful to you for such welcome news. You will do me great good in withdrawing me from this world, out of which I am very glad to go on account of the miseries I see in it, and of being myself in continual affliction."

While this scene was in progress a large, strong-looking man had arrived at the inn close to the castle. His name was Bulle and he carried a case in which was an axe with a newly sharpened edge.

When the deputation had left Mary went through her wardrobe and divided up her money into portions; these she put into packets and wrote on each the name of the one who should receive it. She spent a long time on her knees in prayer and by the time this was done it was two o'clock in the morning of the day she was to die. The execution was to take place at eight o'clock on the morning of 8th February 1587.

At six o'clock she arose. Elizabeth Curle and Jane Kennedy were with her and it was Mary who was the calmest of the three. She commanded them to dress her as for a festival. She wanted them to know that she was not afraid but eager to go to her death.

They dressed her in her kirtle of black satin and her petticoat of crimson velvet; her stockings were of pale blue decorated with silver. The night before Elizabeth Curle and Jane Kennedy had made her a camisole of Scotch plaid and she asked them to see that her body was decently covered after she was dead. They helped her into her widow's gown. The *Agnus Dei* was placed round her neck and the girdle with the cross at her waist. Again she knelt in prayer.

As her friends and attendants were about to follow her into the hall they were stopped by Paulet who would only allow two women and four men to go with her. Those who went were Jane Kennedy and Elizabeth Curle with Sir Andrew Melville, her physician, her surgeon and her apothecary. They were in tears and she, who was calmer than any, bade them not to weep for her. "Rather rejoice," she said, "that you see the end of the long troubles of Mary Stuart."

In the hall a platform had been erected. Twelve feet square and two and a half feet high, it had had a rail built round it. The block and the axe had already been placed on it.

She sat on a black chair while the death-warrant was read. Her gown was removed, and the white kerchief, gold-fringed, was bound about her eyes by Jane Kennedy. Mary Queen of Scots was alone on the platform with Bulle the executioner.

The Queen of Scots murmured: "Into thy hands, O Lord, I commend my spirit".

The first blow cut her head but did not sever it from her body. Bulle struck again and the head rolled away. Bulle picked up the head by the chestnut hair and to the horror of all the head with short white hair fell away from it and Bulle was left holding the luxuriant wig.

There was silence in the hall until the Dean of Peterborough called out: "So perish all the Queen's enemies".

Bulle, reaching for Mary's garters which were his perquisite together with her cross, pomander and rosary, disturbed her little Skye terrier who had crept into the hall hidden by her skirts. He ran out and lay between the Queen's shoulders and head. He would not allow anyone to touch him and refused all food until the day he died.

She was dead after nineteen years of imprisonment – the Queen who would never be forgotten and of whom men and women would write and talk for centuries to come.

There was rejoicing through the country but Queen Elizabeth was uneasy. She made a great show of pretending that she had had no wish to sign the death-warrant. She had not meant the sentence to be carried out; she declared that she was angry that it had been. No one believed her.

Elizabeth ordered that Mary should be buried in state at Peterborough; a gold crown was placed on the coffin which bore her mangled body to the cathedral. Twenty years later her son James I had it removed to Westminster Abbey and buried there.

There were many to mourn her, and many to feel the world was a safer place without her.

She had been born into a violent age and had died violently; she had lived turbulently all the days of her life except during that golden childhood. Never have so many conflicting portraits of one woman been in existence. Who was the real Mary? Her actions reveal a great deal to us, for she is consistent in her generous emotions, her friendship and attachments to those about her. Her fault was that her heart took charge when her head should have been in command. Her life is one long sequence of fatal mistakes. Was she a murderess? That is the essential question. But let us judge her against her times. Look at the lives of those about her, and we find that those who had led the least blameless lives – many of them proved murderers – were the first to condemn her.

She is an enigma, as are most human beings. She is a saint and a sinner; but one thing cannot be denied. She was capable of casting an irresistible fascination on those about her and this has continued throughout the centuries. She was one of the most physically attractive women of her age; so powerful was this attraction that many believed it to come from the Devil. For this reason one of the epithets frequently bestowed on her was that of "The Fair Devil of Scotland".

Bibliography

Anonymous, *Feudal Castles of France*, 1869.

Aubrey, William Hickman Smith *The National and Domestic History of England*.

Battifol, Louis (Translated by Elsie Finnimore Buckley), *National History of France. (The Century of the Renaissance.)*

Black, J. B., *Andrew Lang and the Casket Letters Controversy*, 1951.

Black, J. B., *The Reign of Elizabeth*, 1959.

Bowen, Marjorie, *In the Steps of Mary Queen of Scots*, 1952.

Gore-Brown, Robert, *Lord Bothwell*, 1935.

Buchanan, George (Translated and edited by W. A. Gatherer), *The Tyrannous Reign of Mary Stuart*, 1958.

Campbell, G. A., *Mary Queen of Scots*, 1936.

Cowan, Samuel, *Mary Queen of Scots*, 1901.

Cowan, Samuel, *The Last Days of Mary Stuart*, 1907.

Criss, Mildred, *Mary Stuart*, 1940.

Dakers, Andrew, *The Tragic Queen*, 1937.

Diggles, H. F., *The Casket Letters of Mary Stuart*, 1960.

Edwards, Francis, *The Dangerous Queen*, 1964.

Erskine of Marr, the Hon. Ruaraidh, *The Stout Adventure of Mary Stuart*, 1937.

Fleming, D. Hay, *Mary Queen of Scots, From her Birth till her Flight into England*, 1897.

Francis, G. R., *Mary Queen of Scots*, 1930.

Fraser, Antonia, *Mary Queen of Scots*, 1969.

Froude, J. A., *History of England from the Fall of Wolsey to the Defeat of the Spanish Armada*, 1862.

Gerard, Daniel, *A Sketch and a Defence*, 1886.

Gorman, Herbert, *The Scottish Queen*, 1932.

Guizot, M. (Translated by Robert Black), *History of France*, 1881.

Henderson, T. F., *Mary Queen of Scots*, 1905.

Hosack, J., *Mary Queen of Scots and Her Accusers*, 1969.

Hume, Martin, *Love Affairs of Mary Queen of Scots*.

Kerlie, E. Marianne, *H. M. Mary of Guise-Lorraine, Queen of Scotland*, 1931.

Lang, Andrew, *The Mystery of Mary Stuart*, 1901.

Lang, Andrew, *Portraits and Jewels of Mary Queen of Scots*, 1906.

Lang, Andrew, *John Knox and the Reformation*.

Leader, J. D., *Mary Queen of Scots in Captivity*, 1880.

Linklater, E., *Mary Queen of Scots*, 1937.

MacNalty, Sir Arthur Salusbury, *Mary Queen of Scots: the Daughter of Debate*, 1960.

Mahon, Major General R. H., *Indictment of Mary Queen of Scots*, 1923.

Mahon, Major General R. H., *Mary Queen of Scots: A Study of the Lennox Narrative*, 1924.

Mahon, Major General R. H., *The Tragedy of Kirk o' Field*, 1930.

Meade, June, *Mary Queen of Scots, Queen and Woman*, 1933.

Mignet, F. A., *Mary Queen of Scots*, 1887.

Millar, A. H., *Mary Queen of Scots: Her Life Story*, 1927.

Mumby, Frank Arthur, *The Fall of Mary Stuart*, 1921.

Nau, Claude (Edited by J. Stevenson), *Memorials of Mary Stuart*, 1883.

Neale, J. E., *Queen Elizabeth*, 1934.

Neale, J. E., *The Age of Catherine de' Medici*, 1943.

Odom, Rev. W., *Mary Stuart, Queen of Scots*, 1904.

Parry, His Honour Sir Edward, *The Persecution of Mary Stuart. The Queen's Cause: A study in Criminology*, 1931.

Pollen, J. H., *Mary Queen of Scots and the Babington Plot*, 1922.

Preedy, George R., *The Life of John Knox*.

Rait, Robert S., *Mary Queen of Scots. Extracts from the English, Spanish and Venetian State Papers, Buchanan, Knox, Leslie, Melville, The Diurnal of Occurrents, Nau, etc. etc.*, 1900.

Sichel, Edith, *Catherine de' Medici and the French Reformation*, 1905.

Sichel, Edith, *The Later Years of Catherine de' Medici*, 1908.

Siebert, Margarete Kurlbaum (Translated from German by Mary Agnes Hamilton), *Mary Queen of Scots*, 1928.

Skae, Hilda T., *Life of Mary Queen of Scots*, 1905.

Stephen, Sir Leslie; Lee, Sir Sidney (Edited by), *The Dictionary of National Biography*, 1949-50.

Steuart, A. Francis (Edited by), *The Trial of Mary Queen of Scots*, 1923.

Stoddart, Jane, *The Girlhood of Mary Queen of Scots*, 1908.

Strickland, Anges, *Letters of the Queen of Scots with Historical Introduction and Notes*, 1842.

Strickland, Anges, *Lives of the Queens of Scotland*, 1854.

Turner, Sir George, *Mary Stuart, Forgotten Forgeries*, 1933.

Wade, John, *British History*, 1843.

Waldman, Milton, *Elizabeth and Leicester*, 1944.

Waldman, Milton, *King, Queen, Jack*, 1931.

Williams, H. Noel, *Henri II, His Court and Times*, 1910.

Williams, Neville, *Elizabeth, Queen of England*, 1967.

Zweig, Stefan (Translated by Cedar and Eden Paul), *The Queen of Scots*, 1935.

Illustration Sources

The paintings from the Royal Collection, Nos. 11 and 12, are reproduced by gracious permission of Her Majesty the Queen.

Other photographs appear by kind permission of the following: Bibliotheque Nationale, Nos. 1 and 4; National Portrait Gallery, London, No. 2; Walker Art Gallery, Liverpool, No. 3; Sir David Ogilvy, Bart, No. 5; Trustees of the British Museum, Nos. 6 and 8; National Galleries of Scotland, No. 7; Public Record Office (Crown Copyright; by permission of the Controller of H.M. Stationery Office), No. 9; Dean and Chapter of Westminster Abbey (Photo A. F. Keating), No. 10.

Picture Research by Jennifer Taylor.

Index

113918	Gordon Boshell **THE BLACK MERCEDES**	60p
114043	**THE MILLION POUND RANSOM**	60p
117468	**THE MENDIP MONEY-MAKERS**	60p
105087	Graeme Cook **COMMANDOS IN ACTION!** (illus) (NF)	35p
110927	Terrance Dicks **THE MOUNTIES:** **THE GREAT MARCH WEST**	40p
111052	**THE MOUNTIES:** **MASSACRE IN THE HILLS**	40p
111133	**THE MOUNTIES:** **WAR DRUMS OF THE BLACKFOOT**	45p
103645	G. Krishnamurti **THE ADVENTURES OF RAMA**	35p
11535X	John Lucarotti **OPERATION PATCH**	45p

Animal Stories

107004	Judith M. Berrisford **SKIPPER AND SON** (illus)	35p
107276	**SKIPPER'S EXCITING SUMMER**	40p
118502	Molly Burkett **FOXES, OWLS AND ALL** (illus)	70p
111567	**THAT MAD, BAD BADGER ...** (NF)	35p
109899	Constance Taber Colby **A SKUNK IN THE FAMILY** (illus) (NF)	45p
113675	G. D. Griffiths **ABANDONED!** (illus)	35p
117549	David Gross **THE BADGERS OF BADGER HILL**	50p
109627	Sara Herbert **THE PONY PLOT**	35p†
109708	**THE SECRET OF THE MISSING FOAL**	35p
107861	Alex Lea **TEMBA DAWN, MY CALF**	30p
11017X	Joyce Stranger **THE SECRET HERDS** (illus)	45p
115511	Alison Thomas **BENJI**	40p

†For sale in Britain and Ireland only.
*Not for sale in Canada.